T0133304

DIGITAL SHOCK

Digital Shock

Confronting the New Reality

HERVÉ FISCHER

Translated by Rhonda Mullins

McGill-Queen's University Press
Montreal & Kingston · London · Ithaca

Legal deposit third quarter 2006
Bibliothèque nationale du Québec

Printed in Canada on acid-free paper.

Translation of this book was partially funded by a grant from the Société
de développement des entreprises culturelles Québec (SODEC).

McGill-Queen's University Press acknowledges the support of the Canada
Council for the Arts for our publishing program. We also acknowledge
the financial support of the Government of Canada through the Book
Publishing Industry Development Program (BPIDP) for our publishing
activities.

Library and Archives Canada Cataloguing in Publication

Fischer, Hervé, 1941-
    Digital shock: confronting the new reality / Hervé Fischer;
translated by Rhonda Mullins.
    Translation of: Le choc du numérique: essai.

    Includes bibliographical references and index.
    ISBN-13: 978-0-7735-3114-7   ISBN-10: 0-7735-3114-9

    1. Information society. 2. Computers and civilization.
3. Cybernetics – Social aspects. 4. Digital electronics – Social aspects.
I. Mullins, Rhonda, 1966– II. Title.

HM851.F5713 2006   303-48'34   C2006-901889-8

Typeset in New Baskerville 10.5/13
by Infoscan Collette, Quebec City

Contents

Preface

I count, therefore I am.

The profound crisis in values and in the meaning of human evolution brought about by the revolution of science and digital technology – condemned by some in the name of traditional humanism and celebrated by others with more than legitimate fascination, but with no understanding of its far-reaching and hazardous consequences – provides us with an ideal opportunity to analyse what drives human thought. Any destabilization of received ideas and their logic tends to lay bare the deepest drives of the human imagination, the desire and the instinct for power that propel it, and its mode of societal and logical expression.

This book was first published in 2001, in French. My intention in writing it was to characterize and analyse digital shock at the turn of the millennium – a unique moment of imagination, technological utopia, and magical thinking. But now, in 2006, as we stand at the threshold of this new, Digital Age – which we anticipate will be as important to the evolution of humankind as the Age of Fire – our initial excessive hopes and resistances are ebbing away. It is becoming evident that digital technologies are pervading all fields of human endeavour. We have accommodated many of the resulting changes, and each year our perceptions relating to the digital revolution become more accurate and our fascination with it deepens. The digital shock, far from being over, will increase and expand further. In researching this book, I have learned a great deal about the laws of paradoxical logic and their importance to the formation of human thought. The thirty laws of the digital, which I present throughout this book, are today more authoritative than ever, and their importance will only increase. My research is also intended to assist in the development of a new approach in the humanities based on the critical assertions of sociology and psychoanalysis, and in the establishment of the rudimentary principles of mythanalysis.

Digital Shock is the first in a series of books that consider the birth of a new civilization at the turn of the millennium, its imaginary realm, its quest for meaning and values. Five other works – *Cyber-Prometheus: The Power Instinct*; *The Hyper Planet: From Linear Thought to Dancing Thought*; *We Will Be Gods*; *Society on the Couch: Elements of Mythanalysis*; and *Super Plus: Mythanalysis among the Middle Class* – will follow. In another work, *Colour and Societies,* I will tackle the impulses and behaviour of the imagination in the history of the social uses of colour.

This research will help me to demonstrate the laws of paradoxical logic and their importance in the making of human thought. It will also assist in the development of a new approach in humanities based on the critical assertions of sociology and psychoanalysis, and in establishing the basic principles of mythanalysis.

DIGITAL SHOCK

Prologue

To surf is to hope. Intrepid and anonymous citizen of the Net, have you experienced the captivating beauty of lost isles, swept by the winds of the digital continent, in the middle of nowhere?

I'm sending you this e-mail from Beijing, beyond the Great Wall of China and the Forbidden City.

Publishing directly on the internet is an easily realized dream. And I discovered its joys, but also its depths, when in February 2000 I clicked on the seemingly benign send arrow on my computer screen that was beckoning me to raise a sail of more than 300 pages on the great sea of the internet. With a single click, I cast off the moorings of the book I called *Mythanalysis of the Future*.

Discussing the painting *La Nuit: un port au clair de lune* by eighteenth-century painter Joseph Vernet, musician Hughes Aufray said, "The ships that inspire me to sing are always a symbol of hope. A three-master is waiting to set sail. Are there dreams of a better life on the horizon? These people leave in pursuit of trade or perhaps of a new home." This comment may also be applied to the internet. I think as well of Antoine Watteau's celebrated pre-Romantic painting *The Embarkation for Cythera*, which evokes the urge to travel to an elsewhere that holds as much promise as it does mystery.

In casting off the electronic moorings of *Mythanalysis of the Future*, I wanted to launch a book that would in theory be accessible instantaneously, everywhere, free of charge, twenty-four hours a day. So I snubbed my publishers. It was probably the first instance of publishing a book of this genre – a previously unpublished work aimed at the general public – directly on the internet. I dreamed of a book that readers could critique and comment upon and build on to the point where it would become a second book, parallel to my own. I dreamed of a global community of active readers, effortlessly sharing their ideas and advancing on the manifold horizons of culture and knowledge in varied interpretations of our collective imagination. And yet I had never believed in the euphoria that surrounds digital technology, or in the myth of binding and universal communication as touted by the converts to the new religion of the internet. Neither did I believe in the shared intelligence of a quasi-transcendental elsewhere that Teilhard de Chardin had hoped and prayed for at the end of divine creation, the transhuman consciousness emerging from human interactions – the noosphere. It was a lovely invitation to travel, but for simpletons!

I also had to admit to myself that no one reads more than two or three pages on a computer screen. And if my motivation for publishing on-line was to save our forests, I had to face the fact that if one printed out an internet-published book, one would use a single side of several hundred sheets of paper and likely select a larger font – in other words, this printed book would use twice as much paper as a bound book. It would also require one hour of electricity to run an ordinary home printer plus half a cartridge of ink. Furthermore, the sheets of paper would end up in complete disarray as one read unless they were fastened with a giant paper clip. I had opted for the simplest possible form of publication, eschewing all the extraordinary features of electronic publishing, to ensure that my book could be downloaded quickly without special software using an ordinary modem. And I forwent all sorts of technological wonders, still not widely enough adopted, that would have allowed me to explore a digital aesthetic, to harness the power of intelligent agents, to offer suggested readings and cross-references to research databases and other sites, and to integrate image, sound, and video clips – in short, to exploit all the wondrous creative potential of interactive multimedia technology.

Of course, technology progresses so quickly – we weren't even talking about the internet at the beginning of the 1990s – that ten years from now I won't hesitate to use all the new forms of writing and of applying colour and hypergraphics. By that time, it's likely that one will be able to read a book on-screen as comfortably and enjoyably as on paper; we will be printing books off the internet recto-verso and binding them in pocket format – I'll simply download my pocket e-book and read it in bed, on the beach, or on the subway.

And I am taunted by another type of unease. Every year, new and more powerful computers and software appear. If I am no longer around to regularly transfer the text of my book to media adapted to new formats, then it is in peril of vanishing forever amid technological advancements that would render it inaccessible or unreadable. It is also at the mercy of pirates and hackers who stalk our seas and spread text-eating viruses, internet-transmitted diseases, deadly sirens worthy of *The Odyssey*, and a multitude of monsters as yet unknown. That is, of course, if my book isn't first swallowed up body and soul in a computer crash. Had I myself also aged so quickly, perhaps infected by a computer virus, that I was prepared to renounce my long-time fascination with the digital revolution? I'll come clean: I considered stashing printed copies in a few different places in a bid to survive the slings and arrows of technological time, which ages and withers its products so much faster than the good old Gutenberg era did.

In fact, the battle of new technologies is not waiting to be waged: it has already been won. Its rapid victory affects all fields of human endeavour, at least in wealthy countries (those containing 6 per cent of the world's population), but it will undoubtedly assert itself beyond the technological apartheid that exists in developing countries in much less time than it took for the culture of print to spread.

So it is time to move on to the next phase of appropriation and to resist the hypnotic effect that new technologies exert over us, preventing us from thinking critically. We have to learn to think digital technology, to assert the human versus the machine, to rethink humanism rather than succumbing to the lure of the cathode ray. There is an urgent need for critical philosophy in the digital world – a force that will counter the naive and proselytizing wonderment many of my contemporaries have for the virtual world.

Such a philosophy would help us to avoid much disillusionment and error, not only in our cultural lives but also in our economic and even scientific lives. The universe is not an all-digital simulation. We must return to reality.

The most extraordinary thing about my experience of publishing on the internet – and I mention it to end this e-mail on an optimistic note – was being able to rework the text whenever I wanted. Although published, the text remained open, and I was able to correct it, to delve deeper with it, to re-sculpt it; I could take into account suggestions and objections, new reading I had done, the thinking I did on my walks in the woods. If my book had been published in hard copy by even the most prestigious of publishers, it would have sat in suspension on the bookstore shelf. On the internet, it remains living and open, and I can continue my daily dialogue with it and its readers. I don't have to wait for my publisher to determine whether sales are brisk enough to warrant a new edition before I can rewrite portions of the text or add chapters.

In light of the hundreds of e-mails that I received, of the freedom I had to be both author and publisher of a book available virtually everywhere at no charge, of the fact that I avoided becoming the author of an out-of-print book or one pulped after a year, I would make the same decision today to publish on the internet. However, I must confess that it is very difficult to inhabit a desert island on the eternal sea of the internet, unless that island is noted on navigators' charts. And while everyone talks about the internet, very few surfers stop to read a book on-line, unless it is a popular serial suspense novel. People's reading habits are still very much grounded in paper, and this makes the absence of an editor and a professional distributor keenly felt.

So I began to dream of a hybrid publisher, one who would want to publish simultaneously on paper and on-line. Wouldn't that be the best of both worlds?

THE RETURN TO EARTH

To navigate, you need a port.

It was a wonderful voyage. But to navigate you need a port. And when all is said and done, a book does not belong on the internet. The two media are in opposition. The internet is a medium of electron flow, a dance floor whirling with multimedia hypertext, inhibiting thought. A book is a comfortable recliner in which to rest the body and awaken the soul. Books require reflection and the critical questioning that freezing a word (like freezing a film frame) allows. The space-time of the internet and that of the book are diametrically opposed. This is why the internet will never kill the book; on the contrary, it celebrates it by its very difference. The internet more resembles an ideographic dance of African masks than linear writing. But it is compelling, and it poses new challenges for twenty-first century artists, who must appropriate it for its vast promise, still unfathomed but unquestionably spellbinding.

I was one of the very first to turn my back on conventional publishers and to issue a previously unpublished book of more than 300 pages on the internet, offering it to readers for free. I am now one of the first to make amends by returning to the cult of the book. The book is a medium of thought, the medium most closely identified with the incubation and transmission of thought. It has an undeniable epistemological value as a generator, accelerator, and distributor of ideas.

While I am now publishing on paper, I have preserved the strategy of writing in small digestible capsules as one would for the internet, capsules that are like traces of the digital experience. In any case, I have recognized that the book once pushed aside oral tradition and is now reclaiming its force and necessity in an era when the acceleration of social time requires our bodies and our minds to move quickly and incessantly, to recognize strings of meaning in an instant.

Media influence each other, but they are not interchangeable. We must cultivate them for their differences and their unique virtues. Painting for painting and not for photography. The internet for connectivity, for the network, for the rapid consumption of information quickly erased. The book for slow-moving and circular reflection.

Since the invention of paper by the Chinese 2,000 years ago, and the invention of print by Gutenberg in 1450, the technology of the book has reached a sort of precious and praise-worthy perfection. Here, then, is a book that has been adrift on the seas of the internet for almost two years and was believed lost. It now returns to port with its cargo of spices, experiences, and extraordinary stories.

0: 11 111 010 001

Fascination with the future is blindness to the present.

A GENTLE, YET BRUTAL, REVOLUTION

Since the invention of the computer a little more than fifty years ago, during World War II, computer technology has made tremendous progress – Moore's law holds that the power of computers doubles every eighteen months. But it wasn't until the mid-1990s that we witnessed the true rise of computers as part of the field of new digital information and communications technology. This technological revolution spread so fast that though we talk about it often, we have already forgotten how a phenomenon of such scope could come about so quickly.

As it is with the development of the computer, the US army is credited with the creation of the internet. In 1969, the Pentagon created the Advanced Research Project Network, or ARPANET, a vast network of interconnected computers – a rhizome, or non-linear and decentralized structure – which was absorbed by NSFNET, a creation of the National Science Foundation, in 1986. The World Wide Web was ushered in with the 1990s, when computer scientist Tim Berners-Lee, working at the Centre européen de recherches nucléaires (CERN) near Geneva and at the Massachusetts Institute of Technology (MIT), developed the first browsers. The world is also indebted to Berners-Lee for the standards that rule communications on the Web: HTTP (hypertext transfer protocol) and HTML (hypertext markup language). In 1991, the commercial use of the internet was permitted, and the appearance of the Mosaic browser in 1993 made the Web more user-friendly; the number of Web servers jumped from 50 to 10,000 in a single year. Since then, the internet has been assigned almost as much space in the media as sports news, creating a sudden public appetite for coverage of the phenomenon.

In the meantime, artists of the 1980s invented multimedia (multi-sensory digital technology) and introduced it to the general public through a number of international exhibitions, among them Montreal's Images du futur (1986–96) – which I organized with Ginette Major, and which attracted more than one million visitors. This new advance offered the possibility of a common language – computer binary language – which interfaced image, movement, and sound, coupled with interactivity and then the internet in 1995. It was a true revolution, and it finally brought multimedia and information and communications technologies (ITC) together.

This technological revolution, in place from the end of the 1990s under the influence of digital convergence, which brought computers, telecommunications, radio, and television closer together, gave rise to countless applications in practically every sphere of human activity – among them scientific and military research, education, cultural industries, entertainment, e-commerce, and telemedicine – clearing the path for numerous technological and commercial innovations and bringing these major markets closer together. A number of multinationals followed the example of AOL, which merged with Time Warner in January 2000 and enthusiastically built its business plans around the convergence of networks and content. Digital shock grew deeper with the appearance of dominant ideologies about the information and knowledge society, central to the concept of the new economy, which was inescapable by the end of the 1990s.

Not only did the new economy supplant the old resource-based economy in just a few years, but it also drew considerable authority from its ability to increase productivity, create employment for skilled labour, and reduce the frequency of cyclical economic crises. Above all, however, it derived power from the rapture over globalization and ultra-liberalism, seen as virtues of digital technology and particularly of the internet. Cyberspace was viewed by its authors as a libertarian, transnational zone, one that circumvented government regulations and controls.

As well, due to an abundance of venture capital, particularly in California, business-based research and development initiatives prompted by the media craze for new digital technologies were financed on the spot and on a large scale. The extraordinary ballooning of the stock market bubble and NASDAQ in turn fed the daily interest of the media at precisely the right moment, during the four years that the digital wave lasted. The collapse of dot.com companies, which were born in this atmosphere of misguided enthusiasm, made it possible to restructure and consolidate the sector quickly, to prepare for a second, more rational phase. It looks as though this second phase will be more enduring.

In analysing this remarkable phenomenon, one characteristic of new digital technologies bears emphasizing: unlike that of natural resources, the expansion of technology is independent of geography or geology. A simple private sector or government decision can see it implemented anywhere – in rundown urban areas, in rural areas, or in the desert of Dubai – by attracting financial and human resources through tax incentives and support for job creation. The example of Ireland, a poor country with no tradition of technology that through proactive policies has become in just a few years one of the largest European ITC hubs, clearly demonstrates this. The same applies to the electronic corridor in Malaysia and Bangalore, India. When it comes to wealthy political entities, we can cite the success of Finland; Quebec, with its policies for multimedia and e-commerce cities; Silicon Alley in New York; Internet City in Dubai; the Electronic Corridor in Malaysia; Cyberport in Hong Kong; Multimedia Valley in Shanghai; International Media Boulevard in Beijing; and Ireland, Israel, and Bavaria, with their proactive policies.

Digital shock is therefore the result of unusual circumstances that in the mid-1990s brought together several variables that had an exponential effect: the expansion of computer technology within the military and universities; the invention of ITCs, and particularly of the internet and the Web; the very fact that the digital realm involved remote communication technologies feeding journalists' and the general public's communication fever; the worship of a seductive, utopian imaginary realm; the creativity of multimedia artists; the emergence of the concepts of the new economy and the information society and of ideas related to globalization and ultra-liberalism. Add to this list the frenzied speculation that attracted billions in venture capital to finance innovations and their implementation and, as a result, the daily interest of the media. It was a historical moment of convergence of technology, the military, the universities, the arts, the media, and the economy, along with speculation and irrational fears – fear of the year 2000 bug sprang up immediately among professionals and the general public.

As spectacular and brutal as this digital technology revolution has been, and while its scope is increasing every day, we must remember that in 2001 still only 6 per cent of the world was using the internet. This revolution has created, by virtue of its suddenness and its acceleration, a profound crisis of structures, ideas, and values in wealthy countries and a formidable technological apartheid in developing ones.

CYBERPRIMITIVES

A modernist, futurist revolution? By all appearances yes, since it is based on the heady growth of techno-science, but paradoxically it conveys the most primitive imaginings of the human spirit. We see ourselves as modern beings who have shed primitive mythologies, cannibalism, and black magic. As the children of reason and positivism who have quelled the mumbo-jumbo of the barbarian hordes. As the inventors of a powerful world of science, as capable of beating back foolish alchemy and the superstitions of the Middle Ages and of liberating humanity from its shackles. But what do we actually see around us?

More and more people sport rings in their noses and ears, studs in their tongues and navels, chains on their ankles, wild hairstyles and tattoos of primeval motif. They dance like primitives to the trance-like rhythms of rave and techno music and ingest hallucinogenic drugs. Even adults play at Robinson Crusoe in successful films and reality TV series, or regress to paradise on earth at Club Med. Science fiction films transport us to strangely archaic space-times where good and evil face off on the outskirts of primitive chaos, while under George W. Bush the US builds a space shield and a cybersurveillance satellite network to protect against the forces of evil. Even science invents big bangs that evoke primitive chaos. Video games are the roaming grounds of hordes of devious dragons, dinosaurs, and monsters – players do battle with them like Saint Michael the Archangel versus the demon. We thus find ourselves in a new sort of Middle Ages.

Warlike acts are committed between the tribes of Africa, Asia, the Middle East, and even Europe. Criminal gang members favour studded jackets and embrace a primitive aesthetic of brutal neo-Gothic imagery. The new savages rule the desolate inner cities, and armed gangs control trade in underground parking lots or take hostages and kill peasants and tourists in the Philippines, Colombia, Indonesia, Central Africa, and Asia. Religious freaks and members of the Taliban blow up Buddhas, burn books, and destroy women's jewellery. Islamic fundamentalist kamikazes blow up Arabian markets, mosques, and New York's World Trade Center, whereas fundamentalists of the American Midwest blow up government buildings, kill doctors, and outlaw the teaching of Darwinian evolutionism in schools; others, in Israel and the Arab countries, carry out assassinations in the context of holy wars. In America, young video game addicts orchestrate massacres in their schools, and cocooning enthusiasts hide out in their homes as if in caves, with their fridges, their barbecues, and their guns. Cults are multiplying – worshippers of the sun, fire, life, nature, and mythical gods and goddesses commit mass suicide to become one with the objects of their devotion.

We have lived through the great scares of the year 2000, the big crash and the computer viruses, mad sheep and mad cow, GMOs and global warming – it's reminiscent of the six biblical plagues. All that's missing is the Flood, or its nuclear equivalent. Add to all of this the imaginary economy, the exploitation of the destitute by the powerful, and modern-day enslavement.

FIRST PARADOXICAL LAW
The regression of the human psyche is proportionate to the advance of technological power.

There are also those who preach a return to the source, to natural foods, to ocean paradises; they practise the cult of the body, body-building for men and women, violent combat sports, extreme sports, and adventure tourism. Ice hotels and dogsled races, underwater exploration, and nudism are de rigueur.

Artists echo this neo-primitivism. Stelarc harnesses himself naked to digital technologies and suspends himself in the void with cables, needles stuck into his skin; Spencer Tunick invites thousands of ordinary people to undress and lie down, naked as primitives, side by side on city asphalt; Bériou hides out like a troglodyte in a cave in the middle of France and creates complex computer animations. Museum officials glorify the primary arts.

I, for one, am tired of the discourse of Parisian intellectuals, which is often as sophisticated and academic as it is hollow. These individuals decadently speak for the sake of speaking and engage in turf wars between small local tribes. In order to escape all this, I came to the new world, to a place where an idea is only as good as what it delivers. As Freud amply demonstrated, the human soul is primitive. Jung worked in an old stone dwelling with no running water or electricity – all the better to find the path of our dark archetypes.

All of this suggests a law that could be formulated as follows: The more technology flaunts the power of humankind, the greater the divide between the obvious progress of technology and the regression of the imagination.

The paradox of neo-primitivism is that it manifests itself strongly at the very moment when techno-science prevails. And we discover that neo-primitivism is intrinsically tied to this scientific and technological revolution marked by the digital realm precisely because technology is progressing much faster than our consciousness. More and more, the meaning of the world escapes us. This scares us, excites the darkest drives of our imagination, awakens our demons. The twenty-first century is not a new Renaissance, but rather a second Middle Ages.

After the Stone Age, the Fire Age, and the Iron Age comes the Silicon and Digital Age. A new civilization is taking shape before our eyes that draws an incredible amount of power from the most primitive language we can conceive of: binary code (1 and 0). It is heralded as the knowledge society, and some do see it as the new Renaissance. I, however, believe that the industrial boom of the nineteenth and twentieth centuries gave a new lease on life to the Renaissance, but the present-day digital revolution is actually a second Middle Ages. I will therefore try to shed some light on the challenges of the imaginary realm of digital language, the unconscious mythologies of the dominant middle classes, and the return to magical thinking that techno-science promotes.

Faced with the dangers of this new loss of meaning, we perceive an urgent need to develop a critical philosophy of the digital in relation to the dominant ideologies and the imagination of the middle classes, a philosophy that will allow us to rethink the foundations of our humanism.

WHERE IS THE WORLD GOING? TOWARDS THE YEAR 3000

Why has the future become the imaginary space onto which we project our lives? Where do we stand between the myth of creation and the myth of the future? Who will write the metaphysics of the future? A thousand years on a human scale is beyond the limits of our foresight and imagination. Yet, on the scale of the universe, counted in billions of years, it's a blip. (The first traces of life on our planet are estimated to be 3,400 million years old.)

Our present is a mix of achievement and frustration – in other words, a blend of projects through which we express our desire for more complete happiness and relief from suffering. The best cannot be accomplished in the past, which is why we situate it in the future. The life force that drives us, coupled with our imagination, perpetually spawns new hope, even though history teaches us to look at such hope realistically. How do we understand our current values and the loss of meaning that afflicts us? How do we think about good, evil, and the choices we must make? How do we judge our desire for power critically when time is slipping away from us? We erase the past, we deny the present, and we project ourselves into the future.

AUDACITY

Imagine Christopher Columbus's audacity in asking Isabelle and Ferdinand d'Aragon to endorse the idea that the earth is round rather than flat, flying in the face of everyday experience. And his audacity in wanting to reach the East Indies via the west. And imagine Magellan's audacity in asking Charles Quint to equip ships to sail even greater distances and risking his life to demonstrate that the earth was round through other means: returning to Spain after circumnavigating the globe. The native's poison arrow that killed him on his return trip was not enough to stop the march of time. This great three-year intercontinental sail voyage foreshadowed the audacity of the interplanetary expeditions to Mars, and even more distant destinations, that preoccupy us five centuries later.

THE EARTH SEEMS FLAT ONCE MORE

At the dawn of the third millennium, the world seems more mundane than ever. The earth once again seems flat. Money rules with an iron fist. Accounting computers, commerce and profit, data banks, statistics and quantitative analyses, pragmatism and realism are all subtle tyrants. Poetry no longer sells. But on closer examination, we recognize that irrationality is the incontrovertible master that we must unmask and name. Despite the simplistic, trivial aspect of our mundane world, and despite the unimaginative logic of the material, irrationality breaks out, bursts through the cracks in the dominant discourse of accounting. The social imagination, often the craziest or the most ingenious, spreads everywhere – sometimes even more so in science, business, and the economy than in the arts.

THE DAWN OF A NEW ERA

From revolution to revolution – the Stone Age, the Fire Age, the Iron Age, Gutenberg, Copernicus, the age of electricity, the age of silicon and computer technology – we have believed ourselves part of a revolution that would transform the human adventure. What luck, we say, to have been born at just the right moment in thousands of years of evolution! At the risk of sounding naive myself, I will say that I have no doubt that we are currently at the dawn of a new civilization and that the advent of digital logic and technology is a much more significant revolution than that which followed from the invention of printing. We are entering a new age of humanity: the digital age.

Some maintain that the major inventions and discoveries of the nineteenth century – electricity and the locomotive, the electric ignition engine, chemical transformation industries, antibiotics – had considerable influence on human life and evolution. They also maintain that the new economy of knowledge and computer technology does not hold as much sway as we think and does not call into question the extraordinary power of the old economy. Even the growth in productivity that we attribute to digital technologies seems inferior to the growth that the new processing industries brought about at the beginning of the twentieth century. But those who make this argument are focusing on debatable details and are ignoring the radical paradigm shift that is occurring within the digital realm, a shift that involves much more than adjustments of varying degrees: in the digital realm, our vision, our understanding of the world, our *Weltanschauung* have completely changed, reverberating in our referential values, the way we think, our sensitivities, the way we act, our very humanism.

SECOND PARADOXICAL LAW
Though it appears in gentle guise, the digital revolution has unleashed a radical and brutal force due to its suddenness, its acceleration, its globalizing logic, and the immediacy of its expansion into all fields of activity.

We are experiencing a change in mentality and civilization that is much faster, more brutal, more extensive, and more radical than the rupture of the Renaissance during the quattrocento. Admittedly, the technological revolution has not been bloody. It even seems gentle and rational. But its spread to all human activities is so rapid that in the end it is violent. Its power is said to double every eighteen months, and its effectiveness is such that in all realms of activity – war, science, industry, commerce, art, imagination, politics, private life, and so on – it is profoundly transforming our world forever. For each one of us and for every realm of activity there is a decision to be made: to be or not to be digital. Computer technology imposes a new set of rules. Everyone feels compelled to adopt these rules, the same universal language, the same logic, and the same equipment – whether they be inhabitants of Buddhist India or puritan, capitalist America, members of the mafia or bank employees, scientific researchers, architects, urban planners, teachers, artists, defenders of the environment, military personnel, farmers, airplane pilots, anarchists, protesters, multinationals, democrats, or terrorists.

Computer technology is radical, boundless, omnipresent, immediate. It became pervasive suddenly in the 1990s after four or five decades of incubation and limited sector-specific applications. Its arrival caused heavy turbulence in the realms of stock market speculation and government policy-making, in our private lives, and, above all, in our imaginations.

While computer technology is beyond the reach of more than 90 per cent of the world's population, it nevertheless indirectly imposes its law on even the poorest of human societies. No one escapes it for long. With the help of software and satellites, it can monitor everything that moves or communicates on our planet (witness the famous American spy system Echelon).

Combined with biology, computer technology has become the biotic to decode the book of life – the human genome itself. Who will go higher? Who will do better? Or worse? Digital shock is making itself felt. Digital civilization has barely begun and it is already her-alding its unyielding power and the inevitable transformation of our lives and our destinies.

A PHENOMENON UNPRECEDENTED IN THE HISTORY OF HUMANITY

It is important to understand the scope of the phenomenon of new communication technologies at the dawn of the third millennium. Close to 100 million Americans were connected to the internet in 2000, a number that apparently doubled within a year, which represents half the computer population in the United States. In Canada, more than four million households were on-line in 1998, 25 per cent more than in 1997. It is an explosive phenomenon. The internet is becoming a mass media while remaining a self media; this dual vocation is no doubt one of the keys to its success. This unique new phenomenon is therefore most likely destined for global success. In five years, revenue from the internet has caught up with that of the automobile industry, an industry that has been in existence for 100 years.

> **THIRD PARADOXICAL LAW**
> Digital technologies evolve more quickly than our ideas.

Unfortunately, technology progresses faster than our ideas. The revolution has left our consciousness lagging, the cathode ray screen inhibits our critical faculties, the dance of electronic icons has cast a spell over us, and errant intellectuals suggest that we call this loss of meaning "post-humanism." They see this loss of critical judgment and control as promising a bright future for connective intelligence.

Our era has developed and worships a totalizing and almost totalitarian technological utopia that promises the moon: a cyber–

El Dorado. This utopia lets us dream. It blinds us to all of life's other values and to other possible scenarios of the human journey. Technological utopia has become a dominant ideology, with all that that implies, particularly the alienation of the spirit, the exercise of power by dominant forces, and the exploitation of the dominated.

A CRITICAL FASCINATION

And yet the human spirit is not the extension of shareware, nor is it a computing machine. We can be fascinated by the dawn of a civilization without renouncing our critical spirit or delegating responsibility for our future to software and artificial intelligence. The digital realm therefore induces fascination, and philosophy tries to respond to it with a specific mode of thinking that Salvador Dali might have called "critical fascination." We have to let our-selves be swept along by the tidal wave of new technologies if we are to understand the fever, the innovation, the acceleration, the utopian hopes; we must size up the newness of the phenomenon before our minds can turn to using its faculty of critical distancing and philosophical questioning. I have met philosophers who understand what's at stake in this revolution but who rave about the digital world to the point of losing the very critical spirit they take pride in, who become the ecstatic cantors of the digital world. And I have also met many intellectuals who rant impotently against a revolution that they sullenly look in on from the outside, unwilling to relinquish the protective shell of convictions they acquired in the previous era. Conservatives, afraid of any change that puts their values into question, snarl instinctively like the watchdog who knows nothing about the stranger at the garden gate. But bad-tempered and reactionary objections will soon be wiped out by the breaking digital wave. You have to surf the wave to understand.

1: A Yo-yo Universe

After 500 years of effort to build a realistic image
of the universe, the creation of a contemporary digital simulacrum
marks a return to an idealistic interpretation of the world.

We have never taken reality very seriously. We have always doubted its ontological density. We have consistently substituted reality with belief and behaviour based on magical, religious, and now digital and virtual thought. Four main periods mark the history of humanity. The first is the so-called primitive or primary period. Under the influence of animism, this era narrowed the gap between the sacred and the profane, unifying humans with nature and the mysterious forces that drive it. In order to act effectively on the world, these polytheistic forces had to be appealed to through magical techniques.

POLARIZED DUALISM

Plato conceived of a dualistic universe. The myth of the cave values the eidos, concepts, pure ideas, and idealism, an elsewhere compared to which the real world we perceive is merely illusory, a shadow, an imitation, a pale and imperfect reflection of pure ideas. The wise man must turn away from the real world to contemplate the true world of pure ideas. While the primary universe tied the here and the elsewhere in an animist and naturalist vision of the universe, Plato's idealistic philosophy opposed an idealized elsewhere to a devalued here and now. The dualism was polarized from its beginnings.

This second period in the history of humanity opened the door to monotheistic religions – Judaism, Christianity, or Islam – based on a dualistic opposition between a devalued real world (a vale of misery from which one must avert one's gaze) and a transcendental idealized elsewhere (paradise, perfection). Humanity depends on this transcendental elsewhere, the world of God who created the earth and life. Our salvation lies in the divine. Sacred books explain how the world was created and lay down the values we must hold. We call on God to act on the world. And artists represent this transcendental universe in icons and stained glass so that we can contemplate the transcendental and forget the inferior world into which we are born.

In its own way, Buddhism also contrasts a negation of the real (or apparently real) world with an idealized elsewhere, a fusing light that we can attain when we escape our fallen world. Nirvana.

THE INVENTION OF HUMANISM AND REALISM

The third period that marks human history begins with the quattrocento. The new spirit that emerged during the Italian Renaissance was supported by the Catholic Church, which wanted to humanize religion to combat both the rise of atheism and Cathari heresy. The Church promoted the image of Christ – and God made man – and it commissioned works by artists who wanted to portray a more realistic image of the world. This change in attitude found expression in the invention of geometrical perspective, which represented the real world in three dimensions, through the realism of faces, through shadows of objects and people, through the development of science and technology and experimental medicine as opposed to alchemy, and through esteem for work as opposed to the leisure of the aristocracy. Freud would say that it was the revenge of the principle of reality after a prolonged imaginary escape to the beyond.

This evolution of the Western world brings us to the Encyclopedists of the end of the eighteenth century. But realism is as difficult to construct and sustain philosophically as deism and the belief in a transcendental elsewhere. Realism did not take hold without challenges, without faltering. Philosophers such as Immanuel Kant questioned the ontological nature of reality, imposing on it a priori forms of sensibility. After Kant, realism limited itself to a world of phenomenal appearances.

The nineteenth century was the moment for the affirmation of realism in painting, literature, music, experimental sciences, and the technical arts. Photography, with its objectivity, had pretensions of deposing painting. It was the era of Courbet's painting *The Origin of the World*, which reduced the sacred myth to a realistic and provocative exhibition of the female genitalia. Balzac and Zola brought triumph to realist literature. Then Impressionism emerged, setting itself apart from Realism and favouring the energy created by coloured light over form, even though its preferred subjects were entirely realistic: the outdoors and day-to-day life. Symbolism marked a new anti-realist opposition. Futurism offered a dynamic vision of realism, denying matter in the name of energy and speed. Cubism, in turn, made the vision relative. And the invention of abstract art drew us into metaphysical and introspective languages that opposed all realism. Surrealism also devalued realism, reconstructing elements of reality under the guise of dream. It re-polarized our vision into two worlds, the inferior world of reality, and the unconscious, a superior dreamlike world that governs our relationship with reality.

The de-realization of art would follow – the rejection of art as the production of objects, the assertion of conceptual art against the new realism, launched by Pierre Restany, or pop art, which evoked American consumer society; then hyperrealism, inspired by photography, would mount its attack.

THE END OF REALISM

Realism's moment in the history of painting was brief. Its birth prompted a proliferation of anti-realist movements. It is as though people had a hard time trusting it and taking it seriously. Can this be attributed to our capacity for dreaming? Or to our very real frustrations? We are endlessly seeking to elude reality. We seem incapable of considering it a more important point of reference – more dense and attractive – than the imaginary, the symbolic, or the religious.

THE SUPERIOR WORLD OF NUMBERS

With the quiet revolution of computer technology at the end of the twentieth century, we witnessed the extremely rapid deployment of a new transcendental world: the digital replica of the real world. Since time immemorial, we have sought to escape from the real world and have been on a quest for the ideal, the absolute; we have aspired to the perfection, beauty, and intelligence of another, far more vivid world. We have devoted ourselves to a poetic reverie, like the great mathematicians and apostles of digital languages. Since the Greeks, numerology has been a sort of religion; many fervently believe in superstitions about numbers such as 1, 3, 7, 9, 13, and 69. Realism was hardly a major preoccupation of early or modern mathematicians.

Contemporary computer mathematicians devote themselves to developing a new, unreal, virtual universe that gathers information about the real world to form a computer language and that substitutes itself for the real universe. This noosphere of shared intelligence is presented as the end result of creation – the mundane world seems trivial and reality-challenged by comparison. And this replica becomes our scientific, technological, and economic field of activity, the site of our explorations and, of course, our imaginings, rituals, cultural creations, games and entertainment, teaching – our most important intellectual and financial investments. The real world takes on a negative value, the digital world a positive value. The polarization of dualism has been inverted once again.

The digital simulacra did not come about by chance. It is the unremitting return of the unrealism or idealism that has dominated the history of humanity since its beginnings. During the quattrocento, the transcendental world of the Middle Ages, with its haloed gods and sky-blue and gold backgrounds, was abandoned. After a so-called realist period that lasted some 500 years, we are returning to a new universe that is just as transcendental: the digital universe, which is increasingly ideologically valued, to the detriment of the real world, under the aegis of the new gods of science and technology.

The digital metaphor that computers are building to give us control over and describe reality, or rather to construct it through computer binary language, has imposed itself at the expense of the world of matter.

THE DIGITAL SIMULACRA

The digital simulacra that is sucking us in is simply a new interpretation of the world, but it is the dominant and essential interpretation of our time. It is operational, and it monopolizes the field of expression and activity of the soul: art, science, the economy, politics and social issues, education and communication, television, film and music, and even a supposed post-humanism. This is a new challenge, not just for artists, but for researchers and for philosophers, who question religion and its extravagance, realism and its substance, and who must now question the feverish excesses and the abuse of power to which this new interpretation of the universe give rise. It is not at all a sullen and negative philosophy; it is precisely the opposite – a philosophy that is open to the world and the human journey. Contemporary science is very much a stakeholder in the creation of the *Weltanschauung* of the twenty-first century – at least as much, if not more so than art.

A new paradox needs to be highlighted here: digital technology, born from techno-science and tied to the facilitation of communication, management, commerce, and the economy through its simplistic binary code, has given flight to a transcendental imagination that suggests a new avatar of magic, religion, and transcendental idealism. The digital realm, which poses as an objective, realistic, and demystifying approach to the world and as a mundane form of individual management, is in fact going down in the history of humanity as a return to the irrational, which could be seen as a backward step. This is even more paradoxical since the digital realm heralds itself as a movement obsessed with the future and the unknown.

FOURTH PARADOXICAL LAW
The digital realm, which presents itself as a realistic, utilitarian, and futuristic approach to the world, is in fact a new manifestation of traditional transcendental idealism.

THE LURE OF THE CATHODE RAY

Technological utopia is engrossing, and, like religion, it could take us far (for better or for worse), depending on the use we make of new technologies. We cannot let ourselves be hypnotized by this replica and pass through the looking glass, or take as real and for granted the promises of the new El Dorado.

Neither must we let ourselves fall into the naive illusion of a new religion à la Teilhard de Chardin and start to believe in the cyberculmination of the divine creation of the universe by cyborgs. We must instead rethink critical humanism and update it, taking into consideration the meaning that humankind can bring to these powerful new technologies. We should not allow ourselves to be seduced by the post-humanism that some hope and pray for and that would literally be meaningless, even a return to barbarism. If post-humanism invites us to bow down before the logic and the power of technology, it is absurd – quite simply, a statement of non-thought. It is high time that we question this celebration of a new barbarian magic and develop a philosophical and critical analytical schema that takes into account these new technological challenges and gives them meaning. Nonsense can only be catastrophic with the deployment of the incredible power of digital technologies to come.

2: Artificial Intelligence and Living Computers

Has a 2 been introduced in the series of 1s and 0s?

The first calculating machine – the abacus – dates back a long way and is attributed to the Chinese. Pascal and Leibniz, among many others, also imagined such devices. But it was British mathematician Alan Turing who, at the beginning of World War II, first had the idea of a machine that would process not only numbers but also information – the automatic computing engine, which he saw as an artificial brain. And history should also tip its hat to German engineer Konrad Zuse, who developed the first mechanical brain at around the same time, in 1941. His Z3 calculator was as big as a wardrobe and could calculate square roots. The result appeared on a panel of small light bulbs. At the time, it was hard to imagine what this invention could be used for, and Zuse's patent application, filed in 1936, was turned down in 1967.

In 1943, the American army mandated two engineers from the University of Pennsylvania, John Mauchly and Presper Eckert, to develop an electronic calculator for ballistics calculations. Baptized ENIAC, the thirty-tonne monster, which filled an entire room and consisted of almost 18,000 vacuum tubes, was unveiled to the public in 1946. For each operation, instructions were given to the machine by activating some of the more than 6,000 switches. Then John von Neumann designed the principles of programming and programs capable of making decisions without going through a human operator. The first true computer, EDVAC, ushered in the era of computing.

In *Cybernetics* (1948), Norbert Wiener extrapolates the theoretical underpinnings of an operational mathematical logic and takes on the more complex notions of feedback and circularity, the manipulation of the world through information, and programmed objectives or teleology. Thus the founder of cybernetics envisaged the global nature of the computing vision. The extraordinary history of the development of computing, of its acceleration, its paradoxes, and its illusions had just begun; at the time, no one anticipated the current omnipresence of computer technology.

KAREL CAPEK

The idea of robots, which draws on both tales of cunning genies and the horror of slavery, took shape with Czech playwright Karel Capek's *RUR* (1920). Capek invented androids devoted to work. Since then, the sorcerer's apprentice in us has devised robots with artificial intelligence, potentially capable of becoming autonomous, and indeed even more powerful than humans. The idea gathered steam and became the myth of human superpowers – or the nightmare of computer superpowers.

Artificial intelligence was born. "Since this man had become a mechanism," writes Alfred Jarry in *The Supermale*, "the equilibrium of the world required that another mechanism should manufacture ... a soul."[1] And therein lies one of the other paradoxes of the digital realm.

DEEP BLUE

While the concept of artificial intelligence dates back to the 1950s, it was only in 1997 that it took hold as a symbol in the minds of the public with the victory of an IBM computer named Deep Blue over world chess champion Garry Kasparov. In 2001, Vladimir Kramnik, a new international chess champion, took up the challenge, this time against Deep Fritz, a computer capable of analysing four million moves per second. Shortly before the battle, he said, "Chess is not simply a question of calculations, which is why human beings have a chance against computers. I hope computers don't develop intuition, because if they did, we wouldn't stand a chance."

Of course, the computer programmers who had devoted four years to perfecting the Deep Fritz program had no doubt that the machine would prevail. And for the organizer, Brain Games Network, this match represented "the last chance for human intelligence to assert its superiority over the computing machine." The last chance? It's doubtful.

In the meantime, endless popular fantasies about the power of computers were spun. The year 1968 saw the release of Stanley Kubrick's *2001: A Space Odyssey* (written by Kubrick and Arthur C. Clarke), in which the central character, HAL 9000, a thinking computer, leads the action and becomes psychotic after its programming is corrupted. Since then, computers that in the 1970s were called fifth generation have been identified by a number of gurus and prophets as servants created to simplify our lives, make our beds, cook, clean, keep us company, advise us, or read us a book. And the year 2001 is already in the past ...

MARVIN LEE MINSKY

Marvin Lee Minsky, one of the first thinkers in the area of artificial intelligence, predicted that computers would one day be capable of learning on their own, and that their capacity for thought would be unlimited.

How can we human beings, who know almost nothing of our own thought processes and for whom the brain itself is a mystery, design such a powerful thinking machine? We are driven to do so by the dreams of power that haunt us and that have been fuelled by a few initially quite modest and incomplete achievements in computing. The fantasies created by the accelerating power of the computer have become faster and more promising than computing itself.

COMPUTERS MORE POWERFUL THAN THE HUMAN MIND IN 2020

Ray Kurzweil, author of *The Age of Intelligent Machines* (1990), shows us the potential of the imaginary realm of an inventive mind when it can give free rein to its euphoria over artificial intelligence. His book *The Age of Spiritual Machines* (1999) – subtitled *When Computers Exceed Human Intelligence* – goes one step further with the observation of the exponential acceleration of computer technology. Kurzweil points out that the speed of computers doubled every three years at first, then every two years in the 1960s, and that it now doubles every eighteen months; he believes that computers will match the speed and the power of the human mind by 2020. From this point on, computers will have a sense of humour, will express their own opinions, emotions, and wishes, and demonstrate the same qualities as human thought. Each will have its own personality and its own goals and projects. Your computer could say to you, for example, "I feel lonely and I'm bored. Please keep me company."[2] Arthur C. Clarke, upon the publication of his new novel *The Light of Other Days* and shortly before the dawn of 2001 – the year associated with his famous *Space Odyssey* – said that he subscribed to Kurzweil's prediction and believed that by 2020 the computer would have surpassed the intellectual capacities of human beings.

Kurzweil pointed to the law formulated in 1965 by Gordon Moore, the inventor of the integrated circuit and president of Intel, which held that the size of a transistor should shrink by 50 per cent every twelve months. And we are in fact witnessing a phenomenal miniaturization of transistors. Are the greatest prophets of the future being overly optimistic? At the very least, they are predicting major upheavals.

PHOTONIC CHIPS, ATOMIC TRANSISTORS, QUANTUM WELLS, MOLECULAR AND CHEMICAL COMPUTERS

Photonic chips should make the super-miniaturization of microprocessors possible. By the end of the twentieth century, we had already built transistors the size of a few dozen atoms. Using X-rays, we have succeeded in photolithographing microprocessors on silicon, integrating millions and soon billions of transistors. As well, researchers at Indiana University claim that, thanks to quantum well technique, the quantum computer, which combines the 1 and the 0 of binary code in qubits, could perform requested operations using light and move just a few electrons rather than thousands of them, making calculations infinitely faster.

Researchers at Hewlett Packard are working on chemical microprocessors, futuristic circuits that would multiply the performance of current processes by 1,000 per cent.[3] As a result, we can envisage computers that not only possess extraordinary processing speed and power but also function entirely through a voice interface and manage large multimedia files of image and sound sequences instantaneously.

BLUE GENE

At the end of 1999, IBM announced work on a new computer called Blue Gene, which would be 1,000 times more powerful than Deep Blue (the computer that beat Kasparov) and forty times more powerful than the forty most powerful existing computers combined. It would be able to process a million billion operations a second, with a million processors each performing a billion operations a second.

Blue Gene would generate so much heat that it would require a turbine the size of a jet engine to cool it. But it would be able to simulate the formation of proteins in the human body. The goal? To reach the speed of human metabolism so as to better penetrate the secrets of the human brain and sexuality, as well as to cure a range of illnesses. However, it would take the machine a year or more of uninterrupted processing to analyse a single protein. (Almost 40,000 proteins have been identified, as have some 3.1 billion combinations that enter into the makeup of the genetic code.)

According to Agence France-Presse, an IBM executive predicted that one day people who visit their doctor's office will have a sample of their tissue analysed by a computer capable of determining the cause of their illness; the computer will instantly prescribe the most appropriate treatment based on the patient's genetic combination. This computer, inaugurated in 2005, occupies eighty square metres and stand two metres high.

THE SUPERHUMAN COMPUTER
AND THE SEMANTIC WEB

Prophecies of the superhuman power of artificial intelligence – a concept revisited by IBM in its 1999 ads – partake of the same dream of power that predicted artificial moons for the year 2000. These concepts gratify the market and humankind; they push us to conquer ourselves and the universe; they embody a myth that today seems written on our genes but that would have had no meaning in traditional societies based on vertical or cyclical social time.

The new ambition of Tim Berners-Lee, the inventor of the World Wide Web, is to create a semantic metaweb. His idea, which requires tremendously complex computer processing, involves introducing an artificial brain into the chaos of the Web. His proposal is to attribute hidden codes to key words that display on Web pages to make it possible for computers to instantly decode information that is significant for search engines. Thus, computers could intelligently process information that circulates on the Web and provide us with better access to it.

THE MAGICAL LAW OF THE EXPONENTIAL ACCELERATION OF TIME

Ray Kurzweil dares to compare the rhythm of the evolution of life with computing. From this fanciful amalgam, he derives no less than the Law of Time and Chaos and the Law of Accelerating Returns as Applied to an Evolutionary Process. His analysis leads him to conclude that "evolution builds on its own increasing order. Therefore, in an evolutionary process, order increases exponentially."[4]

Once he has stated these grand laws based on confusion between vital and social processes and on the extrapolation of a bit of, I grant you, spectacular data from the computer industry, Kurzweil harbours no doubt – nor do many Americans, judging from the press accolades and the commercial success of his books – that the year 2020 will be a historical one. It will be the year that computers catch up to human intelligence. From that point on, they will surpass it at an exponential rate.

THE GOOD DIGITAL NEWS ACCORDING TO RAY KURZWEIL

Kurzweil maintains that in order to exceed human capacity and the limits of neural networks, evolution will create human beings capable of inventing a technology a million times faster than the neurons of mammals, which are made up of carbon and extremely slow compared to their infinitely more flexible and faster electronic equivalent.

Kurzweil seems convinced that this is good news, and that artificial intelligence will overcome its last obstacle: biological evolution. Talk about your digital shock! Are we to conclude that the world will become more intelligent? Should people worship this superior intelligence and submit to it for their own good? How will they face the challenge of taming it? Will they have to fight the great central computer that tries to enslave them? Kurzweil's naively optimistic fervour would have us transformed into happy cyborgs.

LIVING COMPUTERS

At the same time, however, in a reverse scenario, researchers at the Institute for Neuronal Computation and the Institute for Non-linear Science of the University of California in San Diego recognize the limits of computer binary logic and are working to surpass them by drawing on the neural feats of life.

Since 1994, researchers from the University of Southern California, joined later by researchers from the University of Wisconsin in Madison, have been working on DNA computers.[5] Their work is based on the fact that DNA operates according to a language with four terms, which is therefore more complex than the binary language of computers, and they want to exploit the remarkable computing and combinatory capacities of the DNA genes using chemical impulses. This state-of-the-art technology involves using biochips, or DNA chips, each of which can hold 10,000 genes per square centimetre, and following the appearance or disappearance of these genes according to a stimulus that determines their respective roles. Biophotonics also contributes to the construction of virtual models of proteins and then to verifying their biological existence – a bit like in astrophysics, where calculations make it increasingly possible to formulate hypotheses about the existence of invisible celestial bodies, the presence of which can be confirmed afterward with very powerful telescopes.

William Ditto, head of the Applied Chaos Lab at the University of Georgia in Atlanta, is among those developing the neurocomputer, or living computer, which integrates living neurons from leeches into computer chips. He believes that the best means to surpass the limits of current computing is a hybrid system, one that combines the living with the artificial, making it possible to introduce a non-linear dynamic capable of taking into account the problem of chaos that binary systems cannot process. Ditto combines methods of using the computer to stimulate living tissue, in particular from the heart and the brain, with non-linear oscillators, which, according to him, build models of intelligence and manipulation of biological systems. By doing so, he hopes to achieve an infinitely greater processing capacity and ability to take into account the complexity of real phenomena, even fuzzy logic, than linear and binary electronic models could ever offer.

Ditto believes that computers perform certain calculations better and faster than the human brain, and the human brain performs certain logical operations better than the computer. A synthesis of the two – in other words, of the geometric mind and the subtle mind – through neurons and binary microprocessors should create an unparalleled capacity for processing and intelligence. This is no small ambition: "Ordinary computers need absolutely correct information every time to come to the right answer. We hope a biological computer will come to the correct answer based on partial information, by filling in the gaps itself."[6] Ditto has still only succeeded in performing additions, but he hopes to create a new generation of computers – leech-ulators capable of thinking for themselves, because the living neurons they contain will be able to make their own connections spontaneously, something which is beyond the scope of computing. Therein lies the difference between the power of the living and the limits of the artificial.

The most astonishing thing is that, on the one hand, Ditto is trying to increase the power of binary computers using a few leech neurons (which are difficult to keep alive, given the heat computers generate), while on the other hand, human beings – with their millions of neurons – are destined to be supplanted within a single generation by faster computers (as Kurzweil would have it). Such a glaring contradiction invites caution. On one side is reliance on the power of nature to surpass computing; on the other is disdain for nature and the claim that the supreme value of technology will take over from life when (in 2020) it reaches the limits of its abilities. We are living in a fantasy world of science and logic.

Of course, we have moved very far afield from the critical spirit that, according to French philosopher Gaston Bachelard, must prevail over the advance of science. In fact, science and technology are increasingly intertwined, and science is not so much a search for the truth as a will to power.

It is remarkable to see the faith that computer technology utopians, educated in mathematics, have in the idea that computers will one day be able to integrate all the data from reality or life – to recombine, predict, or transform all the possible parameters and scenarios of evolution. But the world is not a chess game; it is not a math textbook. Scientific researchers more modest and less naive than Ray Kurzweil recognize its complexity and find it increasingly intricate.

THE MYTH OF ARTIFICIAL INTELLIGENCE

The myth of artificial intelligence assumes that computer technology will be able to factor in and process everything we know about reality. Without this assumption, AI could not lay claim to the power to surpass human thought.

The myth of artificial intelligence pushed to its limit runs headlong into major philosophical problems. It implies that the world can be reduced to algorithms – in other words, to mathematical language capable of translating all natural languages. Natural languages, which are closely tied to social structures, the collective imagination, and the emotions, and which express subtle nuances, will not be overtaken and deposed by binary or even ternary series of computer language. It is terribly presumptuous, if not naive, to maintain that the computer will one day produce a universal and objective language, free of all idiosyncrasy, symbolism, ambiguity, and fantasy, of all desire, magic, and will to power, of all the noise of social communication – in short, a language entirely appropriate for the reality of the world, one that would render the world as it is and that would make it possible for us to understand and dominate the universe. We know, of course, that each language contains an image of the world, that there are as many cosmogonies, or theories of the origin of the universe, as there are natural languages. Even the most mathematical of linguists has never dared such a pretension. You would have to believe that God is a mathematician who programmed the world using IBM and Microsoft computer languages.

FIFTH PARADOXICAL LAW
Once again, human intelligence is inclined to devalue itself and to renounce its own abilities in favour of a supposedly superior intelligence – this time around, the so-called artificial intelligence of the digital realm.

It seems a constant of the human spirit throughout history to gauge its own limits – a remarkable indication of its modesty – and to relinquish its ability to understand the world to a superior intelligence. We invent this intelligence so that we can worship it and call on its infinite wisdom – a dangerous alienation of that very spirit.

Over the course of the millennia, we have given ourselves over to the forces of nature, to magic, to gods and their whims, to religion, to a single god, and – today – to an artificial intelligence that is supposedly superior and capable of transforming us into infinitely powerful cyborgs. One exception seems to prove the rule: the French Encyclopedists' celebration of reason at the end of the eighteenth century. But, to the great displeasure of the skeptics, it took the French Revolution to build a new cult out of it – the cult of the goddess of reason, founder of Western positivism – and to give it legitimacy.

We could also no doubt use our awareness of the limits of our own understanding and our recognition of our inability to unravel the reasons for our universe and our existence to explain our constant tendency to dream of a superior intelligence shaped in our own image, but infinitely more powerful – the provider of the meaning of life, what we need in order to escape absurdity and despair.

In *Artificial Intelligence: AI* (2001), a science fiction film by Steven Spielberg based on a synopsis by Stanley Kubrick, we meet David, a robot programmed to love adoptive parents and to be loved in return; the robot succeeds in this until the parents re-establish contact with Martin, their real son, who has come back to life. Skilfully tugging at the heartstrings and revisiting themes already addressed in *ET*, Spielberg reminds us of the limits of robots and artificial intelligence compared with emotions and human intelligence. And this bears underlining when the reminder is futuristic and comes from a mind as well-informed, passionate, and taken up with technology and dreams of the future as Spielberg's.

3: The Digital Metaphor for the World

The world has become more cyber than real.

IS THE WORLD A SOFTWARE APPLICATION?

Contemporary humanity is busy creating a veritable digital simulation of the real world, which is at once a structure for interpretation and substitution, a universal language, and a means of acting on the world with unprecedented power and effectiveness.

The story begins in the 1980s with the appearance of computer-generated images. Software made it possible to imitate urban and natural environments, the play of light and reflection, the texture of materials, the fluid movement of bodies, facial expressions, and even emotions with great precision. We became accustomed to special effects in film and advertising, effects that made it difficult to distinguish real scenes from digital additions. Real people could be integrated into computer-generated sets or computer-generated people into real sets. Anything became possible; we could no longer be sure of the authenticity of a shot. From that point on, collage, photomontage, video montage, surrealism, and *cinema-vérité* were intrinsically mixable, hybrid, blended.

But this is not why the revolution concerns us. It involves much more than imitating the real world or making simulated, whimsical modifications to it. Rather, it is an epistemological revolution, one that affects our very understanding of the world and our scientific and instrumental knowledge of it. A few examples: our knowledge of the biology of our bodies, of the astrophysics of the universe, of the environment, of the physics of matter and energy, of the genome and of proteins – all of this knowledge has been turned into computer files run in false colour on cathode ray screens. Science is now inextricably linked to digital information and to the software that constructs and processes it. The scientific corpus is now entirely digital and, as such, everything we know and understand of the world is accounted for using digital language. Remove the computer from any lab, and science grinds to a halt, it disappears and with it goes our ability to manage the world. Our computerized knowledge of the world is more true than nature, more real, more credible than our very perceptions. Today's astronomers no longer peer through telescopes. They watch the image of a faraway star reconstructed by computer on a cathode ray screen, sometimes sent from another continent. And the computer reaches the object of observation better than the eye. It also processes it faster and more precisely than the brain.

This digital metaphor is a manifestation of rationalism. It dates back to the Greeks, who also associated music and architecture with it. Archimedes, Euclid, and Pythagoras interpreted the entire world and the soul from the point of view of numbers. In numbers Plato saw the highest level of knowledge and so based the system of the universe on them. The myth of God the mathematician (the book of life is written in geometric characters) has been revisited regularly throughout the centuries – by Boethius, Nicolas de Cues, and Galileo, to name but a few. Leibniz combined the concepts of calculation and logical reasoning more decidedly in what he called calculus ratiocinator: As God calculates, so the world is made.

FORMALIST REALISM

We must also take into account the famous *Tractatus Logico-philosophicus* by Ludwig Wittgenstein, written during World War I, which played a major role in the affirmation of a formal logic of the universe. According to Wittgenstein, logic is transcendental in the sense that it is a reflected image of the world. Logic is the very structure of the world. This isomorphism between the world and the logic of thought should obviously be the key to understanding the world, and computing could not dream of a better epistemological justification. However, this line of thinking centres on what we may call real formalism, which coexists with the real and belongs to British and American Anglo-Saxon culture. Romance-language cultures steer clear of this thinking and do not share the operational pragmatism that has been a tradition since Adam Smith and Malthus. I believe instead that there are as many logics as languages, as many theories of the origin of the universe as societies.

The implicit universalism of logic according to Wittgenstein empties history and sociology of knowledge. Success has been the measure of this illusory and naive simplicity. This unrealistic logic has been well received in Anglo-Saxon capitalist countries because of its very simplicity and its factual symmetry with the logic of management and computer technology. The suspicion that it has aroused in Latin countries – which is also related to the fact that these countries lag behind Anglo-Saxon ones when it comes to computers – has created an obvious disadvantage in commercial competition. But we should not confuse commerce with epistemology.

Plainly stated, the Wittgensteinian utopia reveals the desire for power and conquest associated with the myth of knowledge. Its success reflects the success of a management and commercial culture. The Latin title of the *Tractatus* and the Spinozist parody it contains change nothing: the theory is a perfect example of self-deluding thought with authoritative mathematical/logical window dressing. Its understandable influence on the thought of a computing utopia does nothing to diminish its mythical character – on the contrary.

IS GOD THE GREAT COMPUTER PROGRAMMER?

Without joining the proponents of numerology and arithmosophy in embracing the idea that numbers connect the spiritual and the quantitative, we should place the computing utopia on its historical continuum. It is not a new line of thought, although it is very fashionable and was all the rage at the dawn of the millennium, like the mechanist and organicist metaphors before it. Even the current trend of combining mechanist and organicist metaphors into computing organicism is not new: the genetic codes of life were programmed by the Great Computer Programmer, who saw the world as a book; they can therefore be reprogrammed, a task of great interest to contemporary geneticists. However, I would bet that we'll soon be able to shelve the myth of the Great Computer Programmer along with the myth of the Creator. Such is the way of thought trends that seek an understanding of the world. Ideas and technologies parade through time, each with conviction and passion.

CYBERREALISM OR CYBERMIRAGE?

What world are we living in? The hyperrealist movement in painting during the 1970s offered up images of the urban world rendered with photographic precision, but their perspectives – the closest and the most distant – were perfectly focused, an impossibility if one were using photographic optics. The writing on a store window, the exterior world reflected on its surface, the window display, and the interior of the store would all be reproduced with equally sharp definition.

We can also now refer to cyberrealism. The high definition of digital images created entirely by computer, or cut and paste, attain a realism that our natural vision does not perceive in the real environment. Using the magic of the computer, cyberrealism also makes it possible to pass through walls and human skin. Confusion between the virtual and the real is becoming stronger. The proof is found at the altar of great artistic value, in a painting by Van Gogh presented in 3-D on a giant screen in the documentary *À travers le regard de Vincent.* In this film, the cybermirage is complete: "Enter the painting of Van Gogh through 3-D," blared a 1999 Paris subway ad. Van Gogh is sold to us, betrayed, and diverted from his meaning, and we give him the power to justify the cybermirage by exploiting his cultural legitimacy. He is implicitly presented as a precursor to 3-D cyberperception.

AN ANALOGY THAT CLAIMS TO INVENT A NEW WORLD

With the meteoric rise of science and its technological equipment, we are becoming more inventive, and the human adventure has become more fraught with danger than ever before. Artificial intelligence, genetic manipulation, cloning, and space exploration captivate us, and justifiably so. However, these endeavours will soon tax our ability to adapt to life. What we may call the big bang of the living will also create serious ethical challenges, which will command all of our critical attention and require a new analytical schema; ethics committees and scientific researchers in many countries are currently working on this. Many believe that we are facing a serious problem: we lack control over research lab activities and legal authorization or prohibition of genetic manipulations or biotechnological creations – the scientific, economic, and human stakes of which are high, but the consequences of which cannot be foreseen. And we must make decisions about these potential time bombs in a climate of international competition, which leaves us no room for error and pushes us towards audacity.

This is compounded by the fact that these new possibilities encourage magical thinking. The creative imaginings that arise from scientific research often surpass artistic imaginings. Science is changing our image of the world faster than art is.

The cyberworld that is taking shape before our eyes, the myths that go along it, and the hopes and fears that it arouses bring art, science, and technology closer together to develop new languages, new icons, and new connections with the public. But let's pursue the myth, which goes even deeper. For many ardent admirers of binary code, the point is not to use computing language to reproduce the world so as to understand it as it is, but to create a new one that conforms to our interest and to our desire for power.

SIXTH PARADOXICAL LAW

The digital simulacrum appears not as a new attempt to interpret the universe as it is given to us, an attempt that would take its place in a historical series of analogies – magical, religious, naturalistic, vitalistic, organicist, mechanist, and so on – but rather as a powerful new instrumental device that can radically change the world according to human desire.

This appears to be the first time in the history of humanity that science has moved away from the relatively modest project of interpreting the world to launch a much bolder initiative: taking charge of the way nature, the environment, the book of life, and the brain operate, transforming them to better serve people. Radical changes to the human condition are imminent under the digital realm: artificial intelligence, eugenics, manipulation of species (GMOs), the control of natural phenomena (and possibly the destruction of dangerous asteroids or the control of global warming or cooling), biotics and the creation of bionic humans, cyborgs and robots, the networking of devices for communication that surround us to produce a quasi-magical power, shared connective intelligence, and, finally, a renewal of the universe that was given us, transforming it to conform to the image of human beings. The digital realm aspires to make humans of today something more than bourgeois heroes: cyborgs, demigods endowed with superhuman powers, and, tomorrow, biocomputer gods who will put the finishing touches on the creation of the world.

We are moving from interpretation – involving the magical, religious processes of intercession and processes of industrial adaptation – to will and transformation. Computer language aims for more than just a simple understanding of the world; it is increasingly meant to be an instrumental language for programming life and natural systems – in short, a language of re-creation that evokes the power of the biblical word of God.

WHAT WORLD DO WE WANT TO CREATE?

The following questions must be raised in the face of this trend towards a computer utopia: Do we know what world we want to create? With what values? What goals? And for whom? Who will decide? Intel? IBM? Microsoft? Research labs at MIT? Nintendo? The president of the United States? The pope? Such fundamental philosophical and political questions cannot be dispensed with in the name of binary logic. And yet these questions are far from the minds of cybernetic utopians, who have as much faith in technology as others do in Mother Nature.

THE IMAGINARY REALM OF A REVOLUTION

What imaginary realm is this techno-scientific revolution taking us to, then? Have we become accelerators of power, consciousness, and freedom? Or sorcerer's apprentices drifting towards catastrophe? We must analyse the digital technology revolution, which is founded upon the invasive power of an elementary language. This binary system is extremely simple, and yet it is the most powerful oversimplification we have ever known. Will the human spirit be able to master the speed, the globalization, the genetics, and the complexity that we are creating; can it tame the economic materialism of our era, develop a new humanism, and reprogram our critical consciousness?

HUMANKIND MUST NOT STAKE ITS FUTURE
ON A ROLL OF THE DICE

To paraphrase Einstein, humans should not play dice. The issue of genetically engineered cells, or chimera cells, recalls the fables of ancient mythology, except that it is not confined to the human imagination but occurs within the scientific and industrial reality of our laboratories. The stakes are dizzying. Once again, and more than ever, they involve the best and the worst of medical progress and human madness. Because this is an aspect of the human adventure that we cannot ignore – because we have an appointment with the future, with our evolution, with ourselves – we cannot simply prohibit everything and slam shut Pandora's box. It is opening before our eyes, and we need to sort through it and legislate appropriately.

The creation of a new world necessitates the progressive disappearance of the old. We have learned how to decipher the reversibility, the symmetry, the myths of beginning and end, of creation and destruction, of birth and death. Revolutionary or warrior movements always have a mythical resonance, as have the prophecies or denunciations that give them legitimacy and make them dynamic.

BE WARY OF PREDICTIONS,
PARTICULARLY ABOUT THE FUTURE ...

The digital realm's claim that it is ready to transform the world according to human desire and instinct for power is doubtful. Before we can believe the predictions of futurologists relating to the power of digital technology in the year 2020 or 2030, computers must at least develop the capacity to predict events in the near future. No person or computer can predict events as swift and dramatic as the assassination of John F. Kennedy on 22 November 1963, the May 1968 revolt in France, the fall of the Berlin Wall on 9 November 1989, or the terrorist attacks of 11 September 2001. To date, no guru has predicted a stock market crash, even though these events are tied to basically digital and less complex configurations.

Predictions generated by brilliant and well-known individuals reveal the unpredictability of the world, which no mathematical logarithm or binary system of computer logic will ever master. Futurologist Herman Kahn made abundant contributions to the stream of nonsense published a few years ago about the year 2000. Such predictions may be mere foolishness, but they expose our dreams of power and our fascination with symbols that fire the imagination. In 1967, Kahn and Anthony Wiener predicted the following for the year 2000: widespread use of cryonics; prescribed hibernation periods for human beings; synthetic food and drink; permanent human colonies on the moon and on satellites and interplanetary voyages; inhabited installations and perhaps even colonies under the sea; automated grocery and other major stores; intensive use of machines and robots subservient to humans; personal flying platforms; military technology to control and exploit space; artificial moons and other methods for lighting great expanses at night.[1]

Those who are interested in the predictions of established futurologists and who want to have a little fun will find a beautiful bouquet of illusions and naive ideas in Michel Saint-Germain's amusing 1993 book *L'Avenir n'est plus ce qu'il était*. And, on the subject of miraculous and marvellous computing, let's not forget the president of Digital Equipment's 1970s announcement that there was a market for only five personal computers in the United States and Bill Gates's 1980s contention that 640K ought to be enough for anyone.

Saint-Germain reminds us of the observation made in 1990 by a Bell Laboratories researcher, which Ray Kurzweil forgot to integrate in his exponential growth model and in the law of time and chaos that he decreed, like a new god or a candidate for the Nobel Prize: "For the past 40 years, only one thing has developed faster than computer equipment: human expectations."[2]

BIOINFORMATIC ANALOGIES

Digital interpretations of the world are already commingling with biological references. Those who have exploited the simplistic analogy of the computer seem to have become aware of the fact that nature and life are more complex than binary code. Thus, the king of computing, Bill Gates himself, prefers to use the image of the human body to explain his vision of the new corporation. He compares a company's computer network to a nervous system instead of the reverse, as Kurzweil would have done. According to Gates, such a network is "the digital equivalent of the human nervous system." He believes that corporate nervous systems will advance business at the speed of thought – he prefers to evoke the speed of thought, which is perhaps as fast as the speed of light.[3] Other bigwigs from multinationals now compare their management to the manipulation of DNA and the genetic code of a living organism, which, due to its complexity, no doubt seems more fulfilling than the binary code of computing. In short, Kurzweil's magical thinking was surpassed even before the end of the second millennium.

THE TECHNOCOSM

The metaphysical momentum invested in the dream of artificial intelligence cannot, however, take away from its importance. If we judge a tree by its fruit, we must admit that while the computing metaphor cannot claim to designate the ontological essence of the world, it is still a tool of a power and effectiveness unparalleled in the history of humanity – except by magic.

Pierre Lévy, thinker on the technocosm, sums up this success rather well: "The computerized techncosm belongs to that class of memorable creations the birth of which is perhaps fortuitous, but which, once they have seen the light of day, appear to have the force of destiny: agriculture, writing, the state ... They become entrenched because they are incredible reproducing machines. They spread because those who adopt them are most often conquerors."[4]

4: The Cyberworld: Allegorical Paradigm of a New Civilization

A world so beautiful, so good, so digital!

The digital simulacrum generated by computer language is like a global space for communication, an on-line network of millions of computers belonging to public institutions, private companies, and individuals. Add to this network of networks – also called the Web or the Net – connected by telephone, cable, fibre optics, satellite, microwave, and other means, all off-line digital media, whether magnetic tape, hard disk, CD-ROM, optical disk, or silicon chip. In just a few years, we have built a gigantic device with a very complex architecture that can store and instantaneously circulate billions of binary files. Software, routers, browsers, intelligent agents, search engines, and other devices orient us within this network and let us produce, save, send, download, and display billions of pages of information and images, interconnected through portals, Web sites, data banks, and other repositories, which can be organized into films or musicals, financial or business transactions, video games, e-mail, and whatever else. This space is constantly expanding and mutating; its throughput and speed are increasing exponentially, as is its content. Its power and its novelty stem from a universal code of zeros and ones, the same code used for all the tools and content that it brings together. This is the space that we call the cyberworld.

Through its structures and its content, the cyberworld reflects the real world from which it derives. But the cyberworld is a parallel world, not simply a mirror or substitute world. Because, in addition to reflecting the real world, the cyberworld self-generates, according to its own logic and needs, an increasing amount of previously unpublished content that is unique to it and that breaks free of the constraints of the real world. The cyberworld has its own dynamic. It is growing with a certain amount of autonomy and developing characteristics that are very different from those of the real world. Its space-time, speed, structure, connectivity, and arborescence are a virtual universe that we can enter, losing ourselves in a sort of unreality. The cyberworld is an imaginary realm where we find logic, values, content, and individual and social behaviours that are often very different from those we find in the real world. A sort of dialectic has been established between the two parallel universes based on escape, compensation, complementarity, management, exploration, and opposition.

Clearly, the cyberworld does not have the richness, density, or diversity of the real world. But the life force that it gathers each day is fascinating, and it is taking the form of an allegory, if not a laboratory, of our future. We are now simultaneously living and participating in these two worlds in a sort of hybrid, sometimes schizophrenic, condition that makes our contemporary universe half real, half virtual – a strange social mix. Whereas the storybook universe of Madame Bovary described by Gustave Flaubert was an individual fantasy, the real/digital amalgam that characterizes our new world is turning into a collective fantasy that cannot help but reverberate in our collective reality and bring many changes to it.

Under the influence of the digital realm, human destiny now involves daring astrophysical adventures in the faraway universe and mundane activities, dizzying genetic manipulations and physical misery, artificial intelligence and devastating foolishness, the knowledge economy and famine, magical planetary communications and tragic human solitude, digital democracies and dark dictatorships, electronic wars and massacres by machete, and individual liberties and human enslavement. We are discovering a new world of shadows and conquests, where science and fiction, utopia and misery, liberty and alienation intersect. A world of progress? More like a futuristic primitive world, with its creative intensity and its digital archaisms. This is a riveting moment in the human adventure, one that we are hesitant even to think about because ideas and facts change so fast.

ONTOLOGY OF THE VIRTUAL
OR MYTHOLOGY OF THE REAL?

What we call a virtual world, virtual space, cyberspace, seems either like an imaginary digital space, a simulation of reality generated by logarithms, instrumented and accessible by helmet, glove, remote control, interactive 3-D glasses and screen, or like a network of telematic connectivity between real players. And there are several possible applications for virtuality. It can be a sophisticated technological tool for remote manipulation in science, industry, medicine, the military, exploration, and other fields, essentially through telerobotics, in real but hostile or inaccessible environments (space, the ocean depths, nuclear generating stations, the human body, remote war sites, and so on).

The virtual can also be an imaginary space for games; multimedia film; the building of architectural, urban, or landscaping models; or learning, particularly the learning of techniques that involve risk, such as flight simulation or surgery. As well, the virtual is a cyberspace of internet-based connectivity dedicated to e-commerce, a range of communities of interest, and information and distance education. The ontological status of the virtual therefore varies significantly by case: it can be a simple instrument for the remote manipulation of reality; it can be a simulation of reality; it can be an imaginary world; it can be a space for professional and community communication. In all cases, however, the virtual realm is a place where we invest our desire for power, whether realistic or fanciful. It evokes magic.

Faced with "the desire of the virtual," as it is called by many authors, we would do well to adopt a sociological perspective and to look to art history. We should also add a bit of cultural ecology, humanities, and ethnology to this beautiful virtual world, which is a global culture that tends towards homogeneity, a universal, even totalizing noosphere. We must not forget the reality of multiculturalism, the importance of the diversity of cultural ecosystems, and the relationships of political, economic, and military forces. The simulacrum of this global-tending virtual space will not lighten the weight of desires and reality with a single click or erase the ugliness of the gaps, conflicts, and dysfunction of the world it reflects. The cyberworld is not the ideal and shimmering bubble most of us believe it or dream it to be.

Likewise, it is difficult to take literally this techno-political utopia – this fashionable idea of a connective or collective intelligence, this naive image of the neurons of a planetary hypercortex – that intersects with the hearts-and-flowers utopia of Teilhard de Chardin's noosphere.

The cyberworld is not divine and cannot be deified; it is simply human, and as such it is the reflection of our vale of tears, even when it is watered down, smoothed over, and euphorically coloured using Photoshop. We know only too well that the cyberworld is not a *cache-sexe*, as the French would say – a fig leaf. But neither is it a *cache-misère* – a veil over the ugliness of reality.

CYBERSPACE: A SMOOTH, FLUID, AND PLAYFUL SPACE-TIME?

Digital communication technologies are adept at converging all technologies, promising us a new human power over the environment. This is why the heads of major media multinationals are so taken with business plans founded on the digital convergence of networks, which will allow them to offer the content they control in a variety of forms across media. Convergence harbours the dream of totalitarian power that gratifies their subconscious. The cyberworld gives concrete expression to our wildest dreams of superhuman power in a universe of gadgets. Virtual space-time is increasingly a fabulous and submissive space. It has a strange texture – or, rather, it has no texture at all. It gives itself over immediately and entirely, a smooth and circular free flow, unresisting and neutral. There are no social classes in the cyberworld – no rich and no poor, no obstacles. Nothing opposes the magical click of cyberhumans. Cyberspace is apolitical, and it challenges all objections. It is a seductive space for play and for the immediate realization of our desire for power. The cell phone is the magic wand.

Cyberspace is like a stretched canvas, a space with no depth other than that of light, which points to somewhere else. We move laterally through it using the cursor, scrolling the page up or down, left or right, or we leap to other surfaces also as flat as screens. When the third dimension is suggested in cyberspace, it is only symbolic and has no contour or depth. But the light of the simulacrum of another world, plays the same quasi-religious role it plays when it illuminates the stained glass of a church window and leads the spirit to another place in which we invest our dreams, hopes, and prayers.

THE MYTH OF SPEED

We no longer believe in history. We live in the present. And we have returned to good old chronological time, only now it's under the influence of speed.

Contemporary production lives and dies according to the rhythm of the present. The same has been said of Greek civilization, but the major difference is that the eternity of the present – or of the Greeks' vertical time, or the cyclical time of many other ancient societies – has given way to the event-based ephemera of accelerated time, rapidly consumed and leaving no lasting trace. Chronos is heartily devouring himself.

In science as in business, speed has become the cardinal virtue of time. The University of Orsay in France has perfected an ultrafast camera, Elyse, capable of capturing billions of images a second. A hybrid of a laser and an electron accelerator, it operates in picoseconds, or a millionth of a millionth of a second, which allows it to film chemical reactions and to render them perceptible for the first time. The person who inspired it, Jacqueline Belloni, points out that the picosecond is to the second as the second is to 30,000 years.

Speed is celebrated in the cyberworld; there it endeavours to equal the speed of light. Today's computing still seems slow, but we continue to dream of speed. Bill Gates devoted a book to it: *Business @ the Speed of Thought* (1999). While it is all well and good to hope that computers and communications get faster, we should not confuse the speed of communication with the speed of thought, especially when it comes to education and reflection, which require time.

Relentless academic, professional, intercompany, and international competition finds a compelling symbol in Formula 1 racing or in speedy computers. This attitude is reflected in our incessantly proactive behaviour. Rest has become laziness, a vice; we imagine that anyone who stops to rest before retirement will drop in their tracks, fall to the floor like a spent spinning top. Fast is beautiful. Here's an example to illustrate the power of this new ideology. Insurance provider Belair*direct*, the Quebec pioneer in selling insurance over the internet, sold 1,241 policies on-line in 1998, 5,000 in 1999, and generated several thousand quotes per month in 2000. Its ad announced that it was the first auto insurance company to advocate speed – ten minutes was plenty of time to get an auto insurance quote on www.belairdirect.com.

The inevitable risk arising from the widespread worship of speed in all activities is the development of a social pathology. To a certain extent, chasing time means losing the sense of oneself as the centre of one's own life. That can lead to a destabilization and in turn a de-realization of the self. Plus, the accelerated flow of social time in which we are swept along promotes a tendency to depend upon the entourage to which our agitation connects us; it comes to provide our dynamic equilibrium. The internet opens its arms to us, absorbing us by supporting our proactive behaviour.

Conversely, obsession with speed is also a characteristic of the desire for power. People in power are impatient; they will not wait to have their desires fulfilled.

DIGITAL TIME

Just-in-time: it's the currency of the cyberworld, the virtue that all of its inhabitants claim as their own; it is essentially oriented towards vertical time, or the present. Time has become the very matter of reality, the most significant information that reality has to offer. The future is merging with the accelerated speed of the present. Speed has become an important attribute of contemporary social time. And being in real time is essential. Time prevails over space in the reality of the cyberworld.

Business leaders know that digital technologies are going to restructure the market over and over, but they don't know how. They know that half our current technologies and beliefs will be obsolete within a year, but they don't know which half. They have to make quick decisions in order to position themselves strategically, but they don't know where. The game is becoming incredibly risky, because the investments laid on the boardroom table are larger and larger. The big wheel is spinning as fast as it can, and shareholders are scrutinizing business leaders; they will not forgive a single mistake – they track their stocks daily and panic at the slightest fluctuation. Potentially profitable technological innovations emerge one after the other and constantly change course like a great wind on the internet sea. Bill Gates tells us that to think effectively we must think fast, applying the virtues of computers to the human mind. Should philosophers take part in this sprint too? Will they think better if they think faster? No.

The mythical account of the origins and the destiny of the world, which unfolds in elapsed time, in measurable time, whether it be cyclical or directed, has no room to unfold in our immediate time. It tends to vanish in the present time of events, fleeting and accelerated; it becomes compressed when the future is identified with speed; it is brought closer to current affairs, merging with the present moment.

CYBERTIME

Cybertime is like a whirling top, picking up speed on the spot, veering off suddenly, and skidding to a calamitous halt. The top/cybertime owes its equilibrium to speed, but its movement is immobile, taking place in vertical time. Coming from nowhere, the top has no goal and no meaning; it is going nowhere. We know beforehand that it is going to skid and fall. This symbolizes our time, which erases the past just as one would delete an electronic file – no future. Cybertime, our time, is tragic. It has no past, no future; it is accelerated and compressed and vertical, powered up, ready to explode. Time that consumes itself immediately, time-consuming time, intense, pleasurable time that expires immediately. It's also the basic social time of the dominant middle class, the class without claim to an illustrious and legitimizing ancestry, the class whose horizons were long limited to daily survival and a few immediate pleasures.

This spinning-top time – moving at breakneck speed on the spot, going nowhere – symbolizes the loss of meaning that is destabilizing us, and it demonstrates how the instant is becoming denser. It is the equivalent of a loss of the substance of space. We no longer have a spatial trajectory. Cyberspace becomes ephemeral while it balloons within event-based time. We are witnessing a de-realization of reality.

THE UNIVERSAL TIME OF THE INTERNET

Ericsson and Swatch have invented a universal timetable for the Web to allow users to synchronize their connections. Internet time is different from Greenwich Mean Time. In accordance with this system, which provides one universal time simultaneously around the world, the twenty-four hours of traditional time zones are redivided into 1,000 beats, each one a minute and 26.4 seconds long. We have to adjust new watches and cell phone screens to this time if, for example, we want to participate in a launch party for a new Ericsson product at internet hour 80. The only thing that remains is to adjust our biological clocks by inserting a chip into our bodies so that we will all be on the same global cyberworld time. Isn't that better than using the calendar of the French Revolution?

And what is now called the Web year will be counted in six-month periods, perhaps even three-month periods, to allow for the accelerating pace of change. Time is moving faster than our consciousness, and it seems to have stolen from us all leisure to create a new mythical tale, to support our project of the human adventure.

Time has become smooth. It has no grain, it is fluid and colourless, it has no seasons, no density, no life and death, it has escaped the real world, and us with it: this is why it gives us that delicious shiver of metaphysical vertigo. However, I believe that we will soon adopt a new mythical illusion, catastrophic or tragic, that conforms to the discourse of cults that announce the looming end of the world or promise the fulfillment of our human power – as current science and technology do.

TIME CANNIBALIZES EVERYTHING

Time absorbs and destroys everything, including the electronic arts, which cannot be conserved because of changing multimedia technologies, and which involve a time- and event-based aesthetic rather than the fixed permanence of art in space.

The accelerated pace imposed by the digital revolution (the first computer was created little more than half a century ago) destroys the value of memory and erases history, but it also creates anxiety about the future as compared to the past. The timescape scrolls past windshields and TV and computer screens and is erased as it passes across our rear-view mirrors. Speed fascinates, excites, and arouses fear. It inspires not only violent, dramatic technological works of art but also nostalgic works, those that evoke nature, calm, pleasure, and rest.

This "Chronos syndrome," as it is called, is also the pressure and stress that we are all under because of the acceleration of time. We are fighting against time, like swimmers who struggle against a current that carries us towards the open sea and the dangers of the unknown.

THE GRADUAL DISAPPEARANCE OF HISTORY

Everything changed with the digital revolution. History began to fade. As a result, we tend to cultivate memory to reassure ourselves; we produce and consume information and goods so that we can enjoy our new powers, so that we can maintain the excitement and the anxiety that prompts us to pursue the digital adventure. As artists, we try to master a new, contemporary aesthetic that is more event-driven and that exploits interactive multimedia technology. It may not go on this way forever. We will have to rethink our sense of time and invent a new sense of history.

We must therefore disregard the efforts of ideologically avant-garde artists who strive to mark and make history. Contemporary art falls within the scope of current affairs and no longer within the scope of history. This return to the art of artisans does not denote a crisis in contemporary art, despite what many have maintained. Contemporary art remains socially necessary and paradoxically reconnects with tradition just as we are entering a new digital civilization.

SEVENTH PARADOXICAL LAW
The cyberworld presents itself as a symbolic space of global connectivity that is apolitical, asocial, and ahistorical, but, in fact, it acts as a socially integrating virtual superstructure that gives power and legitimacy to the new middle class, whose image of the world it expresses and whose dominant ideology it forms.

The cyberworld brings together all the attributes of a classic dominant ideology. It is an instrument of social integration that is worthy of its promise of instant and universal connectivity; it denies all social divides and represents itself as a force of global unification; it erases the genesis of social history and offers itself as timeless; through the very structure of its standardizing and egalitarian binary language, and through its decentralized rhizomic, or non-hierarchical, structure, it reflects the ideology of the middle class and most of its equal, interchangeable members. And it promises to bring democratic progress, quasi-magical happiness, and the demiurgical evolution of the universe – to draw humankind together in a societal project and to provide meaning to its destiny.

In all dominant ideologies, there is an alienating symbolic system that benefits the ruling class and that encourages and justifies the exploitation of the dominated. In the structure and ideology of the cyberworld, the share of alienation is particularly apparent; but, by definition, the middle class is in the majority, and its power is therefore rarely disputed. Yet this well-established and consistent political function of cyberworld ideology is the basis for its sustainable development and growth.

It is, however, with respect to developing countries that we should now consider the rise of the cyberworld's dominant ideology of the middle class, which is occurring in developed countries. And it is with respect to these developing countries that we must now think about the dialectic of dominant exploiters/dominated exploited in the context of the digital divide.

THE CYBERWORLD: FOUNDING PARADIGM OF THE NEW DIGITAL CIVILIZATION

The digital ideology that is now taking hold will last for some time. It will be the foundation for a new and powerful civilization. It is a breaking wave rising from a groundswell with a solid social foundation; it has remarkable political and symbolic coherence and it could – barring mishaps – increase in power for centuries to come.

The space-time of the cyberworld is the fundamental social space-time of the new civilization. The cyberworld is like a drawing board on which the architecture of a new civilization is being drafted. The sketch foreshadows the world towards which we are headed. Through a stunning series of experiments, of pas de deux, through trial and error, we are building a social model, we are testing it socially, economically, and politically to reassure ourselves of its practicality. We are participating in the virtual creation of a real project of society and civilization. People are designing this new world in embryo in a strange laboratory of the real; they are programming it, organizing it, designing it architecturally, and colouring it. It falls to us to create the main actors, to write the screenplay depicting their actions and their relationships. People have never before witnessed the birth of a new civilization in such tight real time – it's as if we were in an artist's studio contributing to the first strokes of a major collective creation.

This is why the birth of a new digital world is fascinating for those who dive in and take up the task. The excitement of the moment even justifies much of the over-the-top praise, the irrational enthusiasm, the naïveté, the utopianism, the errors, the illusions, and the primitive regressions. These are surely trifles compared to the fundamental challenges, stakes, responsibilities, and dreams that we must face up to – compared to the incredible astonishment and joy that we are experiencing.

Entrepreneurs, businesspeople, programmers, scientists, politicians, and creators: we are the artist-researchers of this new world, designing it fired by the feverish audacity of great beginnings.

EIGHTH PARADOXICAL LAW
The cyberworld acts as a virtual outline of the new world reality we are developing. It already constitutes this new reality's basic paradigm in real time and its allegorical metaphor.

5: Are We Losing Our Memory?

Memory is life. The future is death. Or vice versa.

FROM THE RECONSTRUCTION OF THE GREAT LIBRARY OF ALEXANDRIA

The Library of Alexandria is a major symbol of human memory, of its ambitions, its heights, and its misery. Before its final destruction, the library – which was founded in 323 BC by Ptolemy I, one of Alexander the Great's generals – housed up to 700,000 volumes (volumina, papyrus rolls) and was partially destroyed (accidentally or deliberately) several times. Around the year 47 BC, during a naval battle outside the port of Alexandria, a fire destroyed parts of the library. Mark Antony, Cleopatra's paramour, offered 200,000 volumes hidden at the library of Pergamum to replace those that were lost. Then, in 391 AD, the Christian emperor Theodore I ordered the great library partially pillaged and burned. Its volumes served, among other things, as fuel for the fires that heated water for the Roman thermal baths. Legend has it that in 642, Arab general Amr Ibn al-As consulted Mecca before ordering what was left of the library burned to the ground. He received this response: "If these writings of the Greeks agree with the book of God, they are useless and need not be preserved; if they disagree, they are pernicious and ought to be destroyed."[1]

Should we remain optimistic in spite of all this? The Library of Alexandria was rebuilt, opening in time for World Book Day 2002.

However, the glass and concrete disc that forms its roof does not symbolize the optical disks of our digital civilization, but simply the sun. This roof will protect the largest reading room in the world, housing eight million volumes, a good number of them devoted to Egyptian and Greco-Roman civilization. And, of course, the new library is connected to the internet.

For a thousand and one reasons, our historical memory has always been fragile. For centuries we have been trying to preserve it by engraving limestone slabs or constructing pyramids; and the scribes of the Middle Ages wore out a lot of quill pens.

TO THE DIGITAL SILOS OF MEMORY

Today, digital technologies are revolutionizing not only our memory capacity, but also the quantity of information we produce. University of Berkeley researchers tried to calculate the volume of information circulating in the world during 1999 alone, taking into account all media: digital, paper, film, disk, TV, magnetic tape, and so on. They arrived at the staggering figure of 1.5 billion gigabytes. What this represents in concrete terms is about 500 times the holdings of the American Library of Congress in Washington, the largest library in the world.

In announcing the age of knowledge, the president of Xerox said that the number of documents available on the Net in 2001 had been estimated at two billion. During the same year, the search engine Google.com scanned 1,610,476,000 Web pages. According to estimates, the production of information is growing by approximately 50 per cent a year, an increase that resulted in more than five billion gigabytes in 2002. In 2006, Google announced that it had digitized and put on-line 4.28 billion pages, which were being fully indexed. Digital storage capacity, taking into account all hard drives worldwide, also doubles every year, while the medium of paper, the use of which is still increasing in absolute terms, is losing its relative importance. The production of information on paper was estimated by specialists at the University of California, Berkeley at no more than thirty-three-thousandths of the worldwide production of new information, while production on digital media apparently increased by about 60 per cent annually. A very large proportion of this annual production of new information appears to be private in nature: 600 times more bytes than public information.

Certainly, the digitization of data now seems an incredible tool for memory and archiving. Genealogy experts are making great use of it, and the Mormon Church has made it a specialty. On Liberty Island, at the entry to the port of New York, where the Statue of Liberty stands, the US government has installed terminals where descendants of immigrants can research the origins of their ancestors. The American Family Immigration History Center at Ellis Island makes a Web site available to the public that brings together archived information on more than 20 million immigrants, and the Mormon Church has established a genealogy site that houses more than 600 million names.

At the same time, digital silos for critical data storage are now being built and offered to companies and governments. In these silos, irreplaceable data is safe from viruses, bugs, hackers, and mechanical failure. Let's just say it's a very profitable initiative for IBM.

MEMORY AND PIXIE DUST

Many such silos will need to be built to protect an enormous amount of information, and this initiative will soon represent an investment of billions of dollars. The worldwide hard drive industry is already valued at $80 billion, more than the annual budget of several countries, while the size of hard drives is shrinking: a hard drive the size of a matchbox currently holds a gigabyte of memory; in the 1980s it would have required a computer the size of a fridge. At the beginning of 2000, IBM was already marketing a super hard drive capable of storing up to 400 gigabytes of data per square inch (or 6.5 cm^2), compared to a maximum of 40 gigabytes with previous technologies. And IBM has announced that it will soon be able to attain 100 billion bytes per square inch. How? By using pixie dust, or ruthenium, a rare metal similar to platinum, inserted between two magnetic layers.

DIGITAL ALZHEIMER'S

But how do we manage this mass of information, which is expanding every day like an out-of-control bubble? How do we orient ourselves? How do we select what is important for our individual and collective memories? And how do we conserve our memory, according to what criteria, and on what media? Is our memory becoming too laden, too bloated, a tad dysfunctional? Does memory obesity destroy the memory? Is the system in danger of breaking up?

Who has not had the irritating experience of losing information from a computer hard drive or an electronic agenda? We become accustomed to it and downplay the drama, telling ourselves that it's not so bad. Life quickly refills the void left in our memory, and random access memory enables us to act and survive. Is there not therefore also a read-only memory, becoming more and more intrusive, in the land of the living? What are we to do with it? Digital technology may find a radical solution to the problem, independent of our will.

DIGITAL AMNESIA

It seems better to leave well enough alone, because this abundance resembles chaos. In 1999, the president of Xerox said that the information highway provides access to so much data and information that we will never be able to absorb it all. And the equation technology+quantity=knowledge has not proven to be true, even if a number of countries believe it and are connecting their schools to the internet – Canada and the United States in 1988, Germany in 2001, France in 2002.

After having happily praised the new digital civilization, we must consider one of its more perverse possible effects: the amnesia with which it threatens future generations. Paradoxically, the more we digitize our cultural memory, the more we risk losing it. The technological power that we trust to better conserve our books, images, films, and musical and television productions is at serious risk of betraying us. Whatever the devout may say, this power is much less secure than paper or the plastic of film and video, the fragility of which we are well acquainted with.

Most Web sites created over ten years ago have been lost forever. We no longer have the means of reading the first CD-ROMs, created in the 1980s. The readers and software of the era no longer exist. And yet we can still read the Dead Sea scrolls, inscriptions in Egyptian tombs, and rock paintings that date back thousands of years. But in ten years time, how will we read an optical disk for which the reader no longer exists? Current software has evolved so far that it won't recognize the language of software marketed in the year 2000.

Laser disks, so highly praised barely a decade ago, have been declared obsolete. And the readers, almost all of which are incompatible between various brands, are now incompatible from one year to the next, even when they share a brand. CD-ROMs, which were highly praised in their turn, are going to make way for the digital versatile disc (DVD), which, in turn, will follow the pace of the market. In any event, twenty years from now they will all be as readable as plastic plates. The optical disks of professional archive centres will meet with the same fate.

NATURAL MEMORY ERASES MORE THAN IT RETAINS

Memory, like the senses – sight, hearing, taste, smell, and touch – is selective, and a large part of its function is to suppress and erase what we don't need, making it easier for us to adapt to the moment and context in which we live. Like computer memory, natural memory has two levels: random access memory, which is always available in real time; and read-only memory, or deep memory, which we must actively search through. Natural memory also has a third level, which is specific to living beings (until now, in any event): repressed memory, which influences our behaviour without our knowing. To my knowledge, no proselyte of the digital realm has yet presented himself or herself as a cyberpsychoanalyst of the digital psyche and examined the computer unconscious.

But let's return to the main function of natural memory, which is to erase 90 per cent of the information that assails us, keeping just 1 or 2 per cent in read/write memory.

ARTIFICIAL MEMORY AND NATURAL MEMORY

Artificial memory, like artificial intelligence, poses serious problems. With each wave of digitization, we choose what seems to be most important and reject nine-tenths of available archives. This choice is made according to the criteria of circumstance and fashion, by virtue of which neither the works of Van Gogh nor those of Rimbaud would have been preserved. And it is the same for the mundane memories of ordinary people, so precious to historians.

Recently I was rereading old letters from my parents and my older brothers, including one that announced my birth in 1941. The paper had yellowed with age, but the letters will still be readable

in a hundred years' time. Today I communicate with my mother
in Paris by phone, and with my sons in New York, San Francisco,
and Hong Kong also by phone, but mainly by e-mail. We never
write letters. The phone and the internet are much faster and more
appealing. Communication has greatly improved. Isn't it marvellous? But what will remain of these exchanges in ten years, let alone
in five minutes? Where will I find a record of the announcement
of the birth of a grandson? And where will this grandson's daughter
find the announcement of the birth of her father? Oh, wonder of
technology! My digital camera and the internet let me see the
photos I take right away and send them out immediately to family
in the four corners of the world. But in a generation, in ten years,
in five years, what will have happened to these magical digital
photos? Unless they are printed on traditional paper, through an
excess of caution that I could barely admit to, I will no longer be
able to look at them because my new computer will not be able to
read them. I treasure the yellowed photos that offer me an image
of my father as he was when he was born in 1899.

Perhaps this is the moment to state a paradoxical law of digital
memory and forgetfulness: The more powerful and sophisticated
technology becomes, and the more immediate, intense, and planetary communication becomes, the greater the danger to memory
of becoming ephemeral, unless it is immediately categorized as
"historical." In contrast, clay footprints of children, like those
found in prehistoric caves in China, can remain intact for millennia. The remarkable paintings in France's Chauvet and Lascaux
caves, which date back to 32,000 and 18,000 BC, respectively,
apparently travelled through time without so much as an alteration
in colour. And clay tablets engraved with wooden stylets from the
Sumerian era, dating back more than 6,000 years, permit us to
read one of the world's first literary masterpieces: the epic poem
of Gilgamesh. We have just discovered the secret library of Nabu-
chodonosor, dating back more than 2,600 years – some 400 tablets
of cuneiform writing housed in a walled-up room the ancient city
of Sippar, in today's Iraq.

Think back to the first microcomputers of the 1980s, to our first
laptops, all dead from premature age within a few years, and compare them to the ancient media that remain readable from one
generation to the next and even increase in value for having
survived the centuries.

Losing our memory at the very moment when social and historical time is accelerating at a dizzying rate is dangerous. Faced with speed, with the unknown, and committed as we are to an increasingly daring human adventure, it is more essential than ever that we cultivate our memory, to know who we are and where we come from, and to remember the lessons of history. It is at the very moment that we most need our memory, faced with a future full of risk, that, paradoxically, we are in the most peril of becoming amnesiacs due to our faith in things digital.

NINTH PARADOXICAL LAW
The more powerful and sophisticated digital technology becomes, the greater the risk that the artificial memory it is meant to protect will become ephemeral.

THE NEED FOR MUSEUMS AND LIBRARIES

Italian writer and semiotician Umberto Eco takes pleasure in denouncing today's democratic museums, through which hordes of supposedly uneducated tourists file, performing a quick visual scan of historical masterpieces that they can't comprehend. And he objects to the flamboyant architecture of these new museums, which creates a diversion from their function of conserving and presenting collections. This is an elitist and highly debatable position. I believe instead that now more than ever we need traditional museums and libraries to protect our memory by carefully conserving the real objects that tell our history; and we need to open them up to everyone. We cannot fall into the cathode ray trap of artificial memory.

But we also have to establish a reliable system of international standards and rules for conserving digital content. The problem becomes clear with the inauguration of more and more virtual libraries. The Gallica Library was launched in 2000 by France's national library, offering the largest collection of volumes on the global network – some 80,000 complete works, and more than 45,000 still images from the fifteenth to the nineteenth centuries, free of copyright, accessible for free on the internet. And in 2006, to compete with Google's initiative of digitize 15 to 20 million books (many from English libraries, including those of Oxford, Stanford, and Harvard), the European Digital Library (EDL) was launched. The BNE will have the participation of twenty-three countries, starting with France, Spain, Germany, the Netherlands, Italy, Poland, and Hungary. In France, however, a decision has been made to digitize and put on-line 150,000 new works each year. They have even devoted a server to – Oh, paradox of the digital realm! – Marcel Proust and *Remembrance of Things Past*. This dynamic is unstoppable. Content indexing will constantly improve until we have a single gigantic, labyrinthine hypertext. The Argentine theoretician Alejandro Piscitelli calls the internet "the printing of the twenty-first century."[2]

Publishers will have to reconsider their positions and start promoting the unique values of paper printed books. We will have to think hard about the challenges of conserving digital content – maintaining it, indexing it, upholding its quality – and ponder its digital architecture. Furthermore, we must consider the issue of intellectual property – royalty payments to authors, and so on. This will be a daunting task, given such new phenomena as Wikipedia, a worldwide multilingual on-line encyclopedia that is written by anybody who wants to create or modify an article. We are entering an age of volatility, of memory obesity, characterized by less and less editorial protection. Paradoxically, in the midst of all this, we may lose our memory, as a fish may drown in water.

UNESCO could take up the task of organizing the necessary consultations and instituting international rules, making it possible to reduce potential risks. We would need to reflect on the selection criteria of archives that are to be digitized. We would also need to ensure that readers and software remain compatible and that digital content is regularly adapted to the standards of new technologies, which should be subject to UNESCO's consent. Then, and only then, could we express confidence in digitization without diminishing the role of traditional media. And we could freely boast about the tremendous advantages of digitization, which allows an unlimited public to consult remotely and under excellent conditions, at any time of day or night, countless documents and fragile archives protected from the ravages of light and human hands.

6: Communication Intoxication

I connect, therefore I am.

What is communicating? Being. What is being? Communicating with the Other. Is it as simple as that? Martin Heidegger asked himself the bewildering question "What is thinking?"; today's compelling question is "What is communicating?" Furthermore, why is there an increase in global communication and a loss of local communication? Why do we believe that communication has invaded the planet? And why are the dream of immediacy and the illusion of transparency in communication associated with digital communication?

Wired zealots believe that new communication technologies eradicate space and time – a grand dream of power, which technology now places within reach. This idea evinces a belief in magic. The current frenzy of communication betrays a technological fetishism, an idolization. Market ideology exploits strong individual motives – it fuses desires to compensate for contemporary society's deficit in interpersonal communication.

THE NOISE OF COMMUNICATION

Communication creates the illusion of a global community in which people can harmoniously join. The field of mediology has been invented to study it. And, in the name of the new goddess of communication, we deny the importance of silence, solitude, and non-communication. We celebrate noise, the explosion of communication, the din of cities and media. And the techno-rhythms of contemporary music echo this.

What has become of communication itself, devised as an exchange, as sharing? What have become of confidences, the intimate murmur, the whispered secret, and personal and private psychological space? We can no longer hear ourselves speak over this planetary caterwauling; it's like meeting a friend in a fashionable, noisy café where we can exchange no more than smiles and banalities because it is impossible to hear the exact words spoken, the nuances and the explanations. Making fun of the great myth of communication that has invaded our world, Jean Baudrillard quipped, "Communicate? Communicate? Only vessels communicate!" And the deluge of individual blogs about anything is astonishing, expressing a vertiginous desire for communication.

COMMUNICATION, DIRECTLY FROM THE FAUCET

Predictions are that telecommunications alone will represent 4.6 per cent of gross domestic product worldwide in 2006. And there will be interference on the electrical grid if research on transmitting internet communications on the electrical grid succeeds. Communications will arrive in our homes through an electrical outlet. How simple! There will be no more need for a second outlet and a second cable. And all of our electrical devices will automatically become communication devices.

But maybe we can do even better. Water is a conductor, and it also produces delightful sound effects. Can we look forward to combining everything in a single network? Will communications flow directly from our water faucets? In France, the Lyonnaise des eaux and the Compagnie générale des eaux have anticipated this evolution, judging from their investment in the internet.

THE INTERNET RELIGION

The desire for communication, which has become an obsession, a basic instinct for many wired fetishists, seems to symbolize the joy of integration into the social body, of feeding from the breast of the planet. It's the desire for love, belonging, participation, and fusion that frees individuals from their anxiety and fear of solitude.

With this as a basis, any manipulation becomes possible. The internet is often the opium of the individual; it fuses the atoms of a ruptured, fragmented society and is individualistic in the extreme. Its content is often less important than the umbilical cord it offers – as Marshall McLuhan said, "The medium is the message."

We have spent too long dreaming of communication as powerful, fast, omnipresent, and at the service of the average person to be shocked by the tremendous growth of digital communications. This feverish communication, this communication intoxication, creates the illusion of restoring a lost social well-being. It reconstructs a new integrating space-time on a planetary scale, paradoxically restoring the three classical elements of space, time, and action.

The internet is instituted social communion. And quixotic communion creates religion, with its priests, rituals, devout followers, feasts, and celebrations.

Desire, multiplied by speed, power, broadband, and the effect of multimedia, creates the seduction and the jubilation of cyberfreedom. Al Gore, former vice-president of the United States, artlessly expressed this dream in political terms while championing the internet at the beginning of the 1990s; he announced a veritable political utopia of universal happiness and democracy regained:

The ... most important principle is to ensure universal service so that the Global Information Infrastructure is available to all members of our societies. Our goal is a kind of global conversation, in which everyone who wants can have his or her say ... The GII will not only be a metaphor for a functioning democracy, it will in fact promote the functioning of democracy by greatly enhancing the participation of citizens in decision-making. And it will greatly promote the ability of nations to cooperate with each other. I see a new Athenian Age of democracy.[1]

INTERNET COMMUNITIES

The internet is a medium that requires the individual to be proactive, much more so than other media, such as telephone and television. It demands individual effort, while television feeds passivity. It requires a technical initiation to more complex knowledge, which assumes membership in a privileged group of cybernauts and introduces us to a new imaginary space – that of the cyberworld.

Effort creates a value, and sharing this value gives rise to a community that is self-aware and able to claim membership in the arena of virtual planetary communication. Every cybernaut feels valued and attached to a group, like a cell to a living organism that provides it with security – the myth of belonging to the greater whole is finally realized. In the solitude of cities and the desert of lost loves, we can dream of no greater consolation. In the context of human aspiration to power over the universe, we cannot conjure a more beautiful utopia.

GOD.ORG AND CHURCH PORTALS

Churches of all denominations know the stakes involved in the internet and have created portals to support the growth of their communities of followers, whether they be Catholic, Protestant, Jewish, or Muslim. In spring 2001, *Wired* published these remarks of a Texan pastor: "God created the internet – he is the one who gave us the ability as human beings to do that. We have a responsibility to use what God's created to reach people."[2] The faithful find useful information – job openings, discussion groups, suggestions and recommendations – on their church's Web site or through hindunet.org, vatican.va, or protestants.org. I encountered the priest from Montreal's Notre Dame Basilica, next-door neighbour to Canada's first electronic café (opened in 1995), on the building site when the café was still under construction. And he saw that the project was good, and he said unto me, "God is also virtual/ real, omnipresent and listening twenty-four hours a day!"

The poster for the Conference of Bishops of France held in 2000 announced: "And God cre@ted ... When man gives meaning to the digital realm." Some sixty French dioceses now have their own Web sites on the Conference of Bishops portal – www.cef.fr – which Pope John Paul II inaugurated during his official visit to France in 1996. Traffic on these sites is increasing: 400,000 visits per month in 1999 and about 1.5 million in 2001. The Protestant Youth of Hanover, Germany, for its part, is increasing the technological innovations for its members at www.ev-jugend-hannover.de.

The cybernaut of any denomination in search of on-line spiritual assistance can now find it at centres that offer spiritual support from priests on-line. However, the Vatican has become concerned and has announced its own "Netiquette," which in particular opposes on-line confession and administration of sacraments. It is a "document for those who use the internet within the Church and for all those concerned about responsible use of this marvellous instrument for evangelizing and pastoral care, for dialogue and teaching

... the internet also offers the Church the opportunity to speak to all countries and in particular those who cannot benefit from the presence of priests. But the sacraments cannot be administered online, neither confession nor any other."

A PLANETARY NETWORK

The digital convergence of information technologies – telecommunications, television, satellite, cable, cinema, and such – promotes a rather totalitarian vision of the internet. It would also make control of content possible, if one day the market economy stops opposing such a thing. Without denying the virtues of digital convergence, we must hope that it does not overcome media diversity, which is absolutely essential for the expression of cultural difference and pluralism of power. Each medium reflects a different structure and image of the world, which corresponds to a different social community.

The merger of America Online and Time Warner at the beginning of 2000 was most certainly a historic symbol of this convergence of new and old media – the internet and television – and of the domination of new over old. Should we be worried about standardization of the world by a dominant communication technology? While it would impoverish human heritage, it is highly unlikely to occur.

THE DEVELOPMENT OF THE MULTI-PURPOSE CELL PHONE

In 1998, as many cell phones were sold as cars and microcomputers. In 2001, in Finland, an extremely wired country, there were already more cell phones in service (three million) than traditional phones; more than half the population already had a mobile phone, and a penetration rate of more than 100 per cent was anticipated for the near future. Nokia, the former paper king, now in difficulty, managed to restructure itself to enter wireless telephony, becoming an innovator in the field; for example, the Nokia Communicator phone weighs only 250 grams and opens like a clamshell to reveal a microcomputer (the device was quickly miniaturized and equipped with more power and speed.)

It is estimated that there were 300 million cell phones in the world in 2005. More and more such phones will have internet terminals.

In 2000 in Finland, 10 to 15 per cent of mobile phones already had internet access. All sorts of peripherals can be added to mobile phones, such as digital cameras that send photos in real time over the internet, or information screens displaying local news; arriving in a new city, we can use our phones to select a hotel, check the weather forecast, and more. Cell phones will also become a substitute for wallets: they will read product barcodes and automatically debit the appropriate amount from an on-line bank account. At this point, we will have achieved the full paradigm of multi-purpose and omnipresent communication in the era of the Net Economy. New models integrate portable video on the cell phone's colour screen. The system will make it possible to develop the portable videophone and a number of mobile imaging services through a decoding chip.

Since 1999, the Japanese company NTT DoCoMo has been producing the i-mode system – which has claimed 20 per cent of the Japanese market in two years – replacing HTML and Java Web languages to provide fluid and fast transmission of all types of standard files on cell phones connected to the internet. This system offers markedly better performance than the European WAP system, and its success gives us a glimpse of a new generation of multi-functional, user-friendly, and efficient cell phones that connect to the internet. We are clearly still at the dawn of a revolution of digital communication tools tending towards multimedia. Now we're hearing about G3: third-generation phones, which – like computers over the past twenty years – appear in a higher-performance model each year.

Young people have overwhelmingly embraced the cell phone. In Canada, 45 per cent of young people had a cell phone by 2000, and 29 per cent planned to buy one in 2001. Sales have been booming since then in developed countries, including China and the Latin American nations. Pagers were also increasingly in vogue (they are less expensive, and a rudimentary coded language makes exchanges possible [235: Problem has been handled; 215: I'm running late; 210: Got your page, I understand]); but they are now being replaced by cell phones. Cell phones are vibrating and ringing more and more often in classrooms.

SATELLITES

A dense network of satellites, currently under construction, will soon provide wide digital coverage of the planet. By 2002, the

Skybridge system, from a consortium of companies in Europe, the United States, and Japan, already intended to have eighty satellites available in low orbit, making it possible to serve 20 million Web surfers simultaneously at minimum speeds of twenty megabytes for individuals and up to 200 megabytes for companies, while avoiding congestion on local loops. The consortium is now developing ways to provide access to interactive broadband services. It is considering geostationary satellites not only of low earth orbit (LEO) but also of medium earth orbit (MEO). A second-generation constellation will include broadband capabilities that imply a large spectrum demand. The competing international Teledesic project, in which Bill Gates is participating, planned no fewer than 288 satellites for 2003: internet heaven. In 2006, the satellite's coverage gets its worldwide extension. The challenge is now to offer more speed, interactivity, and broadband for multimedia services.

Mini- or micro-satellite dishes (which fit in the palm of the hand and cost ten dollars per month) make it possible to receive up to 500 TV and radio stations in the United States. In Canada, we had 220,000 kilometres of cable in 2000, and the annual rate of growth of satellite hookups was 581 per cent in 1999–2000.

THE FULFILLMENT OF
THE MYTH OF COMMUNICATION

Airline companies – beginning with Air Canada and then Cathay Pacific – will soon offer us onboard internet and e-mail services, keeping us constantly connected. To be connected at 35,000 feet and 11 Mbps – what could be more thrilling?

A transparent world in which communication brings everyone closer to everything and shows everyone everything? Omnipresent, multimedia, multi-purpose communications – isn't that enough? No. The fulfillment, the culmination of the myth of communication also requires that it reach the entire population with ever-increasing speed and power. Not to worry: major studies tell us that the transmission speed of telecommunications doubles every 150 days and internet traffic doubles every 100 days. The volume of data transmission is exceeding the volume of phone conversations.

In terms of film, digital projection transmitted by internet and via satellite directly to theatres has begun, and it will soon replace the old 33mm film reels. The images have greater definition, and the system will provide greater flexibility of programming for the public, thanks to the immediate and constant availability of all films on-line and the elimination of the problem of transporting film reels. It will create an insurmountable challenge for Hollywood hegemony. Furthermore, thanks to digitization, advertisers can adapt ads on television and movie screens for each target audience, markedly increasing their profits.

Of course, one might ask why businesspeople would continue to line the pockets of airline companies if they could gather all the information they needed without having to travel and meet with anyone they wanted via 3-D video-conference without leaving the office. And why go out to the movies when it's raining and you can receive any film at home via satellite and order in pizza over the internet? Why leave home when you can shop on-line, visit with friends and family via multimedia videophone, obtain medical diagnoses via internet, and telecommute? All of this assures the mind-boggling success of the digital economy and creates the culture of cocooning Faith Popcorn promised in 1991.

ORAL COMMUNICATION AND INSTRUMENTED COMMUNICATION

This being said, can we claim that communication is better or more intense for a Hong Kong businessman who has a cell phone stuck to each ear than for an African villager who follows an oral tradition? Communication conducted through current technologies is technically very powerful – much more so than the African tam-tam or the smoke signals of Native Americans. But what it gains in distance it loses in psychological proximity. We often talk about the solitude of those who live in cities with 5, 10, and 20 million inhabitants – cities in which people can suffer amid general indifference, where they can die two metres from their neighbour's door or on the subway at the centre of a fearful and uncaring crowd. What kind of communication are we talking about then? How does it compare to the solidarity of rural villagers? Furthermore, compare the fate of the isolated elderly in major cities to that of elders in African villages. Communication is clearly more active, more complete, more accomplished in a social sense in the African example.

And how should we judge the trend of sending text messages of two or three lines with mobile phones? SMS (Short Message Service) lets Peter send a little love note to Julie, or lets Julie remind John to buy a loaf of bread on the way home; it helps us communicate an address or some other useful (or useless) piece of information. Because what's important is staying connected. These text messages, which are becoming a custom, are the symptom of the same frenzied need for communication that sparked the pager trend. Many of us have no professional reason to own a pager; we are not all emergency room doctors or bike couriers. With their short messages, pager addicts engage in style competitions, vying to outdo each other in inventiveness, brevity, and phonetic effectiveness: CU L8R (See you later); BCNU (Be seeing you); XLNT (Excellent!). Communication has become a frantic game and an initiation rite for the cult of the digital. Even the Protestant Youth of Hanover has succumbed, sending its members virtual prayers on their cell phones. One of the group's leaders explained that "Young people can transmit their prayers via SMS to be said during the service that is retransmitted via Webcam on the internet, so that the faithful can follow mass on their cell phones, without even attending."[3] According to the organizers, almost 2,000 people receive mass, the teachings of the Bible, prayers, and sermons on their cell phones via SMS.

AN INEXHAUSTIBLE BODY OF WATER THAT SPREADS

Marshall McLuhan had an intuition. Not only would communication technology influence the content of the message, but for some it would become an end in itself. In this vein, an American surfer from Los Angeles opened a site in 2001 called sendmeadollar.com. He had immediate and considerable success, proving that money is itself a means of communication; the symbolism of this further strengthened the attraction of cybernauts to the system, and his site was named "site of the week" by Yahoo. As a result, the site began receiving some 10,000 hits per day. The surfer asked people to mail their dollars to "The Amazing Site" and gave a post office box number. He amassed several thousand dollars in various international currencies. Others imitated him. A young man from the Netherlands wanted to travel but couldn't afford to, so he launched the site let-me-stay-for-a-day.com, on which he solicited free accommodation. He left on his trip with more than a thousand invitations in his pocket. Internet communication is like a boundless body of water that flows everywhere once the tap is turned on – it floods the planet. Its power is symptomatic of our basic need to communicate; we connect to the flow of communication as if connecting to the energy of life itself. It responds to a profound existential desire, it fills an emptiness, it satisfies a vital instinct. What remains to be seen is whether this flood will pollute or pollinate the planet.

THE NETWORK OF SOLITUDES

The Web is a hunting reserve and adventure land for single people. We could spread a map of the human heart across it, or build on it a virtual temple of Solitude. We observe within the Web forlorn souls visiting discussion groups, passing through portals, and browsing dating sites on a quest for Prince Charming or Ms Right. Threatened by predators in search of naive victims, courageous singles tirelessly seek soulmates. Solitudes endlessly meet and intertwine on the Web; the sites devoted to the plight of the lonely are many, and they offer cybermeetings of all types. Yet wasn't Heidegger right to question the very possibility of human communication?

INTERPERSONAL INFORMATION
AND COMMUNICATION

It seems that the same law applies generally for evaluating social solidarity and communication. The greater the number of people assembled, the greater the danger that the feeling of solitude will grow – unless a mob mentality takes over. And as our remote communication technologies increase, our psychologically close communication decreases. But this is obviously a very general law, one with a thousand and one exceptions. For example, for many older people, more or less abandoned in their seniors' residences, television is an essential link to the social system.

Worldwide networks of digital communication now allow businesspeople to connect to their offices anytime, anywhere, via satellite phone or internet. Retired people connect to the internet to communicate with their grandchildren; their use of this fashionable means of communication makes them seem younger to the little ones, and the technology encourages them to interact with others. To some extent, the network also makes it possible to eradicate the geographical distances that often separate families. Work, school, and the ease with which one can now travel to the other side of the world combine to scatter family members far and wide. It's a good thing that communication technologies permit us to communicate often. But this may not seem like progress when we compare it to the simple oral communication between the members of families who inhabit the same house or village.

TENTH PARADOXICAL LAW
The digital itself constitutes an extremely powerful and universal tool of interpretation and communication, able to express all languages and all manner of content. Because it is also the network for all communication networks, it has imposed itself with immediate and undeniable success, thus confirming McLuhan's paradox "the medium is the message."

We could also express this paradoxical law as follows: Communication technology is the message. And when a technology is a technology of communication – whether the wheel, the ship, writing, roads, printing, the railroad, electricity, the car, aviation, the radio, the telephone, the television, or the internet – it tends to meet with great success.

But what is the message of internet media? It signifies a new, prodigious, immediate, and remote connectivity between human beings and a power to interpret and transform the new world. It a powerful tool of interpersonal communication, of the integration of all knowledge, of the convergence of all technologies, and of effective action in the world. What more could we hope for? Something so powerful cannot be imposed immediately and with complete success. But, this being the case, we should not be surprised that it can found a new civilization, inspire quasi-religious enthusiasm, and fuel utopian hopes.

7: The Internet Tower of Babel

The myth of the Tower of Babel is the first myth of modernity.
It places God as the initiator of the information society,
and it is the founding myth of linguistic and cultural diversity.

THE INTERNET: A PLANETARY HYPERCORTEX?

The faithful of the internet religion believe that digital globalization is the end result of human evolution. They invoke the prediction of Teilhard de Chardin that at the end of the process of creation there will be a kingdom of the mind, of a superior human intelligence characterized by shared knowledge and wisdom. They see the internet as the instrument of this evolution towards perfection and employ metaphors of a connective skin that grows to cover the world, or of neurons of a planetary hypercortex. It's that old nostalgia, that time-worn myth of human unity that will return with the digital realm. Chateaubriand, among others, had already spoken of the dream of a universal society: "The folly of the moment is to achieve a unity of peoples and to make a single man of the entire species."[1]

Is the Web as unified as internet devotees dream? Is it not in fact an ocean on which voyagers immediately lose their way? A complicated cacophony rather than a dream of unifying global connection? Perhaps we could say of the internet what Jorge Luis Borges said about old books:

O Time thy pyramids. This much is known: For every rational line or forthright statement there are leagues of senseless cacophony, verbal nonsense, and incoherency. (I know of one semibarbarous zone who librarians repudiate the "vain and superstitious habit" of trying to find sense in books, equating such a quest with attempting to find meaning in dreams or in the chaotic lines of the palm of one's hand ... They will acknowledge that the inventors of writing imitated the twenty-five natural symbols, but contend that that adoption was fortuitous, coincidental, and that books in themselves have no meaning. That argument, as we shall see, is not entirely fallacious.)[2]

THE INTERNET: METAPHOR FOR THE TOWER OF BABEL?

We could say that the same arrogance, the same will to power that the Bible tells us provoked God when men tried to build a tower that would rise up to meet him, are naively expressed today in the desire to create unified global communication through digital technology. According to the myth, we owe the birth of 10,000 different languages to God. In effect, to put an end to man's inordinate pride in aspiring to reach heaven by building this tower, God acted in a way that foreshadowed our current information society. He did not hurl lightning bolts or unleash other forces of nature to destroy this defiant tower; instead, he created the diversity of languages. Unable to communicate among themselves, the men could not coordinate their building project and deserted the work site. The abandoned tower fell into ruin. This myth involves the punishment of humankind, and we have traditionally interpreted it as being negative. But we should instead look at it as the birth of cultural and linguistic diversity, the will of God, and a heritage that is as precious and as necessary as biodiversity.

Aficionados of globalization also take delight in the fact that the internet is promoting the spread of English as a universal language of communication. We are supposedly witnessing an American cyberunification of the world, progress for one and all. In reality, while the use of English is growing on the Web, it is losing steam. International Technology and Trade Associates, in its *State of the Internet 2000*, pointed out that of the estimated 308 million Netizens, only 51.3 per cent use English (less than half this percentage connect from North America). Of course, 78 per cent of Web pages were still in English, and 95 per cent of them were devoted to e-commerce. But, the report concluded, "as more users come online in Europe and Asia as well as the rest of the world, the internet is becoming multicultural, multilingual, and multipolar."[3]

By 2006, internet development had confirmed this. The expanding array of languages on the Web has begun to reflect the importance of diverse linguistic groups.

According to UNESCO estimates, in 2000, English represented only 65 per cent of content, and this will soon drop below the 50 per cent mark due to the rapid rise of other languages on the internet – mainly French, Mandarin, Hindi, Spanish, Russian, Arabic, Bengali, and Portuguese. Specialists predict that in 2007, Mandarin will exceed the 50 per cent mark in terms of internet content. The Web will soon become a Tower of Babel – in other words, multilingual.

In 2006, UNESCO stated that more than 90 per cent of languages have not yet appeared on the internet, and about 3,000 languages will disappear if we do not work to ensure their survival. It is significant that UNESCO has proposed using the internet to do the job (this, of course, poses a huge challenge for the poorest countries, many of whose languages are purely oral and have no alphabet).

A NEW MENTAL STRUCTURE?

A number of specialists maintain that the internet promotes a new mental structure. Navigating via hypertext and the internet's interactive links is, like the relationship of a glove and a hand, "an inverted reflection of our mental space, a sort of objective shareable mental space," wrote Derrick de Kerckhove, who emphasizes that "the true nature of language is externalized and shared thought."[4] The idea is seductive, but it suggests an overly instrumented notion of thought. In attempting to objectify thought in our external relationships with the world and with other people, we are removing its autonomy from instrumented language, which provides its capacity to transcend social language and to oppose it. The idea of a connective, collective, or shared intelligence confuses the field with the ball that the individual mind throws at it. Even the Lacanian concept of the importance of the Other – that is, of collective and interactive social language as structuring the unconscious – does not deny the fundamental uniqueness of the thought that participates in it. Grammar, syntax, and logic inform thought, and intelligence is based (etymologically) on the image of connections that we establish between things, but the unfathomable source of thought in each of us cannot be reduced to software or to hyperlinks any more than to grammar and syntax. If this were the case, we would think according to the architecture and logic of Office, Windows 2000, or Microsoft Explorer. Our logic stems more from our family and social structure.

In short, this objectified, exteriorizing, or "chosiste" notion of thought is too American, too factual. We cannot turn our mental spaces inside out like the fingers of a glove to objectify the structures of the internet or the cyberworld. To do so would be to submit human thought to the structures of techniques and machines. Reduction to absurdity may help us here. Socrates thought and communicated in the oral mode, not the written, print, digital, or multimedia modes. And I am participating intimately in Socrates's thought in spite of, and across, changes in technical modes of expression. Multimedia, fortunately, cannot change the thought of Socrates.

THE CYBERWORLD DOES NOT COME FROM SOMEWHERE ELSE, LIKE A UFO

The cyberworld has taken root in our countries and in the streets of our cities. To say that the virtual space of the internet is a sort of exteriorized objectification of our mental space is to forget that individuals, although they use the same browsers, have different cultural roots. It denies the overwhelming cultural diversity of our mental spaces.

Societal structures are as changeable as the cultures in which societies distinctively unite. And communication technologies have also changed a lot – from the archaic natural mode of the oral and the gestural to the most sophisticated digital multimedia; both forms coexist today, even in our most technologically developed societies. We still spend more hours a day in the real world than we do in cyberspace. And we must admit that the logical and rigid style of the German language corresponds to a culture, while the light style of the Italian language, with its aesthetic flourishes, corresponds to another culture. There are as many different images of the world as there are languages and cultures.

As the binary logic of computer language spreads worldwide, will it erase these differences and create a shared connective intelligence, standardizing mental spaces, imaginative realms, logic, and cultures? One could argue that thinking together does not mean thinking alike. But thinking according to the same grammar, the same syntax, and in the same words is the beginning of thinking alike. This is the level at which the identity of a culture starts to be forged.

Will the differences between Indian, African, Asian, and European cultures be dissolved into the North American form of thinking? Into Windows 2000? As an ordinary observer, and hardly a prophet, I would answer (as would the vast majority of us) "Never." Even brutal, intelligent, and enduring colonization has never been able to overcome the invincibility of a culture.

CYBERSPACE IS BREAKING UP

Cyberspace is going to split apart like the continents, countries, and territories of the real world it reflects. It is therefore impossible to subscribe to the naive notion – which is far too widespread among digital technology zealots – that the internet and the cyber-world will erase borders, territories, and differences by imposing the same objectified mental space on everyone. The objectified space of whose culture, whose language? American or Chinese? Yours or mine? There are many divergent mental spaces, immutable cultural origins that commingle in cyberspace without being absorbed by it; and it is possible to spend a few hours in an airport without the colour fading from one's skin. The cyberworld will split apart, diversify, and segment into a variety of cultural, linguistic, aesthetic, community, peripheral, marginal, corporate, and imaginative spaces – even if we use the same computer and the same browser to navigate it. Cyberspace will form within itself and increasingly reflect the human diversity found in the real world, because it is the creation and the technical, commercial, and cultural product of the real world.

Experience demonstrates that, at the individual level, virtual space has already split apart and is like a labyrinth. We each choose our own cyberworld with its own bookmarks in the course of our personal navigation. Amid the billions of pages accumulated on the Web there are already as many cyberworlds as there are individual surfers.

THE INTERNET OF CULTURAL
AND LINGUISTIC DIVERSITY

We are seeing large commercial groups seize control of the media convergence of networks, software, and content, but the internet is a web that in theory precludes domination by a central power, and it can encourage diversity in the end. Besides, democracy requires that these monopolies be limited and that a competitive balance among them be achieved.

The internet is not simply a teleshopping centre for citizens who are reduced to the status of e-consumers. It also offers extraordinary potential for developing virtual communities, for the exercise of electronic democracy and the activities of opposing forces, as we saw in Seattle in 1999. The internet is also the place for all self-media and for individual and local initiatives to be heard; it can give a voice to a group, an oppressed culture, a writer, or a marginal cause.

English will compete with thousands of other languages. The success of on-line translation systems will increase at the same rate as the diversity of languages that find new opportunities to express themselves on the internet. While only a small minority of the world's population can connect to the internet, we must also remember that for 90 per cent of this population English is not the mother tongue. The international organizations that predict that half the world's 6,000 extant languages will have disappeared within fifty years are extremely pessimistic – this is highly unlikely. We need to put the debate in a more realistic context. It doesn't matter whether television was invented by francophones or anglophones: today it represents almost every language, as does radio.

ELEVENTH PARADOXICAL LAW
Despite the unifying and globalizing tendency of its underlying technology and symbolism, the cyberworld will increasingly reflect linguistic and cultural diversity and even contribute to their promotion.

Because the cyberworld emanates from the real world that it reflects, however powerful the unifying tendency of its technology and its founding symbolic system, it will not be able to slow the increasing fragmentation of languages used in it, its content, its community of users, and, consequently, its imagination and its values. Millions of people of different cultures who speak different languages circulate on our highways; while they travel the same routes in the same brands of car, they have unique projects and preoccupations. Likewise, a variety of people, also travelling for an array of reasons, meet and talk on planes without assimilating or becoming countrymen.

Globalization is both the naive dream of businesspeople and the exaggerated worry of pessimistic intellectuals. It is a superficial trend, one that will never take hold permanently. Besides, globalization is not all bad – for example, when it comes to the environment, human rights, natural disasters, and so on. And it is unreasonable to oppose the free circulation of ideas, people, and goods. However, cosmopolitanism is not a state that solidifies; it is unstable, vulnerable, and dynamic – whether it be in Hong Kong, New York, Montreal, or Paris. The world is not a computer, merchandise, a global market, or a Holiday Inn, and it never will be. If the globalization trend were to gain strength, then opposing forces would be unleashed. Peripheral conflicts are already arising, and so is a critical global consciousness denouncing environmental pollution, genetically modified organisms (GMOs), multilateral agreements, violence, excessive centralism, and the American desire to bring world trade to heel and reduce world cultures to the level of merchandise.

We must denounce this naive, damaging, and somewhat totalitarian technological utopia, this illusion that we can enter a better, unified cyberspace that would gradually replace the conflict-ridden, fragmented, and unhappy real world. Groupthink systems are dangerous. The fall of the Berlin Wall opened the door to an electronic capitalism that claims to be our saviour and intends to rule the planet – an imperialism that is too sure of itself. As far as its enthusiasts are concerned, we will finally attain the goal of humanity through globalization, hyperliberalism, omnipresent digital technologies, triumphant e-commerce, and planetary communication that initiates dialogue and institutes individual liberties everywhere. We are witnessing an outburst of perverse neo-colonialism, harbinger of false representations, dominated by magical thinking. Like any hegemony, it is already fated to collapse. Let's dream instead of the success of a multipolar world!

ON-LINE TRANSLATION IN REAL TIME

The globalization of the internet also creates a new need. If, out of respect for linguistic diversity, we refuse to adopt English as a universal language, we have to develop tools to understand the Chinese, Arabic, Finnish, and Japanese Web sites to which we will have access. A number of companies are working on this problem, offering on-line real-time translation systems that are constantly being improved and increasing the number of languages they can translate. These machine translation and text summary tools (nStein, a Quebec company, claims to get at a text's DNA and unique meaning) combine dictionaries, linguistic research, intelligent agents (understanding tools), and a capacity for computer processing now available on servers.

LOCALIZATION

The current demand for international communication and the many related markets will have us relying more and more on translation, whether for education, entertainment, or trade – we will need, for example, translated directions for the use of manufactured items. However, respect for cultural diversity and the desire for better translation will compel us to promote high-quality cultural adaptation – or localization – over word-for-word translation. Localization is indispensable, particularly for educational and cultural productions.

8: Generation Net and Internet Culture

Speak Net to better understand one another.

There is much talk these days of a "Net generation." It could also be called generation 0/1 – the generation that reached adolescence at a time when computing forced itself upon our social consciousness with the tumult of the internet, a time when the acceleration of social time disrupted the tranquil rhythm of generations. There is no doubt that this is the wired generation, the Web generation. Its members use the name as a rallying cry for the digital revolution that disrupts our world as we embark on the new millennium. We have therefore come to refer to them as the "natives" – as opposed to the "immigrants," or the older generation, which is working hard to adapt to the cyberworld.

New digital technologies are revolutionizing not only communications, but also the film, television, and entertainment industries, as well as the stock market, commerce, education, and even our private lives. The facts are there, the numbers prove it, the new economy and globalization require it, the knowledge economy prioritizes it, and venture capital has invested ferociously in the internet. The NASDAQ exchange has seen stunning accelerations and irrational feverishness; margin-account investors play on daily fluctuations. For imposing its browser with its basic software, Microsoft was put on trial, becoming a symbol for the revolution – a revolution mounted within a few short years. Newspapers report daily on the internet, and the intensity of that reporting only increased after the 2000–01 NASDAQ collapse.

The revolution fired imaginations and fuelled hopes and fears concerning the new millennium. Trepidation about the "Y2K bug" heightened the emotion. Convinced that computer calendars would interpret 2000 as 1900, we worried that when the new year dawned airplanes would fall from the sky, cities would be plunged into darkness, bank accounts would disappear, gas pumps would stop pumping, and on and on.

Today everything, or almost everything, depends on computers. The digital universe is opening a new era of Western civilization, and the social imagination is experiencing tremors, resonating with the multiple facets of this technological revolution. The Web has become the social symbol of this revolution. In the public perception, the Net generation is identified with playing video games, with searching for homework information on the internet, with attending wired schools, with frequenting internet cafés. This new generation supposedly spends more time in front of a computer screen than in front of a book or even a television.

It is supposedly the generation of Web surfers, of skateboarders and snowboarders. This may be a striking image, but statistics refute it. For, at the dawn of the twenty-first century, there are not yet enough personal computers – let alone computers connected to the internet – to support such a statement. It is not so much teenagers as it is twenty-five to forty-five year olds who have taken up surfing, mainly in their professional environments, but a little bit at home. Computers are still far from being a mass medium like television. They remain the privilege of the well-to-do, of professionals and their children. In 2000, there were many more computers in offices than in homes. And statistics also show that the vast majority of searches on the internet are for practical information – references, technical knowledge, tourism and travel, and shopping sources – information that is not primarily of interest to teenagers. Such surfing is not the kind of emotional activity that identifies a generation. And most Web pages are still discouragingly dull.

DOES AN INTERNET CULTURE EXIST?

We talk about it every day. The internet is now entrenched in rich countries. But does that mean we can say there is an internet culture? It would be difficult to demonstrate that a telephone

culture exists, even though we can describe the social uses of the
phone, the rituals, the most common private or public messages.
This is because the medium of the telephone has not yet attracted
the attention of writers, musicians, or artists – of people eager to
launch new creative endeavours with the magic of the touch-button
keypad and the earpiece. The content of phone use – business
exchanges, mundane personal conversations, the evil empire of voice
mail – is not conducive to creativity; there is no obvious specificity of
language involved. (But this will change soon with the cell phone.)

We could also doubt the existence of a radio culture, even if we
are listeners of so-called cultural programs. Radio broadcasts cultural content, in particular music, but as a medium it produced
few original creations. Its language has its rituals of rhythm and
sound, its suggestive power can be very effective and work on the
imagination, but this is not enough to make it a specific culture.
Television, however, has spawned a specific form of writing, an
aesthetic, many remarkable original works; the frequent mediocrity
of its content does not take away from its cultural legitimacy.

What, then, of internet culture? From the broad perspective of
anthropologists, everything is part of the culture; in this sense, the
internet has growing social uses and an omnipresence in the news,
so it is allotted an important place as an instrument of dissemination and as a cultural object. But does the internet generate original music, art, literature, and film – products that would otherwise
not exist? Does the internet inspire creators to create? Is the internet behind new aesthetic research, new writing, new linguistic,
artistic, dramatic, and musical structures and values? New conceptions of space-time? New modes of interactive participation? New
audiences? The answer to all of these questions is "Yes."

Until now, the uses of the internet have primarily been on the
order of exchanges of information, practical details, e-mail, and
e-commerce. However, we are already seeing literary works, novels,
poems, and essays appear on the internet with original characteristics of multimedia writing. The authors, like Web artists, are
exploring and exploiting writings in arborescence: hypertext links;
the relationship between image, text, sound; the sculptural quality
of icons; streaming video; and the simultaneous interactive participation of several authors or visitors. Since 1985, the French-
language telematic novel *Marco Polo*, or *The New Book of Wonders*,
under the patronage of Umberto Eco and Italo Calvino (which I
coordinated via modem, as public access to the internet took off

only in 1993), involved the daily creation of a collaborative novel by such writers as (among others) Louis Caron (Quebec), Jacques Savoie (New Brunswick), Sony Labou Tansi (Congo), Abdelaziz Kacem (Tunisia), Jacques Lacarrière and Florence Delay (France), as well as artist-illustrator Herménégilde Chiasson (New Brunswick).

Today there are many Web sites of artists who work directly on the Net, some of whom are famous, like Laurie Anderson and Michel Jaffrenou. The number of films created for the internet is growing, and there are already several on-line film festivals, including LeoFest, launched by film star Leonardo DiCaprio. Sites of writers exploring multimedia writing are increasingly numerous, and literary discussion groups are growing in popularity; in the field of music, the growth is phenomenal. Faced with this explosion of internet culture, what are we doing in our respective countries, within our cultural identities? Everyone agrees that the internet is lacking content from cultural minorities – in other words, non-Americans. In Quebec, it has even been suggested that subsidizing low-income families to connect to the internet would be like sending them into American cyberspace.

Beyond practical information or e-commerce (which is available most frequently in English), there is enormous potential in the content market, which, it is said, will soon catch up to, and even surpass, the already impressive digital technology and software market. Major corporations (like Microsoft and AOL) understand this and are buying TV stations and newspaper and magazine groups to feed their communications networks. These networks will soon develop an insatiable thirst for content. Canada, Quebec, France, Mexico, and Brazil, among others, are home to many high-quality cultural industries and high-calibre multimedia companies, but creators for this exploding market will soon be in short supply. Will governments give these companies the means to respond to the demand, or will they leave the field wide open to the Americans? It is now the responsibility of each government, each nation, to include the internet in its cultural budget, giving it the same consideration as music, theatre, literature, or museums.

Creators of innovative content are needed to give the internet its due, to infuse it with nobility and legitimacy in the eyes of the people, who have the fundamental right to access the new culture of our era and appropriate it for themselves. Developing our own internet cultures protects and promotes our cultural identities and languages in the face of the great English-speaking North American collectivity. And this new content could reverberate throughout the internet. The internet was not designed for e-commerce. It is worthy of so much more. Cultures will lose a lot of ground if they do not conquer the internet. They must do so by training creators and by conducting research and development into innovative content; they will also have to ensure that the public institutions that support the creation and dissemination of culture recognize the importance of internet culture. These institutions throughout the world should be creating policies dealing with internet culture and allocating significant budgets to it. We are waiting impatiently for them to recognize internet culture, which they often overlook or underestimate, and to actively support its development.

We don't have to sell our souls to the internet, but we do have to give it a soul. We must create cultures on the internet, and there is no culture without creators.

A NEW DIGITAL CULTURE

Without lapsing into the magical thinking of those who warn of the disappearance of archaic media in the name of everything digital, we must admit that computers and the Web will eventually produce a new digital culture. Western thought, philosophy, literature, and art owe a lot to paper and printing. This shocks nobody; everyone recognizes it. It will be the same with the spread of digital technology. But to reassure the pessimists I will point out that we know how to distinguish between the poetry of Baudelaire and the paper his publisher printed it on and the cathode ray tube by means of which it is broadcast, even if this will inevitably change our sensitivity to that poetry.

After a half a millennium under the dominant influence of Gutenberg, we are witnessing the advent of a multimedia that is reconnecting us with the oral and multi-sensory tradition described by ethnologists. The invention of printing precipitated a radical seizure of learned communication by social elites and the disappearance of regional languages. It also created the immense social phenomenon of illiteracy, with its incalculable political repercussions. In undivided, integrated traditional societies, illiteracy simply didn't exist. Are we to believe in progress when the incredible invention of printing, hailed by one and all as extraordinary progress, resulted in illiteracy on a global scale? (UNESCO estimates that worldwide there are 885 million illiterate people over the age of fifteen.)

THE FUTURE OF THE BOOK AND OF PAPER

Those who worry about the future of the book in the face of the internet's triumph must keep in mind that we are printing, publishing, and reading more books than ever before. The Forest Products Association of Canada clears up any doubts we may have about this: the production of paper for printing went from 946,000 metric tonnes in 1980 to 1.560 million in 1990 and 2.221 million in 2000.

A number of on-line publishers offer an alternative network. In 2000, we saw many on-line publishers appear, even in France – among them oohoo.com (one of the first), cylibris.com, cyeditions.com, manuscrit.com, and publibook.com. And internet portals dedicated to electronic books are springing up. In spring 2001, AOL-TimeWarner launched iPublish.com, a site dedicated to promoting literature; it publishes some fifty books per year and republishes some of the best titles of the Time Warner Book Group, which was bought by the French group Lagardère in 2006. But there are also enormous catalogues of paperback editions and other products to buy on-line at Amazon and Barnes & Noble. Each of these major on-line distributors had sales of about US$3 billion in 2000 – the American book market is valued at US$20 billion. And we are witnessing a great number of endeavours. For example, in the fall of 2000, a science fiction writer created the Baen Free Library, which offered free downloads of books from several different authors. He professed to having based his strategy on piracy: "Losses any author suffers from piracy are almost certainly offset by the additional publicity which, in practice, *any* kind of free copies of a book usually engender, [whether through] public libraries, friends borrowing and loaning each other books, used book stores, promotional copies, etc."[1]

The digital book remains a minute part of the process, entirely negligible from an economic viewpoint. The failure of Stephen King – a best-selling author if ever there was one – in betting on his appeal to sell his thriller *The Plant* serialized on-line demonstrates the difficulties of marketing an unpublished book on-line. In autumn 2000, a King spokesperson told the *New York Times* that

"Even for Stephen King, making people aware that this is out there is a challenge. That is one reason why I am sure that Stephen King would never give up traditional publishing."[2] Not to mention the general lack of enthusiasm of libertarian internet users for anything you have to pay for. Unlike Stephen King, Warren Adler persevered, maintaining a site through which he hoped to sell his own writings for less than the bookstores charged and to become a successful publisher of his own books first on-line and then in paper editions. But this type of initiative is mired in practical difficulty, as seductive as it may sound in theory.

The number of on-line publishers has grown rapidly, and they have a variety of business plans: vanity press, Xlibris.com, iUniverse.com, iPublish.com, PU.net, manuscrit.com, Olympio.com, publibook.com, boodaa.com, alteredit.com, and so on. All have commercial objectives. But, following the libertarian logic of the internet, a German publisher professes to publish with no regard for copyright. On his site, TextZ, Sebastian Luetgert announces: "No copyright, no rights reserved." He claims to be a member of an a.s.ambulanzen Situationist collective and has published the complete works of Guy Debord, as well as the texts of Aragon and other authors. "I am very politicized," Luetgert says. "We can no longer express ourselves against commercial culture through cultural countermeasures. We have to go further, specifically to infringe copyright law, because an individual should not need a credit card to read what he or she wants to on the Internet." He was prepared to move his server to another country to keep it from being shut down: "This is a war we cannot lose."[3]

Such trends may continue on the margins of the e-commerce onslaught, but in the realm of books, the internet will probably never be more than an on-line sales catalogue or a search database that will not replace the paper book. (There are major exceptions – notably, important out-of-print books in the field of research and education; see, for example, "Les Classiques des sciences sociales," at ww.uqac.ca/Classiques_des_sciences_sociales, initiated by Jean-Marie Tremblay in Quebec). But if it seriously tried, fully exploiting the power of digital technology and providing added value, the book would immediately become something other than a book: it would be more of a game, or an interactive exercise, or an on-line multimedia installation.

Interesting on-line publishing efforts deserve mention. An American author with the assumed but legal name of Mark Amerika has created an interactive on-line novel entitled *grammaton.com*, which, in attempting to exploit all newly available software, interfaces, graphics cards, video cards, and sound cards (the reader must invest in sophisticated equipment), offers a new method of multimedia literary production. The novel is presented as an open and interactive work containing some 1,000 screen pages; it uses hypertext links that provide a plethora of stories through which we can immerse ourselves in excitement, delight, or apprehension. The author, who teaches digital arts at the University of Colorado, claims to have surpassed the limits of the traditional book and to be situated between film, literature, and art, making this a very interesting initiative. But he also underlines the fact that he has become "an industry addict," and that the technology of printing on paper now seems to him to have "remarkable stability" – which is not the least of its qualities, all things considered.

Another French author, Renaud Camus, republished on the internet his book *Vaisseaux brûlés*, which was already published on paper, and he claims to have found in this new hypertext version the solution to certain writing problems that had interested him. Many other examples could be cited, including the on-line literary magazine *Metal and Flesh/Chair et metal*, put out by Québécois Ollivier Dyens. Dyens calls his magazine an on-line space rather than a site, thus highlighting the novelty of the spatial and hypergraphic research that electronic writing calls for.

According to an initial judgment of the federal court of New York (rendered in July 2001), a Web site is not a book. In fact, when Random House, the world's leading English-language publisher and a subsidiary of the Bertelsmann group, sued RosettaBooks.com, a small on-line publisher, for having electronically published authors whom it had under contract, it lost. The judge declared that the paper book and the electronic book are not legally of the same nature. And RosettaBooks, which had signed contracts directly with the authors without going through Random House, had the support of the 8,000-member-strong Author's Guild and of the Association of Authors' Representatives (an association of writers' agents).

Is it the medium or the message that is at stake? McLuhan would have agreed with the judge, but Random House has appealed the decision and refuses to make a legal distinction between a book and an e-book. In my opinion, it is clearly a question of derivative rights, which must be part of the initial contract, like the rights for a film adaptation of a novel. Otherwise, the publisher of a paper book cannot claim rights over an e-book any more than it can over the film on which it is based.

BOOKS AND ELECTRONIC PUBLICATIONS

A book is the opposite of a Web site. There are nuances, however. A digital encyclopedia, on videodisc or on-line, has obvious, increasingly indispensable advantages compared to the twenty-six large-format volumes of the encyclopedias of my childhood (plus annual supplements). With a volume of two or three little disks, or one DVD, or the internet, I can now easily access a large amount of regularly updated written and audiovisual information. For the same price (and one day this may be possible), anyone would be willing to buy an encyclopedic or linguistic dictionary in e-book format – one that instantly displays, in high-quality graphics, all research on a word or a name.

Language labs on disk are educationally effective in a way that no book can rival. Scientific magazines on-line make it possible to publish research results without waiting months, even years, which is important when date of publication is competitive. Besides, through e-commerce the internet can contribute tremendously to promoting and distributing books. It already encourages – Oh, the paradox! – the sale of old, rare, and sought-after books: a French virtual bookstore, Chapitre.com, carries some seven million old or out-of-print books for collectors, and it has taken on partners to sell to majors like Barnes & Noble. The internet also encourages micro-editions. Besides, new software makes it possible to efficiently search through large encyclopedias and the vast corpus of texts and images now stored on-line.

American companies like Chapters and Borders also offer to print any book in demand at a regular bookstore, providing access to countless books that no bookstore could stock and that no publisher could regularly republish. No more out-of-print and limited-run books – and all this for a very modest price, because the significant cost of production, distribution, storage, and returns is eliminated.

Can we revolutionize the traditional technologies of paper and ink? Will we stop using paper for the good of our forests? At the Xerox centre in Palo Alto, California, researcher Nick Sheridon has been working since 1972 on creating a new synthetic and digital medium to replace paper, one that is reusable for several successive printings. It is composed of plastic micro-beads, one one-hundredth of a millimetre in diameter, encapsulated and mobile within the minuscule cavities of a thin elastic film filled with fluid. Electrical impulses sent via computer make it possible to orient each of these micro-beads to show one side (black) or the other (white), thereby creating texts or images using the binary logic of the pixels of computing.

According to Sheridon, this medium – called Gyricon – could replace newsprint and many other forms of paper. Since it is recyclable and as inexpensive to mass-produce as traditional paper, it could replace paper for printing, photocopying, and so on. It joins paper's line of succession throughout the ages; "paper" has been limestone, clay, leather, papyrus, cotton fibre, and wood pulp. But formidable technological challenges remain before it can be put to as general and as diversified a use as paper. Gyricon would put at our disposal a synthetic paper that is digitally printable, flexible, and recyclable, but it is passive when compared to plasma screens, which hold greater possibilities. Besides, the paper industry is sustained by the many other domestic and commercial uses of paper, which account for half the annual production.

And what of electronic ink? Joseph Jacobsen, a researcher from Media Lab in Boston, has announced that we will soon have a sort of electronic ink, which, when integrated into the pages of an ordinary-looking book, will make one of 20,000 works saved in a memory card housed in the book's binding appear on the book's cover and pages; all the reader has to do is press a button on the book's spine. The e-book, or the CyBook, can already store thirty 500-page books; the ad for it tells us that it is a veritable portable library. It allows us to carry with us the equivalent of 15,000 pages of books, newspapers, or magazines, and it permits us to increase character size, attach personal notes, and surf the Web with ease. But do we really want to carry 15,000 pages of text around with us?

In 1998, the first e-books appeared – the RocketBook, the SoftBook, the EveryBook, the CyBook – and there are already several brands of cyberbooks in existence; but they will only achieve commercial success when they become as pleasant to read, as beautiful, as physically durable, and as financially accessible as the traditional paper book. Which is as good as saying that there is no danger of this happening anytime soon, and that the advantages that cyberbooks offer over paper books for the same price will have to be considerable if we are to change our reading habits. There are clearly many conditions to be met. In my opinion, the American Electronic Book Newsstand Association, the initiative of the Toronto Public Library to make twenty-four e-books available to the public, and the initiative of the Algonquin Area Public Library in Illinois, which did the same, will change nothing. The sale of electronic books by the American giant Gemstar hit its ceiling at under 100,000 copies in 2001, and the most optimistic forecasts put sales at 1.7 million copies in 2004. Since then, however, most such efforts have failed. Can the new prototype launched by Sony in 2006 at the Las Vegas Consumer Electronics Show – the Sony Reader – actually succeed? This new technology is based on e-ink and reflects natural light instead of being lit from inside; its price is lower, too, at about $400; but this does not change the basic fact that a book must be a book. It cannot contrive to be the iPod of literature. A book is a remarkable technological object, beautiful and cheap. It is in itself a textual screen and demands a specific mental and ideological attitude of the reader. No expensive electronic gadget will ever replace it.

We must not forget that books are not gadgets. If we do, then civilization will have been brought very low indeed. Still, we may see a proliferation of book Web sites through which authors can prolong the lifespan of their works by making additions or corrections directly to the text to accommodate their rapidly changing subject field – be it science, technology, or economics. On these sites, authors can set up discussion forums, display letters from readers, or create a community of involved readers. They can become Webmasters of their own books.

Speed and instantaneity may be values foreign to the tradition of the book, but the value of community is of considerable worth. It is revealing that at the spring 2000 Salon du Livre in Paris, software and e-book distributors were welcomed to a new zone called the "E-book Village"; the same year, the company PlanetExpo created a "virtual book fair" for Montreal's Salon du Livre, organizing virtual booths and discussion forums with authors. Sites like these are very flexible and can reach an international audience, provided that they can gain visibility on the sea of the internet.

Well-known interviewer and host of French cultural TV programs Bernard Pivot has launched a virtual edition of his popular annual spelling championship; and Frédéric Grolleau, also of France, was daring enough to launch in 1999 the first on-line literary program, *Paru TV*, on the Web site paru.com, the success of which was inevitably limited. "It's the only literary program on the Web," commented Grolleau. "It's unfortunate that it's not better known," he added, admitting that his wife had never watched one of his shows in its entirety. "The Internet is very abstract and its format is not user-friendly. A bit of life is lost because of the technology. But something is gained as well. With its freeze frames, it's kind of like a *photoroman*.'"[4]

Just as printing fundamentally changed the tradition of storytelling and oral memory, e-publishing – with its new modes of writing, and therefore of thinking, reading, and distribution – may gradually transform the very nature of books. It may give rise to a new mode of cultural creation that will co-exist with traditional books, a mode that will be far removed from the archaic charm and extraordinary effectiveness of the book that we now know and love. The future of the book-object seems assured in its current form, but we will likely see more and more hybrid paper-book/Web-site editions, with the site complementing the book and influencing it in terms of form and writing, but without ever replacing it. Those who believe that the paper book will soon disappear to make way for the e-book the way the horse disappeared from our cities within a few generations to make way for the automobile make an amusing comparison, but they are comparing the moon and flowers, and there are no flowers on the moon.

VIRTUAL MUSEUMS: DOT.MUSEUM

Earlier, I mentioned the importance of museums to our quest to conserve the memory of our historical heritage. But the proliferation of museum Web sites, even virtual museums, is a remarkable advantage as long as it does not dissuade us from building real museums. The internet may actually provide us with an interesting way to complete our real museums and to answer the objections of Umberto Eco, to the extent that museum sites and virtual museums offer the kind of information about works that we can rarely absorb on a hurried visit to a museum.

It is significant that the International Council of Museums, or the ICOM, was one of the first professional organizations to obtain a category (like .com, .org, or .net) exclusively for museums from the authority that issues domain names: the Internet Corporation

for Assigned Names and Numbers (ICANN). The dot.museum
category is highly symbolic of the cultural and artistic character of
the Web; it reflects the role that multimedia artists have played in
it and the virtual nature of the world of art. It will be a vast international space, open to real and virtual museums, where we will
easily be able to find all extant information on Rubens or Mondrian
and consult collections and archives that are generally inaccessible
to visitors of public exhibitions. It will be a republic of art in the
midst of e-commerce.

NET ART

It is also significant that an institution as established as the Whitney
Museum of American Art in New York City took the initiative in
2000 to organize the first biennial exhibition of modern art to
include Web artists – nine such artists were invited to participate.
The organizers, Maxwell Anderson and Larry Rinder, remarked
that "Artists have always worked in the vanguard of technical developments ... And the same is true for the Internet."[5] Anderson and
Rinder held that the presence of Net art at the biennial would go
down in history. They pointed out that it incorporates very different forms of artistic endeavour, to the extent that they were not
sure whether Net art could be defined as a category, like painting.

Artists' Web sites now number in the thousands, whereas it was
difficult to find ten good ones in 1995. With their multimedia
character, they constitute a category in and of itself, even though
they display incredible diversity – at times leaning towards painting,
at times towards poetry, at times towards film, at times towards
music, video, or photography. It is truly the medium that makes
Net art a new and specific art form. In 2001, the Canadian government recognized the importance of on-line museums by funding
them to the tune of close to $200 million. We must hope that
governments will support the digital arts – Net or non-Net – in
the future to the degree that they support opera: after all, digital
creation is as important as the operatic tradition.

THE FUTURE OF FILM IS
IN DIGITAL TECHNOLOGY

The film of tomorrow will be digital. Old reels will be found only
in film libraries. *Tony de Peltrie*, a short film about a pianist with

striking facial expressions, was the first such feature in the history of digital film. Since it was presented in 1986 at the Images du Futur exhibition in Montreal, the technology has evolved dramatically. A co-director of that film, Daniel Langlois, founder of Softimage, produced a full-length feature in 2001 entitled *The Baroness and the Pig*; it was the first full-length feature entirely produced with a digital camera and intended for large-screen, high-definition digital projection. For his part, George Lucas has announced that his next film will be designed entirely on computer. In 2000, even Hollywood got into the action, disseminating a full-length feature film via the internet: *Titan AE*, produced by 20th Century Fox, was digitized so that it could be sent to Atlanta for a special event. And the next revolution will be digital film distribution by hard disk, satellite, or internet, an innovation that will radically transform the film industry.

In 2000, the Web site icuna.com promoted Web movies – one-minute features, updated every day, to which you could subscribe from your microcomputer – foreshadowing an alternative form of film distribution. In 2000, *The Quantum Project*, a mid-length feature (thirty-two minutes long) that cost $3 million to produce, was the first Web film launched at the Cannes Film Festival exclusively on the internet; it was available for a fee on the site of its producer, SightSound. (The film deals with quantum physics, the internet, and spirituality.) SightSound would like to become a leader in the internet distribution of films. The future of digital distribution depends not only on the development of streaming, a process that makes prior downloading of a film unnecessary, but also on network bandwidth. As for distribution to theatres, the cost of digital projectors would have to drop appreciably for it to challenge the hegemony of 35mm reels.[6]

Disney has already conducted tests on distributing films via satellite to movie theatre chains, a method that could eliminate the cost of copying films, transporting them, and insuring them, while making distribution more flexible. France Télécom is also studying this possibility. Daniel Langlois of the Montreal companies DigiScreen and Pixnet is preparing an alternative network for film distribution via satellite and looking into internet distribution sites, which could bring the old Hollywood distribution machine to its knees.

The internet is now so well recognized by the film industry that the American Academy of Film Arts and Sciences has decided that films already shown on the Web, like those that have already been shown in movie theatres, are not eligible for the Oscar competition. And in 2001 the Cannes Film Festival created an award for Web films, which it presented on the Web site www.monsieurcinema.com/cannes2001. Sites like www.primefilm.com are organizing their own festivals; and a festival of mini-films shown on the Web, entitled 120 Seconds, was launched in Montreal in 2001.

Web-film distribution sites have multiplied, and each does its own promotion. Watching Web movies is barely tolerable now, given the small size of computer screens, but that experience could rapidly improve with the advent of larger digital home TV screens. As a result, we can anticipate the disappearance of videotapes. Blockbuster, the leader in cassette and DVD rentals, is getting ready to move into digital distribution and phone orders.

DIGITAL ACTORS

Many production houses are creating virtual characters for TV shows and the internet. Designed as 3-D computer-generated images, these characters are animated with software that synchronizes their movements, facial expressions, and speech. But more and more of them are being animated using real actors attached to sensors. The actor mimes all the movements and expressions, and the animated figure matches them. The software memorizes gestures so that virtual characters can repeat them on demand.

Video games were the first to offer us animated and interactive characters, but they have remained quite elementary. For film and television, it was necessary to go much further. Made famous by the games she appears in, virtual actress Aki Ross possesses a beauty that is "really" impressive; she launched her film career in 2000 with the hit movie *Final Fantasy: The Spirits Within*. And Swedish artist Steven Stahlberg created Webbie Tookay, an entirely computer-generated supermodel of the Elite Agency. She, too, is very beautiful and very realistic, even though she is digital. Her movements are fluid and sexy, and she wears clothes very well. Her Swedish Pygmalion is planning a big career for her in video games and film, like that of Aki Ross or Lara Croft, who achieved renown through the game *Tomb Raider*. The agent who shepherds Webbie Tookay's virtual career, Luciana Abreu, is a mere human being, but as she told the magazine *Largeur.com*, she is eager to give Webbie an endearing personality.

She is a very happy young woman who buys and uses beauty products. She loves chocolate – which is no problem because she can't put on weight – disco music from the 1970s, and animals, especially dogs. Webbie is interested in environmental issues and is concerned about the world's major issues: poverty, world hunger, etc. She wants to help others ... Of course, she is politically correct, but you have to be to please the majority of people. Plus, she has to be like other models![7]

It appears that the first virtual anchorperson for the Web, entirely computer-generated, was Ananova, launched in spring 2000 by the Press Association of the United Kingdom. She anchors the news like a professional, and her voice is well synchronized. No doubt she is waiting impatiently to join the ranks of flesh-and-blood television hosts like Larry King. A journalist from *Le Monde* admitted that "while not astonishing, the result is convincing. In close-up, Ananova expresses herself with the realism required to make us forget that she doesn't exist."[8] The technological feat is synchronizing the facial expressions and the lips with the words, as well as automatically transforming written news copy into a spoken message delivered by a synthetic voice while maintaining a natural rhythm and intonation.

Many young companies would like to specialize in humanizing the internet, offering computer-generated animated figures capable of conversing with the Web surfer in response to written or spoken requests that the surfer makes using voice-recognition software. This will make virtual visits much more user-friendly, particularly in the areas of e-commerce and on-line education, provided that virtual characters can not only express themselves but also respond in real time, relevantly, and even intelligently. The challenge is to perfect computer-generated professors to host educational products on the internet. Many good artists and imaginative programmers will be needed to achieve this objective, but it's only a matter of time.

A NEW LIFESTYLE

Microsoft has already opted strategically for a totalitarian and global vision of the internet. I am not referring to the accusation that Bill Gates is attempting to eliminate the competition so much as to Gates's concept of the omnipresence of the internet in our activities – what he calls Web-enabling the future. Launching his

Internet Explorer 5 browser in 1999, he announced that he had decided to stake Microsoft's future as much on the Web lifestyle as on the Web style of working. Not only does Microsoft want to become indispensable to the internet, but it also – according to sound business logic – wants the internet itself to become indispensable. This desire drives the company to make investments and acquisitions and to form partnerships with other media. And a New York company now offers internet-connected taxis to enhance our lifestyle, while the airlines are taking control of the internet in the skies. Even in resisting this hegemony, open source code software like LINUX still adds support to the idea of an invasive digital power.

PSEUDO-COMMUNICATION

The mass media in wealthy countries offers so-called global communication in a variety of forms with mind-boggling speed and power using new broadband devices. This contrasts with the increasing impoverishment of interpersonal communication. The dream of global communication confuses quantity with quality, uplifting the technology utopians and exasperating humanists.

Why, for example, would art on the internet be worth more than art on paper? The power of art's dissemination should not be equated with its aesthetic value – unless we make kitsch a supreme value. Why would art produced by computer or telephone be more legitimate than art on a canvas? It could be better or worse. The quality doesn't depend on the technology but on the artist. It is no more the phone or the pencil that makes the artist than it is the screen or the paper; it's what the artist has to say. What makes art created on a computer or on the internet worthy of interest is the fact that it tackles a technological problematic; it explores a new sensibility, a new civilization.

COMMUNICATION FOR COMMUNICATION

Jean Baudrillard was amazed at the sort of communicational ecstasy glorified by the priests of the internet. These advocates of communication for communication's sake, who experience jubilation at being connected to the world, are somewhat naive. They fail to credit the value of silence, solitude, non-communication, the opportunity to meditate in isolation from the noise of the world.

We know that the videophone, which allows you to see and be seen by the person to whom you are talking, never captured the consumer imagination; most people prefer not to be seen when they are talking on the phone. More communication always becomes too much communication, an inflation that provokes the severing of communication – what Edgar Morin calls the "regression of progress."[9] The influx of unsorted, non-hierarchical data – the diluted flood of information to which we are always subjected – trivializes communication. Individuals and companies alike fail to manage it, and it ends up drowning the recipient.

Studies have shown that the success of the internet creates this problem of excess, so that we now need filters and intelligent agents to help us sift through it. A good part of the work of the brain is filtering perceptions of the outside world. Without this function, our ability to adapt to the real world would be impaired – it would be as if we had ingested hallucinogens – and we would not survive for very long. Security, utility, intention, and desire select our sensations and censor anything that is not relevant to our vital requirements. This is precisely the mechanism we are currently lacking in the face of the overabundance of information that (in wealthy countries) bombards us. We are living in a situation of hyperinformation, which undermines our ability to adapt to the real world. Our maladaptation is a serious handicap – one could even call it a social disease. We are submerged in superfluity. Communication has become a sledgehammer that knocks us senseless. It should instead be an art (as it once was) – an art of choosing, of elaborating on what is of concern to us and forgoing the rest.

THE CYBERUMBILICAL CORD OF THE DIGITAL BODY

Despite its alienating triviality, some still choose to celebrate this communicational tidal wave. The religion of communication practised by certain contemporary artists, ingenues of technology, is a delusion. No doubt they believe they are celebrating Mass for the union of the individual and the Great Whole – the social body with which they merge, the family body, the body of the mother. Utopians revere the global brain in which we all share and propose a ritual dance around the golden cyberumbilical cord.

Chats are a more significant phenomenon. But, again, the distinction must be made between insipid chats, in which exchanges are made using onomatopoeia and platitudes, and targeted forums that have a theme. These forums are growing in number, and they draw more and more participants. Through chat forums, buffs of every persuasion share information about their various passions; there is no subject that does not prompt the creation of new forums of exchange between professionals or hobbyists. Aside from these electronic forums, which fulfill a recognized social function of communication remarkably well, there are many others set up to attract men and women, most of them between the ages of twenty-five and forty-five, who are looking for companionship and love.

THE DIGITAL OTHER

According to Lacan, we are in the midst of the festival of the Other. These days, the Other is increasingly the internet, and in fusing communication with the social body, the internet becomes, as Arthur C. Clarke would say, more than the global village: it is our global family. But Lacan would have observed that the Other makes too much noise, deafening us. Unbelief is preferable to this irksome preaching.

In a museum, two telephone receivers are positioned in a 69 formation and two anonymous voices converse. It is an interesting, even a comical gesture, symbolic of the non-place and the absurdity of the dream of communication. Here art is playing its role of being evocative and questioning. But soliciting 500 (rather insipid) messages by implementing a fax network among artists and calling it a historical work because it is part of the Vienna Biennial is no more than an anecdotal amusement. For the ingenue priests of communication, the art is in the connection and the aesthetic is in the click of communication. The aesthetic and artistic value of the messages sent, the richness, the critical questioning, or the expressive power of the content is considered a detail apart from the creation of an impulsive device for communication.

THE MYTHOLOGY OF THE MEGA-MEDIA

Electronic mythology has taken over from Greco-Roman mythology. Zeus's lightning bolts are unleashed on cathode ray screens that we ritually contemplate each day. We are now confronted with a representation of media that turns them into superhuman forces – mega-media – with enormous digital powers – in short, true actors of myth. In his 1995 book *Being Digital*, Nicolas Negroponte proposes that digital man is the successor to Cro-Magnon man and *Homo sapiens*, aptly concluding that "being digital ... does give much cause for optimism. Like a force of nature, the digital age cannot be denied or stopped. It has four very powerful qualities that will result in its ultimate triumph: decentralizing, globalizing, harmonizing, and empowering."[10]

> TWELFTH PARADOXICAL LAW
> Digital technologies are a powerful agent of cultural and spiritual development. They recover, disseminate, and record all previous cultures. They generate new cultural products and ensure their propagation. Computer language leads to a new aesthetic. The cyberworld comprises and institutionalizes a new cultural space-time that is exceptionally dynamic and communicative.

THE SCREEN SOCIETY

But we must add to the list of digital world qualities, or virtues, that Negroponte presents. A fifth goddess presided over the birth of that world: cultural force. Digital technologies offer incredible potential for the creation and dissemination of the cultural products that make the cyberworld a cultural institution, a veritable cultural catalyst and accelerator. And this virtue is even more important because people urgently need to appropriate these new technologies, to infuse them with meaning, to humanize them. It has always been by giving new cultural dimensions to major technical innovations that human beings have been able to adopt them, master them, and extract the best from them. This is the way that we will realize our humanist culture in the digital age, that we will overcome the alienation of humans by technology. By injecting a powerful dose of cultural creation into new digital technologies, we will, once again, have the last word and be able to direct our destiny. This is how what we could call the "screen society," which takes over from the "society of the spectacle" denounced by Guy Dubord, can contribute more to our liberty and less to our alienation.

9: Digital Arts, Multimedia, and Interactivity

Artists introduced us to the new digital world.

WHAT IS MULTIMEDIA?

There are as many meanings attached to the buzzword "multimedia" as there are protestations that it is nonsense. In fact, in the mid-1980s, multimedia revisited the old utopia of the integration of the arts – total art. The Montreal exhibition Images du futur, which I organized with Ginette Major, presented artists' installations every summer from 1986 to 1997; these works combined images, sound, movement, and even public interaction through computer. It had previously been difficult to skilfully blend dance and painting, the violin and charcoal drawing, but new technology had at last made this possible. Multimedia was therefore born with the electronic arts.

At the beginning of the 1990s, the arrival of the first CD-ROMs and the internet in English gave rise to a cultural concern that multimedia seemed to ignore, although it prolonged the first artistic use of multimedia. How would the content industry develop? North American multimedia companies were associated with publishing – with the production of content on-line and offline. This was also the tendency in Europe, characterized by a richness of cultural content and a certain lag in transactional applications on the internet.

THE COMMON LANGUAGE OF DIGITAL

Since then, digital technology has evolved rapidly. Today we are discovering that the fundamental characteristic of multimedia – which makes its exponential development possible – is its technology: digital technology. All new communication technologies, which are infiltrating every field, use the same unit of language: the byte. The strength of the integration of digital convergence is posing a new cultural challenge, one that will alter the contemporary landscape. Whether communication deals with financial data or religion, medical diagnoses or the economy, images, music, science, art, the police, daily life, sex, or housekeeping, the digital mode is becoming a common technology of communication with integrated variations, bringing together satellites, cable, shortwave, the telephone, the internet, TV stations, movie theatres, and more in one immense network. Multimedia is now based on the digital language common to all ITCs. Theoretically, digital content may soon circulate without discrimination.

A team representing the Massachusetts Institute of Technology (MIT) in the United States, the National Institute of Computing Research of the INRS in France, and Keio University in Japan is working on moving the internet towards multimedia. The new Synchronized Multimedia Internet Language, or SMIL, is designed to better transmit images, movement, and sound together.

THE CHALLENGE OF NEW TECHNOLOGIES

Art, then, faces major challenges related to the development of new technologies, especially since the technological revolution has prompted a crisis in the traditional arts, where listlessness and confusion rule. The end of the epic avant-garde, the meanderings of postmodernism, and, above all, the market crisis, have resulted in a widespread acknowledgment of mediocrity. Postmodern contemporary art is in crisis, and very few contemporary works reach beyond the level of anecdote. Through its innovations, which stand in striking contrast to the decaying art of what we should call "post-mediocrity," the digital revolution seems to be delivering a death blow to the fine arts. The digital revolution is precluding the unique art object and therefore the art market. Since the appearance of the first computer images, artists have been developing a digital art space that is interactive, event-based, and ephemeral.

THE RECONCILIATION OF ART AND SOCIETY

The crisis of avant-gardism created an insurmountable divide between art and the general public. Digital art marks a reconciliation of art and society, of art and the middle class, the mass media, and multi-sensory social rituals; it reconnects with the so-called primitive art of ancient times. Cathode ray images are reminiscent of cave drawings, pictographs – indeed, icons. Digital art is collective, playful, and interactive, and it thwarts the status of the modern work of art: there are no longer unique works or objects to collect, there are no longer originals that could justify reproduction, no more unique signatures, no more markets or museums for this art. There is no longer eternity, no longer memory. Each work is erased by the parade of technologies that obliterate what came before. And there are no more art critics for this event-based art that eludes the system of fixed concepts established by the system of fine arts.

Digital art has narrowed the chasm between avant-garde, elitist art and the general public. Initially despised and denounced by orthodox art critics, who recognized the danger it represented, it now dominates the art scene and throws what was the ideological edifice of the classical and modern art system into doubt. It appears to destroy memory, but in doing so it gives greater value to it. We are facing a strange moment, one that bears out the prediction I made in my 1981 book *L'Histoire de l'art est terminée* ("Art History Is Over").

THIRTEENTH PARADOXICAL LAW
Digital technologies have triggered an explosion of new artistic creation, and they reconcile art with society. They restore the primitive social function of art and call into question the classical and modern fine arts system, which bestowed value on the object and on the unique signature and entailed a market, collectors, and museums.

The battle for recognition of the importance of new technologies in artistic creation has been won; digital art has established itself; it will reach the general public more and more; and it will explore our new digital civilization. Unless it models itself on film, which values well-known directors and media dissemination to the general public, digital art is going to become discreet and anonymous, blending into society. And Art, as well as Art History, may well lose their capital letters and become integrated into social life and the cultural industries. In any event, art will probably lose its inflated ideological status. There was no art – in the current overdeveloped sense of the word – in ancient societies; nor were there artists, museums, an art market, or art collectors. In these societies, collective life, its objects, and its rites had a remarkable aesthetic and artistic dimension to which everyone adhered; it also had excellent artists/artisans who worked according to the demands and rituals of society. This may be what the future has in store for us – and sooner than we think. Art is therefore regaining its profound social nature; it is reconnecting with its primary function.

THE ADVENTURE OF SCIENCE

Little by little, digital art is being standardized. And we find ourselves between two crises that are cooling our passion for art. On the one hand, the system of fine arts is in decline. On the other hand, the digital arts, which were an exciting, heroic, and extraordinarily creative adventure in the 1980s and 1990s, seem to have lost their initial momentum, foundering in repetition and giving way to the amusing anecdote. The aesthetic invention that the digital arts indulge in is no longer convincing; the new language of the electronic aesthetic has not taken clear enough shape. We are waiting for the works to speak to us of new structures, new values, central figures in our new digital image of the world – but they don't. We are being offered only cursory, exploratory, and shallow works. In the first fascinating moments of exploration this wasn't a problem, but now we need the Mozarts, Bob Dylans, Erik Saties, Gustave Courbets, Piet Mondrians, Robert Rauschenbergs, Guillaume Apollinaires, Antonin Artauds, Marcel Carnés, and Jean Renoirs of the digital arts. Unfortunately, they are nowhere to be found. While initial works had the merit of novelty, current works can barely persuade us of their importance, let alone their ability to survive. Art is therefore in a crisis at the beginning of this millennium: both traditional and digital contemporary works are disappointing.

As a result, we have become more passionate about science. We are discovering more imagination, daring, and creativity in the scientific adventure than in art. Science is now at the heart of our culture, and the border between art and science is blurring. Like literature and art, science and technology interpret the world, question it, and change it. They demand as much, if not more, creative imagination – think of an astrophysicist exploring the universe – and they make many artistic efforts seem lacklustre and banal. They contribute just as much to forging our social consciousness, our image of the world, our collective imagination, and our sensibility.

Science and technology are surprising us more with their daring new vision than many contemporary works of art.[1] They are finding nourishment in the same humanism, the same myths and utopias, and the same demons. They made the twentieth century one of industrial-scale horror and warlike barbarity, which literature and the arts reflected. But they are also capable of accomplishing wonderful things if we can understand and master them. They are powerful spirits of creation and of the human adventure.

THE VERTIGO OF SCIENCE

The theory of the manipulation and cultivation of the primary cells of human life before those cells specialize and reproduce to become the organs of the fetus, the theory of the origins of the moon – are these not as dizzying, creative, and imaginative as the theories of Impressionism or abstract art? These days, science imagines and art reflects. Increasingly, science forges consciousness and art follows. Art depicts the scientific imagination, in which it finds new inspiration and paths for exploration. While art seems to dissolve in the aesthetic dimension of our environment and our communications, the myth of creation is moving towards science.

It follows that science has become techno-science, creating its own technology of scientific research. This research makes scientific advances possible and gives them direction – it even determines them. Techno-science is a theatre of the instrumented imagination, a domain of inspiration, creation, and collective dramatic art. Andrew Grove, president of Intel, understands this perfectly. Closely observing the efforts of his researchers, he compared the software industry to the theatre, "where directors, actors, musicians, writers, technicians, and financial backers are brought together for a brief moment of time to create a new production."[2]

ART IS EITHER ICONIC OR IT IS NOT

In the portraits of the Sun King or in the music of John Cage, the artistic expression of the myth of creation changes and is renewed. In earlier times, art was monotheistic. Each artist and each work of art was unique. Uniqueness guaranteed artistic value. In the cybersociety that we are entering as we embark on the third millennium, the cathode ray images of electronic art will become reminiscent of primitive pictographs. Should we be surprised? Progress in art does not exist, even if this is what avant-garde ideologues would have us believe.

Art is not found in the fetishism of the object or in its market value, but in its collective symbolism. The most fascinating function of art has always been the creation of icons that condense each society's world image, that translate the values and the structures of the society the artists belong to, whether they are expressing themselves through computer, paint, or clay; on a canvas, the Web, a screen, the wall of a cave, or a mask.

The sky is falling, and the world has lost its reason. We are submerged in the unknown, in the free flow of human thought. Time itself flows on, and days, years, battles, victories, and lives drift past. We are trying to escape the flood, to free ourselves from it long enough to gain perspective on our situation, to comprehend our place in the universe. Seeking flat rocks for safe footing, we attempt to cross the raging river of time that seems intent on sweeping us away. We need to pause, to rest, to snatch a moment to concentrate if we are to more rigorously and expressively elaborate the major trends of human thought. From such pauses come the exceptional books that punctuate and deeply influence our history. We build libraries for these books, this flesh of our spirit. And we build museums for the masks, sculptures, icons, and paintings that have marked the great eras of our civilizations and reflected our changing image of the world. These institutions protect our memory and allow us access to it.

Within this flood of images, sounds, references, and dance steps, how do we orient ourselves? How do we ascribe meaning without first isolating and then concentrating on certain moments? The cinematic freeze-frame has become indispensable to those who are struggling to grasp what is happening, who are striving to decode our new civilization. The freeze-frame – that instant of immobilization, of respite for gaze and thought – is the very nature of the icon.

Art, like literature, is either iconic or it isn't. Icons appear to us as visual condensations that symbolize an aesthetic and a theme – the structures, values, and main references of the society that produces them. They refer to the great myths of that society. They become major social referential images. Iconic status can apply to a painting, a sculpture, a work of architecture, a city, a musical composition, a film, or a choreography.

> FOURTEENTH PARADOXICAL LAW
> The more that digital arts destroy the stable visual space of classical art and explore the accelerated and destabilizing flux of time and the circumstances in which we are caught up, the more they will lean towards iconic expression, thus renewing links with the tradition of primitive arts.

Now that the digital simulacrum has engulfed us, destroying fixed space and image, it is time for artists to apply themselves to deciphering the figures and matrices. While movement and multimedia installations increasingly dominate contemporary creation (as the sequential, ephemeral, interactive, and elusive flow of digital arts is imposed), we must not only analyse the narrative structure but also try to freeze the frame, as the film critic does, and find the images that the director and the cinematographer have composed for each film sequence.

It's the same in the cinema of life, even when images accelerate and submerge us. The artist must learn to decipher them. We do not have access to the creator's notes. An artistic language that corresponds to this flow needs to be proposed and developed. The challenge is the same as the one faced by the artists of the quattrocento, the cubists, and the Italian Futurists. To decode the flux of the world is to invent a new language. And this is how the challenge of art is formulated, past and present, even if digital tools change the way the cards are dealt. More than ever, we need stable points of reference, fixed images to help us understand our new world and orient ourselves in it while social time accelerates and the technological revolution overwhelms our consciousness.

In the past, natural landscapes were the decor of our lives. Today we have digitized landscapes, diagrams, and curves. Today's art must take into account the digital simulacrum, just as art of the past had to take into account the influence of religion, or of realism. It is useful to remember that ancient or classical art did not ignore the power of numbers, beginning with the Italian perspective and the geometry of the golden ratio. We could cite Nicolas Poussin, the first classical painter to endeavour to paint foliage realistically; he rendered the number 333 in little brushstrokes in an attempt to suggest the detail of leaves. But, more significantly, music – and ancient music in particular – has always been a digital and abstract language, built on the frequencies of tones and half-tones and on rhythms. Artists already know how to make numbers sing and cry. In music, narrative efforts (for example, opera, or the music of Wagner) or realist efforts (for example, noise music) remain exceptional.

We could perhaps distinguish between two traditions in artistic creation: on the one hand, the digital tradition, which has existed since the Pythagoreans in architecture, the golden ratio, music, the rules of poetic versification, and the rules of pictorial composition; on the other hand, the narrative tradition, which we find especially in literature or cinema, but which is also sometimes implicated in other arts – dance, in particular. These two traditions, digital and narrative, are both based on the myth of creation, which evokes the origins of life, either through numbers or narrative, and which is the very structure of all knowledge. And artists, like scientists, are striving to decode the universe.

10: Artist-Researchers and Laboratories of the Future

"I do not seek. I find," said Picasso.
But artists, beginning with Picasso himself,
do not find – they search.

All cultures have been, are, and will be dominated by their myths of creation, which they draw from their very depths, and which they introduce like a set of answers to the inevitable question of the meaning of existence.

DISCOVERY IS INVENTION

Artists, at least those who count, are researchers who either glorify a moment of civilization, project themselves into the avant-garde of their time, or express its decadence with force. For them, to create is not only to imagine and perceive, but also to develop the sensibility of their time, a new image of the world, and the aesthetic language in which to express it – in other words, to invent. Picasso remarked that a painting goes through a series of destructions during its creation. Discoveries do not just appear before us, ready-made: we imagine them, invent them, construct them.

ARTIST-RESEARCHERS

Great artists are catalysts and cultural accelerators. The contribution of artists – musicians, filmmakers, painters, sculptors, dancers, designers, and architects – to the creation of new social practices, sensibilities, representations of the world, and the search for individual and collective identity is at the heart of all civilizations. And yet this contribution is generally recognized only after the fact. Critics accused the Impressionists of being mere dabblers before their vision of nature and daily life became essential to us. In fact, their analysis of the way the eye perceives colour, dividing it into tiny strokes of vivid hue, was fundamental to the development of the four-colour offset printing process. In 1856, master photographer Félix Nadar, friend of the Impressionists and the bohemians, founded the Society for Artistic Photography (portraits, reproductions, stereoscopes, posthumous portraits), a limited company supported by wealthy investors. In 1861, when he filed a patent for artificial light photography, an art form and a huge market were born. The Lumière brothers and a carnival showman named Georges Méliès created the film industry. Then the great French, Italian, and Hollywood directors offered us a new image of our society, one that continues to wield its influence over us.

In fact, the notion of the "artist-researcher" was adopted by Montreal's Hexagram Media Lab. I developed the initial concept and helped to shepherd the project between 2000 and 2002 at Concordia University in affiliation with the Université du Québec à Montréal.[1]

LEONARDO DA VINCI AND GOETHE

I could list more examples – point to the Greeks, the Egyptians, the Italian Renaissance. Leonardo da Vinci, creator of the *Mona Lisa*, took pride in his talents as an engineer and inventor of machines of all descriptions, and he devoted much of his time to science, in particular to dissecting human cadavers. The German poet Goethe was also a renowned naturalist, the father of an important theory of colour, and an accomplished statesman. Le Corbusier, one of the most famous architects of modern times, spent his mornings in his painting studio, which he considered his basic research laboratory, and his afternoons at the drafting board. Ocean explorer turned filmmaker Jacques Cousteau was infatuated with the undersea depths; he started the diving oxygen tank industry by having such a tank developed for him by engineer Émile Gagnan (who has been unjustly forgotten).

In 1965, Korean American artist Nam June Paik turned the first light video camera, the Portapak, into an individual communication tool like the simple camera. He used it to record Pope Paul VI's visit to New York City in a very free, artistic style; he then screened the film for patrons of a marginal New York café lavishly named Café à Go-Go. In so doing, he inaugurated a social practice that would have major artistic and commercial repercussions. The video camera would soon be adopted by other artists and by countless amateurs eager to record their vacations and family activities.

And it was again the multimedia artists of the 1980s – those unheralded pioneers – who launched the contemporary multimedia industry, which has become so prominent with the dawn of the new economy and new communications. In Quebec, innovative artist Guy Laliberté created the Cirque du Soleil, which now mounts productions on every continent and has resident troupes in Las Vegas and Orlando. Daniel Langlois founded the multinational company Softimage, originator of 3-D computer animation software – the software used to create the dazzling special effects in such films as *Star Wars: Episode I – The Phantom Menace, The Matrix, Titanic, Men in Black, Twister,* and *Jurassic Park.*

VISIONARIES

These artist-researchers are the innovators of our society – its possible consciousness, to use the expression of sociologist Lucien Goldmann. They can intuit the future, create new models of communication, behaviour, perception, urban planning, even morality and economy. The importance of artists as explorers, enlighteners, and guides to new social trends – which they can identify before others or even manufacture – is generally overlooked. They are ignored during their creative lives and later glorified in museums, movies, and history books. Couldn't we do better? Couldn't we furnish these artists – given their role in determining the future of society and developing its social, industrial, and commercial activities – with the means to unleash their energies and talents and conduct their vital research?

Artists invent tools, imagine new representations of the universe, and create the languages of tomorrow. They are researchers by nature and by definition. Those who use new digital technologies are explorers, decoders, and mediators; they make it possible for society as a whole to appropriate the new technologies. The artist-researcher has therefore become an increasingly important player in our society and in the current knowledge economy.

LIKE SCIENTIFIC RESEARCHERS

Like scientific researchers, artists question evidence. Also like scientific researchers, they observe the real and give free rein to the imagination in recombining known elements and building hypotheses; they explore these hypotheses systematically through experimentation. They question their own perceptions, logic, tools, and expression. They question the codes and models of usage. Working across disciplines, artists search for inspiration in models borrowed from music or natural science, film or biology, computer science or Buddhism, the language of dolphins or astrophysics. Scientific researchers do the same. Like scientists, artists are more interested in errors, contradictions, subconsciously deliberate mistakes, chance, and vague intuitions than they are in entrenched discourse and established truths. Mathematicians who develop new computer languages are of a similar disposition. And Einstein's provocative statements reflect that disposition as well. Gaston Bachelard refers to this phenomenon in his famous work *Le Nouvel esprit scientifique* – it is how geometry and penicillin were created. Wassily Kandinsky is purported to have invented abstract art when he propped a painting against the wall of his studio on its side and the next evening was astonished to see a work of art he did not recognize.

The Santa Fe Institute, where Nobel Prize-winners, artists, and philosophers gathered in the mid-1980s, made a significant contribution to twenty-first-century science by questioning the linear and simplistic rationalism that had dominated science since Newton and Descartes but that had become unsuitable for modern scientific research. These people studied concepts of complexity, chaos, unpredictability, discontinuity, intuition, fuzzy logic, ambiguity, dynamics, and spontaneous self-organization. And yet these concepts and values have prevailed since the nineteenth century among artist-researchers. Quantum physics is more fuzzy and imprecise than Impressionist painting ever was, and yet it is full of promise. The artist's creative imagination is more like that of the scientist or the entrepreneur or businessperson than we have cared to admit.

We need to examine our prejudices in this context. Innovations like interactive television, wearable computing, virtual spaces, artificial intelligence, and robotics were the province of artist-researchers and programmers long before businesspeople even thought of them.

The brain's two hemispheres link creativity with action. With this in mind, Derrick de Kerckhove writes: "It should come as no surprise that artists vie with military researchers ... The paradox, of course, is that society grants the military lavish funding for its R&D and the art world lives on crusts."[2] By recognizing the value and the fundamental role of our artist-researchers and fulfilling their financial requirements as we do those of researchers in science and technology, we will change the new knowledge economy and our future. We will build a powerful force of research and development and strategic innovation for the new industries of multimedia, and more.

SCIENTISTS AND ENTREPRENEURS ARE ALSO ARTISTS

Like great artists, important scientists and entrepreneurs are creators with capricious imaginations. After arguing for recognition of the importance of artists to our new economy, it is only fair that I acknowledge that great scientists and great entrepreneurs are also creative, imaginative, incorrigible, and as deserving of our admiration as artists. Furthermore, I maintain that artists and scientific researchers should recognize each other, get to know each other, and work together more often.

Are artists the only ones who stray from the beaten path, who shun current practice, who seek alternatives to what is being said, painted, danced, written, and filmed? At the risk of deflating the overblown artistic ego, I would answer "No." As Gaston Bachelard clearly demonstrated, scientists also behave like free, imaginative, wayward spirits, even if their scenarios and workplaces are different. If this were not so, then Pasteur would never have imagined and then discovered microbes with his microscope, and Fleming would not have discovered penicillin in the cultures he grew in his poorly maintained laboratory. To discover is to invent.

In order to invent/discover a cure for cancer or AIDS, the researcher must have insomnia, seek out other ideas, read a mystery novel, dare to change a hypothesis. What is astrophysics if not a poetic invention? Biotechnology, patents on life, cloning, GMOs, artificial intelligence, quantum physics, and global warming often move beyond the realm of the imagination into that of science fiction.

THE CREATIVE IMAGINATION IN BUSINESS

In the 1960s, David Rockefeller wrote a book called *Creative Imagination in Banking* in which he described his success in the field of finance. In 2000, another successful businessman, Bernard Arnault, published a book about his luxury business empire entitled *La Passion créative.*[3]

Everyone knows that dot.com entrepreneurs search tirelessly for a niche or a new idea, whether it be a technology, a gadget, or a service. Entrepreneurs in general have always done this. The Quebec-based Bombardier Incorporated got its start in 1942 when J. Armand Bombardier jury-rigged a tracked vehicle that could drive on snow. His company has since become the third-largest manufacturer of airplanes in the world and one of the largest in train transport. Entrepreneurs are also obsessed researchers: they seek to create new needs and therefore create new markets, new products, and new sales techniques at the risk of losing their shirts, like proper artists.

Andrew Grove, president of the multinational Intel, is so conscious of the inherent oddness of the entrepreneurial spirit that he wrote a book about today's business world entitled *Only the Paranoid Survive*, bringing to mind the Paranoid-Critical Method advocated by Salvador Dali.[4]

ARTISTS, CRAFTSMEN, AND TECHNOCRATS

In his preface to Patricia Pitcher's *Artists, Craftsmen, and Technocrats* (1997), Henry Mintzberg remarks that Pitcher "shows in a pointed, deep study of a large financial institution how the Technocrats killed what the Artists built and the Craftsmen protected."[5] Analysing the psychological and behavioural characteristics of these three categories of actors within companies, Pitcher underlines the visionary, imaginary, and creative capacity of artists and their ability to change; she contrasts this with the repetitive mindset of technocrats, whose rigidity renders them incapable of meeting the challenges of today's world. She adds that artists, in their inevitable opposition to technocrats, need the help of craftsmen, who, though not visionary, can understand and implement artists' visionary ideas and who have the flexibility required for success. This is the direction that managerial ideology is currently taking – it is calling upon emotional intelligence and stressing the importance of shared creativity for multinationals and small businesses alike.

> **FIFTEENTH PARADOXICAL LAW**
> Although the digital realm is based on a simplistic and reductive binary language – 1 or 0 – the resulting new information society depends on imagination and creativity, which henceforth will comprise the principal capital of the new economy.

The imagination is increasingly important as we move from a resource-based economy to an information- and communication-based one. In Quebec, natural resources represent no more than 3 per cent of the GNP, and even in Dubai, United Arab Emirates, oil represents no more than 10 per cent of the GDP. We are moving from natural resources to human resources and human capital. It is often said that innovation is to the new economy what production was to the old – in other words, its engine of growth. Jeremy Rifkin highlights this in his 2000 book *The Age of Access*: "Intellectual capital ... is the driving force of the new era and much coveted. Concepts, ideas, and images – not things – are the real items of value in the new economy. Wealth is no longer vested in physical capital but rather in human imagination and creativity."[6] We must therefore forge a true culture of creativity, imagination, and innovation in action.

Our new civilization is obsessively oriented towards the future, the unexpected, the new, the imaginary, and the creative. We don't know where we're going. We have to react fast; we no longer have a model, so we have to be dynamic. Large California companies have departments for researching new products, forecasting trends, and collecting business and technological intelligence, and they know that you need to invent and launch at least ten money-losing products before you can find a single successful one. These companies are not afraid to pay artists without assigning them a specific function; they give artists access to technologies so that they can imagine and invent according to their whims. They are banking on a solid, profitable idea – a *very* profitable idea – arising from these artists' meanderings.

IMAGINING TO ADAPT

Allan Greenspan, the very tiresome chairman of the US Federal Reserve Board from 1987 to 2006, demonstrated his awareness of the economic role of innovation when he said that we are experiencing "a period of technological innovation that occurs perhaps once every fifty or one-hundred years."[7] Because of the acceleration of social time and the frenzied and competitive atmosphere we live in, we must learn to constantly readapt ourselves, our companies, our technologies, our financial institutions, and our scientific methods; to constantly question our habits and our certainties; to constantly begin again without necessarily having the time to verify our actions. Our entrepreneurs are always in action, and we expect them to be faster than everyone else, better prepared, and visionary. We do not allow them to make mistakes. Amazingly, realism in business now consists of knowing how to imagine and demystify, to ascertain the reality beyond words, habits, prejudices, worries, and hopes – it consists of being able to imagine a strategy for conquest.

This explains why the well-established and prudent Caisse de dépôt et placement du Québec – a financial institution that manages funds for public and private pension and insurance plans – created in the early years of this decade a new fund for cultural small businesses and announced the creation of Impressario, an investment service for projects costing less than $2 million undertaken by companies in cultural industries. This is how one of the institution's officials justified this initiative: "Two major directions guide this action: the recognition of ideas, creators, and producers, and contribution to the development of companies."[8]

AND BUREAUCRATS?

Governments, the public service, and even judges also need to rise to the challenge of the imagination. They are being asked to move away from the much-decried traditional model of the techno-structure and the bureaucracy and adopt new values. This is a big challenge for them, because they must respect constitutions, laws, jurisprudence, and regulations while grappling with a growing number of new questions. How can a balance be maintained between established legality and the realities of our new civilization? What risks are acceptable? They must also take into account the potential for problems with labour unions, which function in accordance with regulations forged through protracted struggle; union members often object to decompartmentalization, destabilization, and the questioning of modes of employment and the standardization of professional roles.

Bureaucrats must design new regulatory models that allow for an equitable decision-making framework while balancing the general interest with individual needs. They must also consider the dynamic of change, because regulations cannot be modified every six months; and they must realistically re-examine rules, numbers, and company risk. Thus, laws and regulations on the Web present serious challenges to governments and courts. Cyberspace is a permissive territory that accommodates an increasing volume of human activity and commercial transactions. All of this should be subject to democratic law, posing an enormous challenge for public administrators in the real world. At the very least, cyberspace is a practice field on which we can learn how to adapt to the new while protecting our precious democratic values. On this field we can also rethink humanism, law, and the role of the state.

We will inevitably experience future shock, to use Alvin Toffler's term. And the shock of the digital affects all of us, including the state and its bureaucrats. We are perpetually out of step. We need to create administrative research and development think-tanks.

THE LABORATORIES OF THE FUTURE

A number of countries, inspired by the model of MIT, have decided to create laboratories of the future under the influence of the new digital technologies. These countries are convinced that creativity and imagination have become the raw materials of the new economy. Such labs will draw not only on the expertise of artists, scientists, and technological innovators, but also on that of entrepreneurs and financiers who speculate on NASDAQ and must deal with company mergers and venture capital investors. Everything must demonstrate vision, imagination, and audacity, given the novelty of the world, the technological revolution, the new economy, globalization, and the progress of artificial intelligence. On this basis, labs of the future aim to bring together creators in a common research and development project, drawing on their talent, intelligence, and private and public capital. Because, as Rifkin points out:

We are making a long-term shift from industrial production to cultural production. More and more cutting-edge commerce in the future will involve the marketing of a vast array of cultural experiences rather than of just traditional industrial-based goods and services. Global travel and tourism, theme cities and parks, destination entertainment centers, wellness, fashion and cuisine, professional sports and games, gambling, music, film, television, the virtual world of cyberspace, and electronically mediated entertainment of every kind are fast becoming the center of a new hypercapitalism that trades in access to cultural experiences.[9]

New digital media seem to be a crucial area for investigation because they are central to our new digital civilization and they have applications in almost every field. But their success depends on the fast-growing cultural industries, interactive television and computer-generated characters, television advertising, the design of Web portals and pages, e-commerce virtual stores, the video game industry, theme parks, virtual museums, fashion design, wearable computing and interactive textiles, and scientific visualization.

On its own, the content market will probably surpass the already massive sales of the communication technology market (equipment and software) and will create tremendous demand for qualified and creative producers.

ARTIFICIAL INTELLIGENCE AND NANOROBOTICS FOR THE DISABLED

The laboratories of the future must concern themselves not only with perfecting creative technologies but also with human beings themselves. It will be important to develop interfaces between images, music, and movement; and between tactile, auditory, acoustic, olfactory, visual, motor, and even cognitive sensory stimulation.

Thanks to advances in our understanding of the areas of the brain that play a decisive role in the diversity of our activities; thanks to nanotechnology, to robotic miniaturization of digitally controlled peripherals such as microphones and cameras; thanks to interactive textiles and solar or body-energy sensors, the disabled can lead more normal lives. Just think that in China in 2006 the Chinese Federation for Disabled Persons had 60 million members – a huge problem and a huge market. The disabled can be digitally rigged for improved vision, hearing, or mobility. Researchers have already succeeded in helping the deaf hear and the blind see using auditory implants and micro-cameras connected to the brain. Even though synthetic vision and hearing are still rudimentary, these breakthroughs in digital technology show great promise.

Technological innovations that combine robotics and artificial intelligence support our obvious duty of human solidarity, but aside from assisting people with disabilities, they have many other applications in all sorts of professional and artistic fields. All this research will respond to countless challenges for our new civilization and have huge economic stakes.

11: The Promises of Convergence

The return of the myth of unity is inherent
in the digital universe.

FROM DIVERSIFICATION TO CONVERGENCE

In the beginning of 2000, convergence was very much in style. It was inspiring corporate business plans, municipal mergers, globalization, and even the new life sciences. It was prompting investment: financial, political, and even epistemological. But from the perspective of 2006 we know that this was not any more durable than the trend towards diversification that preceded it. Twenty years ago, diversification was all the rage. In a cycle of successive crises, large companies sought to protect themselves by putting their eggs into different baskets. They split their acquisitions between new, profitable but risky sectors and established, secure sectors like real estate. Diversification is still the business model for holding companies, Japanese groups that have businesses in a range of sectors: biotechnology, transportation, agri-food, cars, televisions, computers, vacuum cleaners, and newspapers and television stations.

Diversification reinforced the concept of the entrepreneur as corporate owner/financier whose credibility was based not on specialized skills in a particular sector, but on general talent as a visionary and financial manager. This ideology spread, becoming evident in the sciences, which were now praised for their multidisciplinary nature, their opposition to specialized, fragmented knowledge. This new way of seeing heralded the rise of a larger, more international concept of the world and of business. Some multinationals remained unchanged, but many others, after resounding failures brought on by diversification, sold off what they weren't able to master.

Diversification also resulted from an effort to adapt to accelerated change. Major corporations like Seagram, the world leader in spirits, concerned about a drop in revenues, turned to the entertainment, music, and film industry, purchasing Universal Studios and Polygram. Bell Canada, which was losing its monopoly and saw its profitability threatened, bought newspapers and television stations (and even contemplated acquiring the Montreal Canadiens hockey team). In doing so, the company employed a new approach: convergence-oriented diversification, involving an attempt to digitally master media technologies and content simultaneously.

THE NEW PARADIGM OF CONVERGENCE

The fashion was turned on its head. For five years after the turn of the millennium, all we heard about was convergence. This new paradigm was universally dominant: our context was the new globalization, and merging was the thing to do. This was particularly striking with the TMTs: the technology/media/telecoms.

The historical kickoff for convergence was the buyout of Time Warner (12.6 million customers) by AOL (25 million subscribers) on 10 January 2000, which was approved by the Federal Trade Commission. Microsoft and Disney adopted this strategy, followed immediately by many others, such as BCE, Rogers, and Quebecor in Canada, and (in the year 2000) Vivendi-Seagram-Canal+ in Europe.

The idea of convergence owes much to digital technology. The technologies of production, post-production, and distribution can now become a vast field of multimedia and interactive communications common to computing, the telecoms, the internet, television, radio, film, and video games. This convergence has created the illusion that it is possible to control major international markets – in short, to create commercial empires, to reduce costs, and to recycle content. This notion – based on the American dream of a vast on-line free trade zone, tax-free for e-commerce – is not to be taken lightly, because of the increasing number of Netizens.

THE MYTH OF CONVERGENCE

The imaginative force of convergence lies in the eternal myth of unity. Nothing more effectively sums up this trend towards almost magical convergence than the extreme connectivity of domestic life. Witness a technology like Bluetooth, which provides an intelligent connection between your toaster, bathwater, garage door, fridge contents, television programming, medical monitoring, financial management, and your subcutaneous silicon chip implant.

However, upstream from this universe of gadgets and multi-purpose interfaces resides a fundamental reality: distribution network owners want full control over large sources of content and services, without which networks, which are very expensive to develop and maintain, would have nothing to offer. Reciprocally, producers of content and services want to exercise ownership control over distribution networks. Since large companies like to buy smaller ones, it is necessary for an enterprise to hold onto its position in the face of international competition and steer clear of predators. This results in integration, either horizontal (for example Wal-Mart or Hewlett-Packard/Compaq) or vertical.

However, convergence is still largely theoretical, limited mostly to the financial integration of owners, to a basket of mixed fruit. The horizontal integration of networks among themselves and the vertical integration of content with networks remain to be seen. Therein lies an enormous, perhaps insurmountable challenge. The Bluetooth convergence, which we've heard so much about since 1999, has been very slow to materialize. The question is: Do we really need this convergence? Do we use the twenty-seven features of our voice mail, or the feature that allows us to program 312 numbers into our cell phones, or the one that lets us adorn our computer screens with millions of colours? The answer is clear: No! The human being is not ready to become *homo convergens.*

Is convergence possible? Some insist that it isn't. What is technically possible is not necessarily commercially possible, because technology moves faster than social practice. We cannot presume that markets are the direct and immediate product of technological change. We have to move from the human/machine coupling to a more refined analysis of supply in relation to the customer's expectations and real needs.

CONVERGENCE IS EXPENSIVE!

It is unrealistic to assume that it is economical to deliver content on a variety of digital media, such as traditional and on-line newspapers, television, radio, Web sites, and phone screens, because this presupposes specialized human resources and expensive technology. In effect, it's added value that businesses want to offer customers in giving them access to all the information they could hope for, anywhere, anytime, under any circumstances – at home, in their cars, at their workplaces, or at play. And customers would not necessarily be inclined to pay a fair market price for the flood of information to which they would be constantly subjected. They would likely get sick and tired of this surfeit and seek to escape it. Why would I want to play tennis at home, in a restaurant, in the street, in a car, twenty-four hours a day, even if technology made it possible? Instead, people will probably choose a single medium, the one that technically and aesthetically offers the best performance and is most suitable to their purposes, and they will abandon the others. Companies that make substantial investment in convergence will inevitably face financial losses.

And think of journalists. Will they want to become multimedia reporter/analysts and wander about with their laptops, their internet-connected cell phones, their digital cameras, in order to satisfy their employers and supply every distribution channel for the same salary and the same copyright? The unprofitability of on-line newspapers – even the interactive *Wall Street Journal*, with its oft-cited success, is still not turning an easy profit – and the stock market collapse in tech stocks at the beginning of the millennium, as well as difficulties related to copyright, have led certain media companies to suspend on-line publication. On-line advertising has been identified as the culprit; its failure to quickly materialize contradicted the optimistic forecasts that circulated during the stock market speculation on dot.coms. The prestigious *New York Times Digital* laid off staff due to losses of close to US$50 million. Media magnate Rupert Murdoch did likewise at News Corporation; Michael Eisner, head of Disney, closed Disney's Go.com portal after losses of more than $200 million; and CNN, NBC, and Knight Ridder have slashed in their internet divisions. According to statements made to various press agencies by an expert at the research firm Jupiter Communications, the outlook, which seemed unlimited, had suddenly become very pessimistic. In fact, among others, Jupiter contributed greatly to the unrealistic prophecies, probably to satisfy its clients, and it could be held responsible for such huge commercial errors and financial losses.

> **SIXTEENTH PARADOXICAL LAW**
> As the digital convergence of the media becomes more established, we rediscover the irreducible specificity of different media and the social uses that distinguish them.

Technologically speaking, the battle for convergence is not yet won. Technique compatibility has not been achieved – far from it. And yet convergence has become a slogan of the digital age and the refrain of media entrepreneurs. Convergence will only have a commercial future if, paradoxically, it respects diversity and the specificity of industries, technologies, media, social practices, and cultures and abandons naive magical thinking. The markets will sound the next alarm for those who invest massively in convergence, and the return to reality will be expensive and painful.

Thus, it is unrealistic to plan to redistribute newspaper content on cell phone screens. Rethinking the format, the display and search software, the design, and the means of adapting content to the telephone would cost a fortune. This type of distribution, except for certain information of a practical nature, will probably not coincide with market demand for some time. And the possible success of a home delivery system via internet of the major newspapers in a format standardized for office paper will not change the nature of the problem. Companies that are trying this, like NewspaperDirect, are targeting a real but narrow client base – ship passengers, guests at large hotels, marginalized cultural communities, students, diplomats living abroad – not a very broad business plan.

Likewise, Web TV projects are riddled with problems, given how great the opposition is between televised media (flow media, offering passive and collective consumption and pleasure) and the internet (stock media, involving individual initiative, work, difficulty). Applying the models of television to the internet would be a step backwards, and the desire to transform TV into the internet is naive. It makes no more sense to create television on the internet than it does to have the internet on television or radio on television. These industries and these media do not address the same audience, do not share social practices, do not have the same content or use the same journalists – even if everything is digital. Content, aesthetics, programming, audiences, and journalists are different. Digital technology will not alter this fact. Even in all-digital industries, future success will come from seeking out the specific virtues of each medium. The only exception – although it is not really a convergence – is the Blackberry, a multi-functional mobile telephone that has an agenda, a pad, and an internet connection for text messages. The industry is trying to create a market for a new phone each year – an ever more powerful device that offers connections for images and TV programs – but so far it has only managed to produce one that is still expensive and heavy and that appeals to a limited market (3 per cent of mobile telephone users worldwide in 2006).

To date, the only commercial success of convergence is suspect: the convergence of publicity between media of a single owner, which rapidly becomes abusive and irritating to audiences.

DIGITAL ESPERANTO

We must try, however, to perfect a universal and extremely fluid digital language that will not only allow computers to communicate with each other (this has already been achieved with HTML) but also permit all types of digital files to intercommunicate (whether they be text, graphics, or sound), as well as all types of terminals, computers, television receivers, personal digital assistants, cell phones, and home appliances. There is hope for the new XML language developed by the W3C – the World Wide Web Consortium – and the Japanese company DoCoMo, in particular, wants to take on the challenge of developing it further.

THE INVINCIBLE FORTRESS OF HUMANS

Through its very technology, convergence is imposing itself. But this convergence may not be sustainable – or desirable. Convergence is clearly an issue that is specific to technology and the business world, and we know that human beings are not as convergent as technology, even though some entrepreneurs may dream of such a human evolution. Humans prefer diversity of content over convergence of communication technologies. Digital convergence contains a dream, a seductive force, a technological and commercial utopia, but human beings are somewhere else. Somewhere other, we hope, than at the final stage of technological logic and the economic process, somewhere other than locked inside a fortress that even the power of the digital will be unable to penetrate.

Multipurpose use is the naive expression of a myth – that of the magical and the all-powerful. We need to stop inventing gadgets that we can hold in the palm of the hand, that we imagine can do absolutely everything. It's just far too naive.

The split of AOLTimeWarner, which was considered exemplary in 2000, and the quiet resignation of its initiator, Steve Case, in 2004 reflects the failure of such a utopia.

12: The Libertarian and Ultraliberal Digital Realm

The internet is an ideological battlefield
for libertarians and ultraliberals.

Without dwelling on the providers of multimedia interactive internet sex, we must look at sites that incite hatred, racism, and violence, which no one can really control. At the dawn of the third millennium, the internet is still a veritable Wild West, fearing neither God nor man.

The internet offers us access to everything – every imaginable human perversity, papal masses, and on and on. Hacking government sites has become a sport, organized crime has embraced the internet, and it's the place to go if you want a recipe for constructing a bomb – "Hate school? Here's how to issue a fake bomb threat, and here's how to build a real bomb." With fifteen minutes of research, you can find ten Web sites that explain how to stage a massacre.

A Republican candidate for the presidency of the United States, multi-millionaire Steve Forbes, no doubt wanted to pass for a modern man when, in 1999, he announced his candidacy first on the internet. The internet faithful, people who have invested their dreams in this technology, envision communicating with the entire world. They have succumbed to technological fetishism. They need to be reminded that the world is not a cybersimulation. The world is not electronic. The communications dispatched by all the new digital technologies throughout the world do not constitute the world.

A CYBERSPACE DECLARATION OF INDEPENDENCE

In the eyes of optimists, the mythical investment in media is considerable. They imagine themselves aboard the caravels of the conquerors and explorers who are transporting us to the New World, the cybercontinent. They believe that they have reawakened the fundamental American desire to push towards a new frontier.

In 1996, John Perry Barlow of the Electronic Frontier Foundation proclaimed the "Declaration of the Independence of Cyberspace" in order to oppose the American Congress, which wanted to legislate against violence and sex on the internet.[1] Since the internet's beginnings, the libertarian will that favours the new cybernetic space, that defies regulation and readily accepts the risk of abuse in the name of individual freedom of expression, has manifested itself through its main apostles – people like Douglas Rushkoff, who now curses the internet's evolution towards e-commerce.[2] In the internet they see the Wild West, but they don't want a sheriff to deal with. They see a new frontier, an electronic continent discovered by cyber–Christopher Columbuses. Their vision of cyberspace is idealistic and virtuous; in it, evil, crime, and e-commerce are kept at bay.

FREE SOFTWARE

The Free Software and Open Source Association is promoting free software on the Web.[3] Their initiative involves revealing software source codes so that everyone can contribute to the development of applications; use of this software is therefore free. In so doing, these defenders of free software are expressing their resistance to software that multinationals like Microsoft seek to impose. Linux, on which Linus Torvalds of Finland started work in 1992, is a prime example. This protest aims to safeguard freedom and free communication from commercial techno-structures that try to profit systematically from the new global communication network by setting up private toll booths – such activity made Bill Gates the richest man in the world within a few short years.

HACKERS AND PROTESTERS

Computer hackers, the pirates of the internet – or crackers or phreakers, as they are sometimes called – the Richard Stallmans, the Phiber Optiks, the Vladimir Levins, are enemy number one of multinationals like Microsoft, not to mention the banks and the Pentagon. They will go down in internet history as genius cyberdelinquents. Kevin Mitnick, the most notorious hacker, confined to a maximum security prison since his 1995 conviction for causing such companies as Sun and Motorola to incur losses of us$80 million, is considered a cyberterrorist by the American justice system and a martyr by his admirers. He was even accused, wrongly it seems, of having infiltrated the NORAD Center at the Pentagon, an act that inspired the film *War Games*.[4]

Other hacktivists, like Ken Thompson and Denis Ritchie (inventors in 1969 of the Unix system), Steve Wozniak (who founded Apple with Steve Jobs), and Linus Torvalds, have reintegrated into the system as libertarian computer programmers and expert consultants. Hacking continually takes on new forms that challenge the internet's market techno-structure. Music bore the brunt of this, with the MP3 and MP4 compression and download system. The story has no end: it unfolds at the pace of technological developments. The Cult of the Dead Cow, one of the best-known hacker groups, launched Back Orifice, which attacks Windows 2000 and can constantly metamorphose because it is available as open source code software. Another computer virus, Injustice, merits mention here because its name is indicative of the protest mentality that inspired its author. It spreads via e-mail, causing no damage. It takes the form of a message of support for the Palestinians. In its March 2001 announcement of the new virus, Computer Associates reported that this was the first time they had seen a virus of this type used to spread a political message.

Even though some viruses are launched by fanatical computer programmers intent on testing their talents as if they were playing a game, most viruses are the product of a spirit of revolt against a powerful system. In the young hacker's eyes, we have drifted out of a libertarian project and entered one with commercial ends and control. We must therefore expect that many more viruses and worms like Code Red (which hit in the summer of 2001) will infect Microsoft's prevailing applications and Web sites of major institutions and set off red alerts in government offices. Code Red erased sites and displayed the signature "hacked by Chinese," creating a red herring and mocking the seriousness of political games. Was this not about crashing the White House? Organizations of French farmers also used the internet in their fight against major distribution networks, which they accused of exploitation. Paysans.com offered natural products via the internet at very competitive prices: beef, chicken, vegetables, fruit, and cheese – all guaranteed organic.

The protest also finds inspiration in the denunciation of communication that has become a commodity and a means of manipulation. The spirit of commerce has cast a spell over the cyberworld. This commercial hijacking of communication that buys and sells itself and tries to seduce in order to sell feeds an insatiable desire for consumption; it also offers excitement and countless toys, amusements, and distractions. Communication has consequently become a veritable potion to induce social euphoria. Alienation is as possible as freedom with digital communication's libertarian mechanisms or cynical empires – or whatever else we may call them.

Thus, there are many new-generation cyberanarchists who dream of creating a cyberspace alternative to the real world because they believe that constraints and limitations on individual freedoms are unacceptable. The Napster experiment of providing free access to music was a symbolic act. It was also a tremendous success, even if some saw it as a vast pirating enterprise that exasperated commercial distributors and robbed artists of their royalties. The idea that underlies this type of initiative is widespread: on the internet, access to everything should be free.

Should we see the internet as an El Dorado? At the very least, it is a recurring dream as utopian as the Marxist dream of abundance in which each would partake according to his or her needs after the proletariat took power and the communist society was built.

FREENET

It was this very dream that motivated twenty-three-year-old Irish programmer Ian Clarke to launch Freenet, which he had worked on as a school project while a student at the University of Edinburgh.[5] In the name of anarchy, Clarke designed a system that makes it possible to store and distribute any material or information anonymously, without being subject to any law. Freenet.sourceforge.net is in fact a network that has no easily identifiable centre and has been designed to avoid all control. The system works using peer-2-peer technology: a network of computers that are always turned on and through which files are constantly moving at high speed. Users do not need to reveal their identities, and Freenet requires no central maintenance system. Entirely open, it spontaneously generates its development and has no leader or owner who could be prosecuted. The anonymity of its users – as a user, you know only the identity of the person who forwarded the message to you and the person to whom you will in turn forward it, but you do not know the primary source of the information you are circulating – presents a big problem for those who want to regulate the internet. Clarke acknowledges that Freenet could become a major worldwide network and help Netizens from countries that are subject to strict controls, like China, achieve freedom of expression, but that it could also be opposed if it were to encourage criminal practices – for example, if it were employed to launder money for international terrorism or to aid sexual predators.

THE LIBERTARIAN DREAM

This ideology is, for better or worse, typically American. It expresses a staunch political will to defend individual freedom, which is one of the founding principles of American democracy. In the name of such freedom, firearms are sold virtually without restriction in the United States. The ideology also corresponds to a lifestyle that refocuses on the individual, which is a broad trend of our era. The basic principle of this lifestyle is clearly defined in *The Popcorn Report*, published in 1991. Cocooning. Faith Popcorn's notion of people in their private fortresses – refocusing on their individual selves, on their private space, their local freedom, their quality of life, physically secure and equipped with a barbecue – was very influential.[6] This egocentric tendency encompasses several preoccupations: education, health, the immediate environment, and respectability or puritan morality. An abstraction of the conservatism of half the American population, the concept of individualistic cocooning ties in with the idea of the rhizome and the internet network. We should not be surprised that the idea found a logical extension in the growth of e-commerce, which makes it possible to have anything sold on-line delivered to your door. People no longer need to drive to the mall, load up a cart, and haul home the groceries. Thanks to the internet, they can stay at home with their loaded guns, their barbecues, and their great big fridges full of food.

FROM COCOONING TO THE GLOBAL VILLAGE

Cocooning joins the long line of McLuhan's prophecies about the coming of the global village. This vision corresponds to the twofold movement that the internet and all digital communication networks have inspired. On the one hand, the internet, unlike mass media such as television and newspapers, is an individualistic, proactive media that intersects with the vision of refocusing on the individual, or cocooning. On the other hand, it suggests a globalizing network that crosses national borders and cultural and linguistic divides and that offers us a technological utopia of a united digital cyberplanet, where we will be citizens of the world, cybercitizens, e-consumers in a vast cyberdemocracy fed by shared intelligence.

Individualist ideology took hold in the nineteenth century with the rise of bourgeois ideology, and it gained new momentum with the growing power of the middle class – a class that saw itself as a juxtaposition of free individuals. As a reaction to the individualist fragmentation of society, we are now seeing the re-emergence of the myth of unity, which has existed in our social imagination throughout the ages. There can be no doubt that the paradigm of the internet has contributed substantially to this. The same trend can be seen in science, politics, economics, and entrepreneurial ideology. Likewise, the power of new media (phone, radio, television), which McLuhan believed both promoted the globalization of humanity and made possible a re-centring on local identities, reached its apex with the internet.

Free trade and the unification of major international markets is now the order of the day. The example of the Common Market and the European Union is contagious. The North American Free Trade Agreement (NAFTA), Mercosur, and the Free Trade Area of the Americas (FTAA) initiatives followed. This ideology of free trade has found support among those infatuated with e-commerce; in the name of free trade, Americans are actively defending the concept of a cybermarket without taxation. Allan Greenspan, chairman of the Federal Reserve Board for so many years, presents this unification of markets as a source of newfound prosperity.

The very concept of globalization radically expands the ideology of free trade and hyperliberalism into a political dimension and emphasizes the practically planetary interdependence of peoples, their interests, their values, as well as the environmental and epidemiological threats that could affect us all. The zealots of globalization claim to favour more liberty, democracy, education, and prosperity, and they believe that the new communication technologies are essential to their cause.

A TWOFOLD OPPOSING MOVEMENT AND A GAME OF BALANCE

We are witnessing under the symbolic sign of the internet – which simultaneously inspires, encourages, and reflects these major structural and ideological trends of our era – a twofold movement, the movement of the global village. On the one hand, there is refocusing on the individual and a growing egocentrism; on the other hand, there is the prospect of increasingly powerful global unification. This is the framework for our actions as much in our communication networks as in our political vision, our economic efforts, and our entrepreneurial activities. In fact, one of the challenges that we currently face is to establish operational connections between these contradictory and distant poles. We have to put intermediary structures into place, operational relays, in all of these fields.

SEVENTEENTH PARADOXICAL LAW

The digital realm favours a fundamental and dynamic new human equilibrium that valorizes opposite poles: even as globalizing tendencies are expressed, tendencies towards fragmentation assert themselves in opposition. On the social level, this translates into an intensified repositioning of the individual in the heart of a communication network oriented towards globalization; and on the political level, into the identity-oriented repositioning of small social groups (villages, communities, regions, countries) facing global groups (federations, large continental free trade zones, international organizations).

What political science shows us is that democracy cannot be exercised on a planetary scale, except for certain functions that are governed by so-called universal values (designated according to the ideology of the most powerful), such as peace, respect for human rights, humanitarian efforts, conservation of a global heritage, and coping with natural disasters.

Readers of Aldous Huxley and George Orwell know that in the genre of science fiction, the large central computer takes on great power in any global political organization. At a certain point, management will become too complex for human beings, and we will have to put our trust in a central artificial intelligence. Are we tempted by this nightmare scenario? We know that the exercise of democracy involves political structures of a reasonable, human scale that are capable of taking into account concrete problems, cultural and linguistic diversity, and the roots of our identity – the values and reference points that we all need.

In the cyberspace of the internet, we are likewise witnessing a rapid structuring of the labyrinth of digital information. Major centres are being created, and techno-structures are taking control; powerful players like AOL, MSN, Yahoo!, Google, and Bertelsmann have entered the game. Regulations are emerging. The flow of information is re-centering on portals, subgroups, and dominant and less dominant shopping centres. Soon, cyberspace will reflect political, economic, and commercial real life, with all of its conflicts and relationships of force. It is only a matter of time and of technological progress: intelligent agents and electronic syntax are going to put intermediary structures into place – buffers, local communities, the platforms for debate and local exchange that we need. Cyberspace will increasingly be socialized and structured in the image of the real world. So much for magical technological utopias. How could we ever have believed, except under the influence of our recurring myth of joyful rediscovered unity, that cyberspace, like a cyber–El Dorado, would escape reality?

DEMOCRATIZING
AND REGULATING CYBERSPACE

Because it reflects our societies, cyberspace must be regulated and subjected to the rule of law. Political democracy is the fruit of

centuries of struggle and progress, always uncertain, always in need
of reinforcement. Democracy is still the privilege of a few countries.
The democracy we have built through valiant effort we must also
apply to the internet; the liberty of the individual must be respected.
We must balance the nearby with the distant, the macro view with
the micro view, global authority with individual or local initiative.
This can only be accomplished by creating intermediary structures.

THE OTHER WWW: WOMEN WEAVING THE WEB

There can be no democracy unless women are equal partners with
men. Some predict that women will increasingly be the weavers of
the Web. The three *W*s of the World Wide Web will take on a new
meaning: Women Weaving the Web. Statistics show that half of
Netizens worldwide are women; according to Media Metrix, they
represented 50.4 per cent of Netizens in the year 2000, an increase
of 126 per cent in a year. Women fifty-five and older are also very
interested in the Web: their use grew by 110 per cent in a year.[7]
Women surf, meet, share their experiences, and create solidarity.
They often do not appreciate the technological aspect of the Web
as much as men do, but they have a greater appreciation for the
human and communications aspects of it. Men say that women like
to talk; the Web gives them an unlimited opportunity to chat and
to seek the information that is meaningful to their daily lives.

According to studies by Nielsen Media Research, NetRating, Taylor
Nelson, Sofres, and others (the subject is important for e-commerce),
women frequently visit sites that are targeted at them. Even Microsoft
created a portal for women (www.womencentral.msn.com), and
women meet in cyberspace at sites like women.com, ivillage.com,
cybergirl.com, femina.com, webgrrls.com, wwwomen.com,
voiceofwomen.com, oxygen.com, as well as women's Webzines.
While men still make up the large majority of on-line consumers,
the female consumer is much sought-after and long-awaited.

Furthermore, women hold an increasing number of positions in
dot.com companies, including executive positions. Several studies
show that their numbers doubled between 1998 and 1999, even
though they were still in the minority, particularly as presidents. In
this regard, cyberspace seems to be less sexist than the real world.

The provocatively named Webgrrls, who have created women's
internet communities in several countries, have encountered

difficulties and are in the process of reorganizing. In Montreal, they are now called the DigitElles and are part of the international women's support group DigitEve. This community honours women who work in digital technology and new media and pushes for the recognition of women in cyberspace. Digital shock has therefore spread to women as well: Webbinettes, Internennettes (a French site), and "digital women" are mounting the conquest of cyberspace.

<h2 style="text-align:center">CYBERSPACE: AN EXTRATERRITORIAL
OR MARGINAL SPACE OF FREEDOM</h2>

For those who have a hard time integrating into their social milieu, cyberspace can be a refuge. Real civil society tends to impose well-defined social roles and status on all of us. It is difficult to escape the classifications of sex, age, civil status, skin colour, profession, and even lifestyle. The new generation does not necessarily subscribe to these constraints, or to the rigid edifice of social values that supports them. Cyberspace can therefore be seen as a libertarian space where everyone can circulate anonymously and post freely, using only a first name or pseudonym – identifications that do not necessarily correspond to gender or sexual orientation. We can express ourselves without censure, with tremendous freedom – the freedom of the anonymous cybercitizen of the virtual world – according to our opinions, political positions, or fantasies. And in cyberspace we can meet and talk with other cybercitizens who are just as free.

If one faces hostility in real society as a result of skin colour, one can exchange it; one can make friends or flirt on the internet with those whose skin colour is politically valued. Those who have followed convoluted paths through successive immigrations, or who are cut off from their roots and have not integrated into the new civil society, can see themselves as citizens of the world or citizens without a state; they can view the cyberworld as an imaginary country where anything is possible. This is the position taken by philosopher Pierre Lévy: "I am a Jew (by birth and religious tradition), Tunisian (by birth and for a portion of my musical and gastronomic culture, etc.), French (language and educational culture), European (for the ideal of a supranational, pacifist and multicultural political entity), a Quebecer (by choosing to belong to francophone

America), Canadian (an immigrant to Canada), philosopher (by vocation), professor (by profession), Buddhist (through meditation), and so on."[8] Lévy has clearly adopted cybercitizenship as well.

A person with physical disabilities feels just like others in cyberspace, where people move about lightly, like spirits, unencumbered by a body. Cybercitizens have no face; they can navigate in a mental universe where the physical is erased, where everyone's history can be forgotten. They can enhance their standing, be what they dreamed of being. They can experiment with a parade of identities and explore their implications in exchanges with other cyberworld citizens. Studies show that male and female homosexuals are more interested in the internet than the general heterosexual population is. The civic space of the cyberworld becomes a place of redemption, of exploration and experimentation, a place where changing identity or gender is possible, a place where escape from a hard-to-manage or disappointing reality is possible. Users can become dependent on this place of freedom if the daily return to the real world is too painful. But this risk must not cause us to overlook the positive aspects of a liberating virtual universe.

COMMUNICATION AS MERCHANDISE

One of the pioneers of the digital dream is Douglas Rushkoff, an American writer for hip 1980s magazines that promoted the internet counterculture. In 1994, Rushkoff published his influential book *Cyberia*, but he now criticizes the course cyberspace is taking.[9] He believes it has become a shopping centre where money, business, venture capital, and profit are the sole topics of discussion. The dream is dead, he insists, completely perverted by the quest for money. In his eyes, the internet has become a rip-off. He is not alone in denouncing the demise of a magnificent project of human communication and democracy, a vital endeavour battered to death by the demons of business. And yet, was it not venture capital that made technological research and development possible and supported the spectacular rise of the Web and of digital communication technologies? Rushkoff was naive to think that digital technology would create a paradise, a romantic space for the realization of the dream of liberating communication. Digital technology does not have intrinsic libertarian or liberating values.

... AND AS A SPACE OF FREEDOM
WITHOUT FRONTIERS

Leftism survived computing capitalism's power grab and has gone on to lead the battle against communications multinationals in the name of freedom. Some reject the leftist utopia but still aspire to access the internet, also in the name of freedom. In 1999, Reporters Without Borders reported on some forty countries whose governments are creating virtual borders to stop the free circulation of ideas for political or religious reasons. Reporters Without Borders reviews the situation each year. North Korea has prohibited the internet; because there is no service provider or server, the internet simply does not exist in that country. And Saudi Arabia and China are among the countries most determined to control their digital borders. Saudi Arabia, whose culture is foreign to the internet, only authorized access to it in 1999; it protects itself by stringently filtering content and origin. It is worthy of note that once filtering was established, Saudi women, who still do not have the right to drive a car, were permitted to go on-line. There they have discovered a world outside the Wahhabi kingdom.

And while we can say that in China the Great Wall is cracking because of the internet, which is increasingly tolerated, the same cannot be said of other fundamentalist countries, which are often the poorest. The Chinese government attempts to maintain control in spite of everything, and in 2000 it proclaimed three laws in quick succession to curtail expression. As a result, Guo Qinghai, a thirty-six-year-old bank employee and cyberdissident, was sentenced by a Ganzhou court to four years of prison in 2001 for having disseminated articles promoting democracy on the Web. Many find themselves the target of such prosecutions, even for "crimes of opinion" committed outside of China: Lu Xinhua was arrested in Wuhan for criticizing Chinese president Jiang Zemin on foreign sites. The fact that Yahoo! gave information to Chinese authorities in 2005 about its Chinese users, and Google's 2006 agreement with the Chinese government to censor their research engine in exchange for being allowed into China, have sparked much debate in Western countries.

In 2001, in Iran, religious authorities closed down 400 cybercafés as elections approached. The satanic American Web experienced

remarkable growth after the election of reformist president
Mohammad Khatami, but the ayatollahs regained control of newspapers and the internet. And the Taliban of Islamabad prohibited
the use of the internet in order to prevent access to "vulgar,
immoral, and anti-Islamic" material, the Afghani News Agency
reported in 2001. They denounced not only the internet itself, but
all things "obscene, immoral and against Islam" found on it.[10]

Still, we should note that the same internet allows many people
with disabilities access to information; it enables them to communicate and to join the working world. Furthermore, the same internet made it possible for globalization protestors to converge on
Seattle in 1999 during a meeting of wto member countries.

ON-LINE CYBERACTIVISTS

The Quebec Summit on the Free Trade Area of the Americas
(FTAA), held in April 2001, provided us with an opportunity to
judge the scope of the internet's growing role in supporting a
worldwide critical consciousness. As demonstrations took place in
Quebec City, many Netizens spoke out against globalization
through petitions and declarations on protest sites. On the French
site www.archinet.fr, the protest was already well underway. The site
www.marchedespeuples.org was at the centre of the virtual protest
– it was far less risky for protestors to vent their feelings there than
in the streets, as tear gas, pepper spray, and water cannon have yet
to be adapted for Web use. Political protest sites are multiplying,
and they deal with all current issues. There are also sites for
humanitarian causes, for human rights, for the liberation of political prisoners, for or against abortion, against the death penalty in
the United States, and many others.

A CYBERNETIC SOCIETY?
LIBERTY OR ULTRALIBERALISM?

The ideology of the new economy is tied to the ideology of globalization and to that of the communication-based utopia of an immediate, almost standardized, and transparent space-time, where
money and bytes circulate fast and furiously over high-bandwidth
networks. Plus, money itself is becoming electronic. Is this the
realization of Norbert Wiener's cybernetic model, according to

which society functions as a circular information system that is automatically self-regulating? The model of the new economy is very similar to this.

It remains to be seen whether the information highway will stay libertarian, in afocal rhizomes, without centres of power, or whether it will become a series of Roman roads. Imperial Rome built such roads to extend its conquest to the limits of the known world, and so all Roman roads led to Rome. The internet is a multipoint web that envelopes the planet but precludes a centralist ideology; this web is libertarian, or potentially ultraliberal. This is the fulfillment of the cybernetic vision. In his theory, Wiener included the concept of manipulation of information, which makes it possible to rule – in other words, to control. The question is, therefore: Who will manipulate? Everyone, as a naive communications democracy utopia would have it? Or the most powerful? Will it be the empire of virtue, the Athenian agora of equal citizens, or the empire of force?

The cyberworld is presented as a vast world that is plugged into the values of the future: democracy, economic growth, technological progress, and instantaneous communication. But it might simply be an empire of the rich – an empire that could spread rapidly by taking advantage of the void left by the collapse of the Communist empire since the fall of the Berlin Wall. The ultraliberal utopia could be as dangerous as the Marxist utopia was; it, too, has menacing expansionist designs.

Libertarian and ultraliberal seem to be two contradictory poles of the same concept of liberty, as it is laid out by the utopians of individual liberty or by the utopians of capitalist thought. And it has become a major democratic issue, one that could be expressed as our eighteenth paradoxical law.

EIGHTEENTH PARADOXICAL LAW

Cyberspace has become the political playing field of two opposing conceptions of liberty: on the one hand, a libertarian utopia; and on the other hand, groupthink – the hegemony of ultraliberal ideology.

13: The Digital Angel

The battle is already raging in cyberspace
between the digital angels and devils.

PART ANGEL, PART DEVIL

In 1999, the Florida-based company Applied Digital Solutions (ADS) developed the Digital Angel. This silicon chip, or cookie, the size of a grain of rice, can be inserted into any object or under human skin, putting its host in constant remote communication with surveillance systems. The chip could be used to monitor a person's health, security, and movements. ADS tells us that the Digital Angel seems destined to become the interface between the human and electronic networks; the company is convinced that its product will be in great demand. "Big Brother is watching," warned George Orwell in *1984*.

THE BRIGHT SIDE OF ELECTRONIC MONITORING ...

Global positioning systems, or GPS, for geopositioning via satellite, already make it possible to monitor cars and trucks and to quickly locate a distress signal and perform a rescue. They could soon be keeping everyone constantly linked to the entire global communication and information network. A car radio station can already set out an itinerary in real time. In the near future, a mechanic will hook your car's computer up to the internet for scheduled maintenance or to identify the cause of a problem in order to repair it. It is conceivable that while you are driving your car, your radio will warn you that you are approaching roadwork, that you are speeding, that you need gas, that you should stop at a certain restaurant, that you've had too much to drink to be driving, and so on.

... AND THE DARK SIDE

We are witnessing the acceleration of the digital telecommunications industry, which promises a thousand and one benefits. However, it also offers countless services that we don't need – or, worse, that could soon become a network for monitoring an individual's movements and communications, as once only God himself could do. We have learned, for example, that the police are now able to re-create a suspect's movements, even long after the crime, thanks to the geopositioning of the suspect's cell phone, which emits signals when on, even when it's not in use. In fact, a new system, the mobile positioning system, or MPS, is currently available for cell phones.

Dataveillance or cyveillance systems are also under development. Surveillance camera networks in urban centres and in companies, listening devices for electronic communications and voice-mail boxes, devices for checking e-mail exchanges, cookies placed without the user's knowledge in computers or internet messages to study user behaviour (already in Windows 98 and Pentium III processors): these constitute the flip side of technological progress because they are a direct threat to our privacy. If we're going to talk about angels, we also need to talk about the many digital devils out there.

Reality is starting to resemble fiction, particularly the prophetic fiction of George Orwell. Blue Eyes, the sensory technology developed at IBM research laboratories in Almaden, California, makes it possible to complement voice commands with a visual dialogue between humans and computers, but it also opens the door to a new generation of devices to monitor our every move, both at home and at work. Sweet liberty – what more do you have in store for us? Unlike British professor Kevin Warwick – who actually experimented on himself with the device – must we wait to have chips implanted in our bodies, eliminating the need for keys or codes to open the doors of our homes and cars, to establish our identities, or to pay for our purchases? This very chip could place us under constant cybersurveillance …

Furthermore, your boss or your wife can discreetly install a snooper no bigger than a USB drive between your keyboard and your personal computer and register without your knowledge any data or message that enters via your keyboard. And this snooper can be read, printed, memorized via a Windows NotePad – it's that simple.[1]

THE DIGITAL AMBUSH

The Internet has become as dangerous as a dark street at night. Jayne Hitchcock, the aptly named Maryland writer who became the victim of an Internet harassment campaign as the result of a dispute with a literary agency, can attest to this. Cyberpredators managed to get hold of her identity on the Web, as well as those of her friends and members of her family, and she was bombarded daily with obscene messages. There was also the case of the New Yorker who accessed the digital files of the 400 richest Americans (as listed by *Forbes* magazine) – Steven Spielberg among them – and obtained their private addresses, credit card numbers, banking information, and more.

Most internet users still hesitate to use their credit cards on-line – hundreds of thousands of numbers are stolen on-line each year. We also know that a number of companies and brokers systematically accumulate supposedly confidential information about each of us. For example, data mining makes it possible to find out about a person's lifestyle – the type of activities he or she engages in, as well as purchases and favourite forms of entertainment – from credit card transactions, phone calls, and type of Web searches performed. These companies secretly sell their lists, despite American privacy protection laws passed in 1999 and 2000.

The commercial potential of such devices is already being exploited for targeted advertising. You are sports-minded, frequent Japanese restaurants, travel a lot, garden, and buy books or large quantities of alcohol or medication: your credit cards and your internet browsing reveal all of this and more, including things that are less politically correct. Don't be surprised if you receive targeted advertising in your personal e-mail and your mailbox or are solicited by phone. Even humanitarian and charitable organizations exchange information: simply send a cheque to one of them, and you will start receiving mail solicitations from others. This is probably just the beginning of a new, powerful, invisible marketing method based on the digital traces you leave (data mining).

An anonymous message reminding us of an unfortunate reality is circulating on the Web: "These days, if you're not careful, any idiot who knows how to push buttons can get into your computer and take control of your hard drive without you knowing." Someone could therefore impersonate you, sending e-mail or making purchases, and then harass or blackmail you. If this lack of security is not resolved soon, it will create a big problem for the internet. It is currently much easier for a professional to empty your bank account with digital tools than with a crowbar.

The simple fact that companies use wireless systems to connect their computers makes them vulnerable to industrial hacking. Even though they protect themselves from hackers with firewalls, it's not hard for a hacker to connect to their internal networks without their knowledge and capture files by going through the hubs that connect wireless computers. All he needs to do is position himself a few hundred metres away with a laptop equipped with an antenna, inexpensive software like Wired Equivalent Protocol (WEP), and an Ethernet card.

FROM SOCIAL INSURANCE NUMBER TO TELEPHONE NUMBER AS ID

We are being told that soon each of us will be given a phone number at birth. This digital telephone identification will replace our current health insurance and social insurance numbers. Great news! At last! And what a change in symbol – from an identity based on illness to one based on communications. (A new symbol for illness?)

THE FIFTH ESTATE: COMPUTING FOR GOVERNMENTS AND LARGE COMPANIES

Smartcards and public databases also increasingly represent serious threats to democracy. Government mega-databases created to manage every citizen's health, tax, and police records are added to a variety of other files: each person's banking history, kept by financial institutions, with a black mark for each late mortgage or credit card payment; the files of insurance companies eager to know people's driving or medical histories; and the files of companies that want to understand the lifestyles of their customers in order to better target their advertising. These databases are a major, direct threat to privacy.

The cross-referencing of these files, which can occur at any moment without our knowledge, is child's play for public administrations. And criminal intrusions into them are frequent – there was a recent case in Quebec in which criminal gangs once again infiltrated the automobile insurance service, likely resulting in several assassinations. And these files are growing by the minute. What we call e-governance – the governmental network of public services offered to citizens and companies – is a double-edged sword, because as it makes things easier and reduces costs, it also contributes to the computerized knowledge of all social actors.

The intelligent vision system (Smart Vision) combines software with surveillance cameras, making it possible, for example, to immediately spot unusual behaviour in a sea of people in motion. In an airport or a subway station, a person moving in the wrong direction or stopping in a corridor will be detected and subjected to closer surveillance. These systems can also compare police photos of wanted people or those deemed undesirable with the images recorded by surveillance cameras. Public opinion supports these developments. The question then becomes whether society will tolerate the violation of individual liberty in the name of improved public security. In fact, surveillance techniques are becoming so intertwined that it will soon be impossible to escape them. As Reg Whitaker points out, there is no more big brother but rather a whole lot of little brothers who see everything, know everything, and endlessly report on our activities.[2] Privacy International, an association that fights these abuses, hands out the ironic Big Brother Awards to denounce companies that develop such remote surveillance systems.

BORDER CONTROL IN CYBERSPACE AND ANONYMITY

Zero-Knowledge of Montreal and Anonymizer of San Diego have developed software that protects the anonymity of Web surfers.[3] Surfers can visit sites or send messages without leaving an identifying trace, which ensures respect for their private space in cyberspace. As University of Washington law professor Jeffrey Rosen explains, it involves covering your own tracks or leaving traces in invisible ink. Aside from Freenet and Freedom, which also allow you to register under a false identity, there are other techniques, including software that hides a confidential message in the encoding of a harmless image or in a seemingly ordinary piece of text; the presence of this message is imperceptible, and only the recipient has the decryption key.

Cybercriminals can therefore hack without risk. As a result, locating political activists, hackers, even cyberterrorists and criminals has become a major challenge for the police of the virtual world. Governments and legal authorities will likely want their cybersovereignty over their national territories to be respected. For example, China or Iran will want to be technically able to block messages from foreign Netizen protesters. And when the French government obtained a court ruling prohibiting Yahoo! France from selling Nazi paraphernalia on-line, the decision had to be enforceable. At first, Yahoo! falsely maintained that it was technically impossible to specifically block access to a site for a particular category of Netizens – in this instance the French – but it later had to comply with the judgment.

One solution came from a Quebec company, BorderControl. Its founders developed a search engine that scans the Web for the twelve-digit sequences that identify a site. The company uses the engine to build a huge digital databank of the world's servers, URLs, and IP addresses. All that remains to be done to create a protected area within cyberspace is to block access to a category of addresses. Likewise, by scanning server addresses linked to the delivery of a message on the internet, we will be able to trace the geographical origin of the source message.

All of these techniques for detection or camouflage will have to improve and fight it out among themselves, and we can anticipate that a lot of expertise and money will be invested in them in the future.

THE BIG PLANETARY EARS

But that's not all. Since the 1990s, the United States, Canada, England, Australia, and New Zealand have collaborated on deploying the Echelon system under the aegis of the National Security

Agency. This system scans all the information circulating worldwide via satellite and perhaps on networks (private phone and data, fax, internet) looking for a certain number of keywords, such as "terrorism," "bomb," "attack," and so on; it then selects onscreen messages that contain references of a sensitive nature. The stated objective is to fight terrorism, but the reality – denounced by some – is related to scientific, industrial, political, and other forms of espionage. After seven months of research, a Council of Europe commission of inquiry concluded that "the existence of a global system for intercepting communications ... is no longer in doubt"; and "the purpose of the system is to intercept ... private and commercial communications."[4] Europe has therefore decided to start developing its own surveillance system, called Galileo, despite American resistance.

Satellite surveillance systems that can pinpoint objects measuring less than one metre and follow their movements only reinforce this splendid system. Is it too much to hope that the enormous amount of information collected will be unmanageable? Yes – this underestimates the processing capacity of computers. If a simple, commonly used search engine like Google is able to detect 35.5 million Web sites and pages that contain the word "love" in 0.07 seconds, we shouldn't kid ourselves.

The computerization of our societies is one of the biggest threats of our new civilization. It is unfortunately still taken too lightly by those who are its targeted victims, and public authorities and business-world denizens obviously see only the advantages and are pushing to expand their databases with more determination than discretion. This question has become an urgent one for any self-respecting democracy, but public debate is overdue.

It is true that the internet also encourages the development of a critical global consciousness – so-called alterglobalization – and increasingly mobilizes the young who object to the way it is evolving. The Global Forum on Fostering Democracy and Development through e-Government, held in Washington in 1999, Brasilia in 2000, Naples in 2001, and Marrakech in 2002, brings together not only government representatives from forty countries but also thousands of activists against globalization and computer control by governments. There were 20,000 to 50,000 demonstrators in Naples, mobilized via internet on the Agenzia di Comunicazione Antagonista Web site (its name alone speaks volumes). We must not underestimate the ability of our democracies to self-regulate when it comes to computer control, but the challenge is immense and pressing.

TOWARDS UNIVERSAL ELECTRONIC CONTROL: WORLD WATCH WEB

"Who watches whom?" worried Netizens might ask. The way has now been paved for a universal and extremely powerful system of digital control of citizens and of the circulation of goods and ideas, thanks to search engines, intelligent agents, cookies, and the intersection of databases with a network of satellites. It is still difficult to legislate when it comes to these new issues and to distinguish between sanctioned, well-intentioned activities and crimes. There is no greater threat to the relationship between consumers and on-line companies than the threat to confidentiality.

We must not merely blame private companies. Governments also use this insidious practice. According to a 2001 investigation by the CBC that tested 600 government sites, one in ten planted cookies in visitors' computers (without their knowledge, of course) – contravening official policies for the protection of the privacy of citizens. Web sites use not only cookies – which we can regularly throw into our computers' trash receptacles – but they also use e-mail with hidden files attached. These are capable of touring the recipient's hard drive undetected and informing the issuer about the habits and lifestyles of its customers.

Furthermore, it is hard for citizens to refuse to sign authorizations for financial background checks. Those who do refuse will not receive the mortgage they are applying for, or they won't be able to open a bank account. Databases created this way are likely to be cross-referenced with those of insurance companies, health services, tax authorities, and marketing firms. Every abuse, public and clandestine, is possible, and abuses will occur more and more often if we don't put a stop to them by passing strong laws and deploying digital tools and deterrent penalties. The same digital technologies we sing the praises of can threaten democracy and individual freedom, and we are facing serious violations of privacy, which are presented to us as inevitable.

These technologies encourage the proliferation of cybercrimes and hacking, as well as exercising strict control over the circulation of goods. For example, these technologies will make it possible to associate a hidden code with every digital file and to monitor its circulation and use. A pirated music file could thus be located and destroyed remotely. The internet, which initially appeared to be a libertarian space of adventure, will paradoxically become a space under high digital surveillance where the digital angels and devils will wage a fierce battle.

NINETEENTH PARADOXICAL LAW
The digital realm, which presents itself as a space for individual and commercial freedom that eludes control and even encourages piracy, has in fact the technological potential to become a space for the most radical digital control we can imagine: all information circulating and the profiles of users can be traced, situated, and kept on file.

Science fiction, which perhaps premonitorily cultivates the myth of globalization, is already exploring the chip that will be implanted in people's shoulders at birth to serve as identification, an electronic wallet, a multi-purpose key, which will provide access to our medical files and make us locatable by satellite if we are lost or trying (in vain) to disappear in the great expanse of the new world. Because cyberspace is likely to become more and more transparent. Too bad for those of us who appreciate the odd shadow.

14: Cash and Digital Economics

Money has become the digital fluid of the economy,
and it irrigates the imaginary realm of many
of our contemporaries.

CASH IS DIGITAL, AND VICE VERSA

Jeremy Rifkin observes, "From the beginning of human civilization to now, culture has always preceded markets."[1] It's interesting that he makes this observation at a moment when we talk of nothing *but* the economy, which is becoming an arena of amazingly simplistic, one-dimensional thought. The gloating utopia of digital capitalism seems to have taken over from the defeated utopia of communism.

The new economy, or the knowledge economy, is built – as Nicholas Negroponte has suggested – on information and the production and circulation of bits, while the old manufacturing and industrial economy depended on atoms and natural resources.[2] Information is money, we gleefully announce. Bits are now the substance of our commercial exchanges. They are associated with wealth. Entrepreneurs have become information brokers, cash-digital bankers. In the digital age, money is electronic, and it is the raw material of the new economy. The monetary and the digital are two sides of the same coin.

A JITTERY DIGITAL ECONOMY

The value of products and services is increasingly based on immediate information and rapid speculation. Time is money and therefore the source of more and more stress. The space-time of the new economy is a virtual space and an instant time for a very sensitive cybereconomy (e-business, e-economy). The stock market, always pulsating, echoes in the economic imagination. It listens to itself, psychologically prepared to exaggerate its own moods and thus accelerate its movements.

As a result, the economy has become jittery and volatile, evolving at the speed of electricity, whereas the flow of money in the old economy – based on work and raw materials and slow systems of communication – was more impervious and therefore much less active. The new economy is more vulnerable to human uncertainties and fantasies, to the vagaries of speculation, events, imaginings, and gambling by the main players. In fact, it is so vulnerable that within it money is more than a unit of measure and exchange: it has become oxygen.

AN INCREASINGLY IMAGINARY ECONOMY: THE I-ECONOMY

We live in our imaginations, the poets say. Economists of the Net economy also live in the imaginary realm, but they don't even know it. The stock market valuation of large companies managed to climb by a factor of 1,000 in a few months and drop as much within a few weeks. Digital technologies are also, paradoxically, psycho-technologies; they make the digital imagination beat like an adventurer's excited heart. Psychologist Robert McIllwraith has pointed to the role of feelings in the economy, reminding us that economics remains a social science, in spite of its sophisticated mathematical tools.

Emotions have become very important to the economic behaviour of players in the new digital economy, while statistical tools are now ineffective in the face of new situations. And the digital economy is increasingly of the imaginary order. Therefore, what we call the electronic economy (e-economy) we can actually call the imaginary economy: the i-economy. Its drives and the extent of its fluctuations stem from its unreality, its de-realization. This is because the new economy is based on the production and exchange of information and no longer so much on merchandise – bits and not atoms, says Negroponte. The information and concepts that are exchanged do not circulate in tankers or freight trains but in the immaterial form of electronic files.

This dematerialization of the economy encourages not only its fluidity and acceleration, but also its volatility and, consequently, the grip that the imagination can have on it. The value of a loaf of bread or a house is easily ascertained; the object is there, visible and perceptible. But what is a concept worth? What is a fantasy or a vision worth? And where is it? What guarantee is there of the ownership rights that are attached to it? What about its lifespan? How are the units of account for an imaginary economy established when that economy is more exposed than the traditional economy to the squalls and the panic and the enthusiasm of speculators?

"While controlling the exchange of goods characterizes the age just passing, controlling the exchange of concepts characterizes the new age coming. In the twenty-first century, institutions increasingly trade in ideas," says Rifkin.[3] Solveig Godeluck underlines this: "Since [the Net economy] is based on confidence and detached from the real economy, it is at the mercy of rumour and manipulation. We are indeed entering the era of information capitalism, but it is fraught with risks and dangers."[4] Should it come as a surprise, then, that gambling takes up more and more space in the i-economy? When currency circulates at digital speed, imaginations heat up and hearts race with get-rich-quick dreams.

This digital stimulation ensures the success of on-line e-brokers such as eBay, E*Trade Financial, Yahoo! Finance, MSN Money Central, AltaVista Money, and Virtual Stock Exchange. These sites, not unlike on-line casinos, let anyone play the market daily for a minimal commission, doing nothing to alleviate the craving for imaginary wealth. The imaginary economy is also infected, feverish, as evidenced by the popularity of on-line stock market simulation games (for example, TradersPlay.com, MainXchange Stockgame, Marcopoly).

Shareholders increasingly respond like owners rather than entrepreneurs. They carefully consider monthly financial results – the numbers – and ignore the reality of the operations and human resources on which these results are based. This reality has been overwhelmed by the arithmetic-based logic of immediate profit. The digital fluidity of the imaginary economy stokes its event-based dynamic and speeds up trades. Money irrigates the economy, making the imaginary realm of the digital pulsate.

TWENTIETH PARADOXICAL LAW
The monetary and the digital are two complementary forms of the same language of numbers, which becomes the raw material of the new economy.

We also use the term "Net economy" for this new economy that no longer hoards and that has replaced the traditional nest egg with the Web. Bill Gates, the world's richest man, accurately sums up this new vision of a fluid economy based not on raw materials and natural resources but on the rapid circulation of electronic information: "Part of the goal here is to take all the transactions, all the business understanding ... and really get those into digital form. So, you could say it's a transition from what is largely an offline economy to a very real-time digital online economy."[5] According to Gates, even the domestic economy will move from the hard disks of microcomputers to cyberspace.

ULTRALIBERALISM

This new economy has a religion – ultraliberalism – to which all virtues are ascribed. It expresses a sort of economic law of nature: competition, which would be dangerous to thwart through artificial state controls. It ultimately promotes employment, the enrichment of the middle classes, the development of poor countries, democracy, and the circulation of people, ideas, and merchandise – nothing less than world peace and planetary progress. It is difficult to oppose the great principle of the free movement of people, assets, services, and capital, but we must not forget that the freedom of some cannot be had at the expense of others. Freedom should not be enjoyed only by the strongest, and so it requires democratic management, regulation, restraint. Ultraliberalism tends naturally to uphold the law of natural selection, the law of the jungle, the law of the predator. Who would have thought that we would build global relationships between peoples according to the harsh law that compels brother to turn on brother, even in the paradise of America?

Of course, ultraliberalism is uncomfortable with state regulation. If the natural law of the economy were to be seen as superior to the reason of the state, we are told, then there would be fewer states and the world would be a better place. Under the banner of economic freedom, the new masters of the world have replaced states; they are the multinationals, or, as we should call them, the transnational corporations. They rule the market society, wage ruthless war on each other, and share territory – like wolves. In this global market democracy, some die of indigestion, others of hunger. The price of a computer is eight years' salary in Bangladesh and two weeks' salary in the United States.

In this business democracy, we are no longer citizens of the state, but consumers, users of commercial products and customers of companies. I'm not suggesting that this is the end of the world; I don't think that we need to shed tears over the ignobility of capitalism, but this is a world we will have to discipline if we want to find something in it for ourselves as free subjects.

AMERICAN SUCCESS

Although it experienced a slowdown in 2001, on the threshold of the new millennium, the United States is a model of economic success that has been unequalled for a long time. It has seen eight years of uninterrupted growth, with an annual growth rate of 4 per cent to 6 per cent; full, or almost full, employment (official statistics put the unemployment rate at 4.25 per cent); controlled inflation (less than 2 per cent); a long-term federal budget surplus; and peaks on Wall Street and NASDAQ that stand as a model for ultraliberalism. The Clinton presidency was dubbed the "Eight Glorious Years," a reference to the post-war (1945 to 1975) economic boom in France known as les Trente Glorieuses ("the thirty glorious years"). The collapse of NASDAQ and the stock market valuation of digital technology companies have led to a consolidation and restructuring of the more viable companies. The success of the American economy – the made-in-the-USA prototype – has given rise to new theories, in particular the idea of lengthening economic cycles. It has also prompted us to ask – in light of British economist A.W. Phillips's sacrosanct principle of the non-accelerating inflation rate of unemployment (NAIRU) – how the unemployment rate can drop below 6 per cent without inflation rising again. We have also begun to question whether the massive military expenses stemming from George W. Bush's desire for imperialistic hegemony and preventive wars will devastate the American model.

E-PARADISE.COM

The new economy, according to this recent American model, is based largely on information, as opposed to the old economy, which was based on production. What we call the Net economy, the cybereconomy, or the v-economy (virtual economy) has seen meteoric growth, stimulating the imaginations of future buffs. In 1998, Michael de Kare-Silver declared the Net economy the final achievement of human happiness. Cocooning, he predicted, would take hold completely, since, thanks to e-commerce, abundance could flow effortlessly to our homes – all we had to do was click. Then, to prevent us from becoming sad, solitary consumers holed up at home, the grand masters of commerce would redouble their efforts to lure us to an artificial paradise: the new shopping centre. Inspired by Walt Disney theme parks and discount shopping centres – Disneyworld meets Wal-Mart – these blissful places promised to fulfill the myth of happiness:

Suddenly there's more time for family and friends. There's the opportunity to relax, pursue hobbies and have more quality leisure time … Visits to large shopping centres will grow in popularity. It will present the opportunity to see a complete range of products with all the leading suppliers and distributors represented. There will be special areas … for leaving young children with highly trained staff in superb facilities. There will be a wide choice of places to eat, meet friends and socialise. In the bigger centres and malls there will be additional social and entertainment facilities – for example, with sports and fitness clubs and movie theatres … [It will be] the total shopping experience … [and it will] excite consumers so they still want to visit, despite the temptations of electronic shopping.[6]

Two competing temptations and delights are no doubt better than one in the quest for perfect happiness. De Kare-Silver's vision appeared quite plausible at the time: in 1999, internet companies were worth on average 220 times their profits – a first for the stock market. But this is no longer the case, you say. True, but it could happen again. And to get the ball rolling in that direction, free internet connections are now being considered. If it happens, there will no longer even be a ticket wicket at the gates of e-paradise.

MARKET DEMOCRACY

Marx said that we would finally achieve happiness after the communist revolution. He embellished the myth by suggesting that there would be great heaps of merchandise from which each person could draw according to his or her needs. Now Marx's promise appears to have been fulfilled by e-commerce and the major shopping centres of the new economy, which have brought together the two driving forces of American democracy: the consumer industry and the entertainment industry, the religion of consumption and the cult of distraction.

However, the Marxist utopia of the nineteenth century was no less naive and simplistic than its twenty-first-century e-capitalist alternative, which is aiming, once again, to conquer the world; it wants to annex all ideas to its own dream and attempt to legitimize itself through the supposed virtues of ultraliberalism (which proponents call "market democracy"). By contrast, Marx claimed to speak in the name of social justice. But the chances of achieving market democracy are not much greater than the chances of achieving social justice.

THE ECONOMIC BOOST PROVIDED BY NEW INFORMATION TECHNOLOGIES

The American government is trying its best to find legal means to funnel the global empire of wealth from the new economy into the United States. The US secretary of commerce, noting that e-commerce doubles in volume every year, was not afraid to say that e-commerce has seen growth beyond expectation and will become the main growth factor in the American economy in the twenty-first century. Having as early as 1998 reached more than $300 billion in sales, the internet seemed destined for geometric growth. Alone, it already exceeded the GNP of Argentina and almost equalled that of Switzerland. After only five years of commercialization, the internet matched the sales figures of the American automobile industry ($350 billion), an industry that was built up over a century. Forecasts were that by 2006, half the people employed in the United States would work in information technology industries. Of course, it never even approached this peak, and the "forecasts" were revealed to be vague euphoric statements. Even before the end of the twentieth century, 50 per cent of American economic growth was attributed to information technologies (in France, this figure was only 15 per cent). It is interesting to note that the drop in the price of electronic and communication equipment (computers, phones, faxes) may have reduced the inflation rate by one point.

A NEW PRODUCTIVITY

Another significant aspect of this new economy is that it is sustained by a transformation of work. It requires less physical force and manipulation and more intelligence and innovation. While this initially creates unemployment, it substantially increases the quality, quantity, and speed of production through automation. Productivity has taken off, rising 2 per cent per year. New technologies have become powerful engines of economic growth. Yet often in the new economy an investment of $100 or $200 million will create only about twenty-five new jobs – this is the price we have to pay. Yet somehow unemployment remains limited, particularly in the United States.

Stock market quotes, as well as daily monitoring by thousands of shareholders, have also influenced the management of public companies, which flaunt the profitability of their leadership to their investors in order to ensure their professional legitimacy and future. A listing on the stock market reorients companies, for better or for worse, towards profitability. Some companies, however, choose to invest large sums up front to capture the largest possible market share right away, thus putting themselves at risk of losing money in their first years. Amazon.com is one of the very few that succeeded with this strategy. Finally, the removal of customs barriers in a broad free trade zone makes it possible to increase sales in new markets.

A DUTY-FREE CYBERZONE OF ELECTRONIC COMMERCE

The Americans plan to create a vast free trade area – a duty-free cyberzone. The Magaziner report, approved in 1997 by the US government, is explicit in its recommendations on this matter: for e-commerce to spread at full capacity, "governments must adopt a non-regulatory, market-oriented approach to electronic commerce, one that facilitates the emergence of a transparent and predictable legal environment to support global business and commerce. Official decision makers must respect the unique nature of the medium and recognize that widespread competition and increased consumer choice should be the defining features of the new digital marketplace."[7]

THE NEW HEROES OF OUR TIME

The ideology of entrepreneurship is now the cornerstone of the dominant ideology of the middle class. The entrepreneurial spirit, the valorization of hard work, dominates our era and, along with the scientific and technological spirit, it inspires our new civilization. (For the record, the leisure society heralded in the 1970s was stillborn.) In Japan, praise for hard work is not new; for a long time, Japanese companies have given meaning to the lives of their employees, absorbing their time and their thoughts. In the West, the entrepreneurial myth is rooted in the spirit of capitalism and in Protestantism, as Max Weber has shown.

What is new is the celebration of the entrepreneurial epic. Our heroes are now the conquistadors of hypercapitalism. In the media, much space is devoted to them; the science of entrepreneurship has become a hot topic. The covers of best-sellers bear this out – in 2001, I noted these glorious titles in airport bookstores: *Wisdom of the CEO, The Book of Business Wisdom, How to Become a CEO, How to Think like a CEO, The Millionaire Next Door, Power: The 18 Laws, The Heart of a Leader, The Mind of the CEO, The Tools of Leadership, The Guru Guide to Entrepreneurship, Managers and Mantras, Titans: How the Canadian Establishment Seized Power, When Corporations Rule the World, The Seven Steps to Nirvana (Strategic Insights into eBusiness Transformation), What It Takes to Be #1, The Future of Leadership,* and *Leadership from Within.* A body of literature for businesspeople who spend time in airports preparing to conquer the world.

THE RISKS OF THE DIGITAL ECONOMY

Great technical innovations have always caused speculative fever and major collapses – witness the railroad and the automobile. A group of players will eventually stabilize and restructure things, making it possible to reach cruising altitude. The misfortunes of the American dot.coms simply confirm this rule, and now the repercussions of flights of digital enthusiasm are also reverberating in people's imaginations – and in the economy.

There were such high hopes for the new economy that entrepreneurs were given access to easy money and didn't have to worry much about immediate profitability; many speculators borrowed heavily to get rich quick on the stock market. We could have predicted what would happen when the bubble burst: the market would crash, and the consequences would be global. Crisis factors included unlimited currency speculation and stock market speculation that grossly inflated the value of companies – even those operating at a loss. The crisis occurred in spring 2000, but the international economy remained unscathed.

THE SHOCK OF SPECULATION

On the evening in 1995 that it made its debut on the stock exchange, Netscape was worth US$2 million, though it had yet to turn a profit. In 2001, Nortel, the world's leading supplier of network equipment, saw its share price plummet from C$124 to less than a dollar in just a few months. And many other equally important companies, such as Cisco, Lucent, and Softbank, also lost 90 per cent of their market value. What happened?

At the beginning of the period of intense excitement over digital technologies it was so easy for California dot.com entrepreneurs to obtain venture capital that they became niche hunters: all they needed was a new idea for products or services and the beginnings of a business plan. The 2001 documentary *Startup.com* by Chris Hegedus and Jehane Noujaim tells the story of two young Net economy entrepreneurs, Kaleil and Tom, who, in November 1998, founded govWorks.com, a company that enabled people to pay taxes and fines on-line. The filmmakers followed the young entrepreneurs, camera in hand, all the while working on the financing for their film. They managed to obtain about $700,000 from their distributor for a shoot that would last a year and a half. For their part, Kaleil and Tom collected $20 million in six weeks and raised almost $60 million in venture capital in a year and a half. The stock market crash was fatal to Kaleil and Tom's enterprise, but Hegedus and Noujaim have gone on to make other films.

A CALIFORNIA DOT.COM IS EASILY WORTH A DUTCH TULIP BULB

Such impulsiveness is not unique to the Net economy. In 1630s Holland, the tulip bulb trade came down with a speculative fever that produced equally surreal results. At the time, a rare tulip bulb could increase in value by 100 to 200 per cent in a few months and be traded for more than the price of a house on one of Amsterdam's chicest canals. In 1636, speculation reached its peak, and in February 1637 there was a devastating crash. So, we should not look for the causes of the dot.com crisis in the nature of digital technology but rather in ancient dreams of sudden and spectacular wealth and power.[8]

As Derrick de Kerkhove points out:

There is, without a doubt ... a sort of required path that, beyond a critical threshold of virtualization, makes us give up the safeguards of established models and put ourselves to the task of building an alternative domain, divorced from reality. This model becomes essential and grows from its own strength to the point where the de-realization becomes too obvious. We then suddenly come back to the models that not long ago we rejected. Swept along in generalized disrepute, the start-ups as well as the stars of the Net economy find themselves in difficulty ... With the help of passing fashion, we enter the stage of disenchantment, of "Net ennui." The birds of ill omen who had resisted the Net because they could see no good in it, and who predicted its collapse, are now rejoicing.[9]

MIND-BOGGLING PROJECTIONS FOR E-COMMERCE

This feverishness in the imaginary realm – which gave rise to euphoric arithmetical projections at the turn of the century – was reflected in forecasts. The methodological bases of these forecasts were often uncertain and contradictory, but the forecasts themselves were almost always overly optimistic, and they were echoed daily in the media. E-commerce seemed destined for spectacular growth.

Its value was predicted to approach $380 billion in 2003, compared to an estimated $48 billion in 1998. In fact, according to the Boston Consulting Group, it only attained $44.5 billion in 1999 and $65 billion in 2000 for all of North America, Canada included. In 1999, it was said that e-commerce was already being transacted in 30 per cent of US households, that Canada would soon reach this level, in 2000 it would be Germany's turn – then England's in 2001, Japan's in 2002, and France's in 2003. The entire planet would follow: e-commerce was already in its adolescence.

In fact, the evolution has been much slower than predicted, even for business-to-business (or B2B) e-commerce. As far as retail (B2C, or business-to-consumers) is concerned, apart from a few exceptions, it has not lived up to its promise, and it will take much more time, perhaps years, for it to create the new consumer habits it depends upon. In 2005, in Canada, online sales reached $40 billion, which still represents only 1 per cent of total revenues of private companies, according to Statistics Canada. Its development also assumes that virtual stores will become more appealing. Everything still remains to be done in this respect. We are even witnessing a falling off of e-commerce due to the difficulty of handling requests and transactions on-line, the difficulty of getting reimbursed, and local taxes and customs fees, which can easily double the price of an on-line purchase from another country. The gurus of e-commerce must accept the fact that retail e-commerce will not kill off business in stores, and on-line purchases will still represent only a small proportion of total consumption – probably in the order of 10 per cent, at best – and this consumption will occur only in sectors that lend themselves to it, like electronics, books, music, travel, and tourism.

IS MONEY MADE ON THE INTERNET?

As I have said, Amazon.com's business plan, which inspired many dot.coms that have since collapsed, was based on an initial deficit investment that was intended to allow the company to grab a healthy share of the market out of the gate. Despite the disastrous results of this strategy for many of the companies that undertook it, there are signs that some will survive. In the field of on-line travel services, the two American leaders, Travelocity.com, a subsidiary of the Sabre electronic reservation system, and Expedia.com, a subsidiary of Microsoft, are finally turning a profit after five years of losses. And Priceline.com, whose sales strategy is based on what the buyer bids and not on what the agency offers, also forecasts that it will move out of the red. Of course, these agencies target the general public rather than businesspeople.

Here is a key to success for e-traders: base on-line e-commerce on a network of real outlets. This makes it possible to amortize losses, to capitalize on brand reputation, to give consumers the opportunity to shop first on the Web in order to narrow down the options before making their purchases in a real store where they can see what they're buying. All of this will increase customer confidence.

A SLOT IN YOUR TELEVISION?

Will there soon be slots in our TV sets into which we can insert a credit card to make on-line purchases? And will our purchases be delivered faster than the speed of light by teleportation? Those who don't believe in this are condemned to disappear. In 1999, accounting firm Arthur Andersen and the National Association of Wholesaler Distributors announced that those distributors who had not integrated e-commerce would be out of business by 2003.

It is likely, in fact, that the Net economy will undergo major expansion. We have already seen such transformations in the past. However, they almost always materialize slower than expected. And they don't necessarily involve the entire planet or even all of American society, in which the old economy still generates the majority of employment – fortunately so, for those who have not studied computer science or who have little education. We must not forget that the American economy functions in car gears, while in developing countries it functions on foot or bike. We must not forget that the old world, which is more real than virtual, has many unique charms.

Fundamentalism, whether religious, right wing, or left wing, is reinforced by the globalization of this dominant ideology combined with American imperialism. In the eyes of fundamentalist groups of very different cultures, Uncle Sam is the Satan of a civilization devoted body and soul to money. And G.W. Bush, in turn, has declared war on the axis of evil.

The law of the natural economy and its supposed benefits has been a mythical reference for centuries. The rich always find that

the economy works because it has served them well, and they want
the same for others. Never before has this idea been so predominant. But if the free development of the new economy and its
expansionist principles intensifies in rich countries, it will result in
human catastrophes in the poor ones. It would be disastrous to
apply America's values and culture to poor countries. It's is all too
familiar: we would once again witness the depraved effects of
colonial capitalism. Combined with the ideology of globalization,
the imperialism of the new economy is the updated version of
nineteenth century colonialism.

THE SWING OF THE PENDULUM AGAINST
THE WILD WEST ECONOMY

We must anticipate a swing of the pendulum: money freedom (for
those who have it) threatens to trigger anti-economy sentiment in
the civilization that is now being born. The ideology of economism
is much too one-dimensional, obsessive, simplistic, and inequitable,
and so an active critical consciousness will soon spring up to
counter it. Excess breeds excess, and this avid economism will soon
precipitate a scandal of inequality and exploitation. A serious financial crisis is all that is needed for many to lose faith in the goddess
of the new economy. Humanism and the great spiritual questions
will re-emerge in the wake of these excesses and the next stock
market crash. Unfortunately, we can forecast it.

Globalization and the new economy are not irresistible myths;
they are neither irreversible nor the inevitable outcome of
progress. It is naive to believe that they lead to the liberation of
peoples. And the politics of the International Monetary Fund, an
organization that has become a symbol of the magical thinking of
the new world economy of developed civilizations, have shown that
globalization is an instrument of economic violence committed
against the weak of developing civilizations, entirely legally.

We will realize that money obscures the spirit; that the myth of
the new economy has been the machine for mighty wars; that it
perpetuates the law of the strongest; that it has contributed little
to the worldwide growth of democracy or to the development of
two-thirds of humanity. We should rethink economic relationships
so that we can, for example, begin to manage the planet's water
supply – blue gold – according to principles of equity and human

need rather than subjugating it to the merciless relationships of economic power in the developed world.

MONEY: THE UNIVERSAL TRANSFORMER

The supporters of the new economy and globalization maintain that money could be made a global unit of communication. Money is perhaps the most universal language – more universal than English. It is also the most basic form of symbolic exchange, just as bits and atoms are the basic units of computing and matter, even though it also takes on many added symbolic values. Money establishes the interchangeability of all gestures, objects, and values, even the most dissimilar, the most contradictory – sex as well as God's mercies. It is like water in that it makes everything circulate by oxidizing it. It is the universal factor, connector, and transformer. It is therefore the cornerstone of the new economy and globalization.

MONEY: THE ZERO DEGREE OF HUMAN SOLIDARITY

When the community bonds of close communication – the feeling of belonging to a village, a neighbourhood, a region, a nation – come undone, when borders are abolished and states erased in the name of the new market and global democracy, when citizens are no more than consumers, when management wins over politics, when globalization results in the atomization of the human masses, there is only money to connect individuals. Money is therefore the most basic form, the zero degree of human solidarity. That says everything about the absence of meaning that today confronts us. In ordinary situations – excluding widely covered natural catastrophes, uprisings, or political crises – we are now experiencing a major decline in social solidarity. Egocentric individuals must find meaning in their own lives. The best possible interpretation that we could give to this is that money's dominance demonstrates that humanity has attained a level of autonomy and maturity that allows people to be simply consumers of the world. But that's not the case at all. We all need to belong to a social group, the culture of which infuses our lives with meaning and value, brings us closer together, supports our collective projects. The money-based zero-degree form of meaning is psychologically and practically impossible to sustain. And we cannot forget that money's ambivalence is anxiety-provoking; money is also an instrument of death.

TWENTY-FIRST PARADOXICAL LAW
Monetary flow is both the degree zero of human solidarity and the accelerator of the imaginative economy – the i-economy.

15: Global Utopia and Digital Apartheid

The progress of machines is more apparent
than that of humans.

THE PLANETARY UTOPIA OF THE INTERNET

It is difficult to share Nicholas Negroponte's vision of the internet
as "creating a totally new, global social fabric" unless we first recognize that at the beginning of the twenty-first century this fabric
encompasses only 6 per cent of humanity.[1] It is also difficult to
agree with philosopher Pierre Lévy, who has been lured by the
sirens of the internet. He maintains, with startling optimism, that
"by the end of the first decades of the 21st century, more than 80%
of human beings will have access to cyberspace and will use it
daily." From this he infers that "a concrete idea of humanity is now
developing." To him, the Web represents "an immense virtual village," with streets, highways, businesses, offices, squares, and cafés,
and the computer is the means of transport. Furthermore, "cyberspace is the ultimate metropolis, the world metropolis"; and "the
solitary planet is being constructed by the web and its virtual economy. The development of the web 'is' the process of the awareness
– and the realization! – of the unity of mankind."[2]

While Lévy points out that in other respects the concept of unity
does not mean the end of inequality, the electronic solidarity that
he predicts is hard to credit in a world in which conflicts and social
rifts are multiplying. And how are we to believe his prediction that
states will disappear and we will have a single global currency when

national identities are awakening throughout the world in response to the excesses of globalization? According to Lévy, it is no longer America but rather cyberspace that will reign benevolently over humanity. Those who oppose this vision are hand-wringing, schizophrenic, backward-looking types who, "rather than promoting a positive vision of the future spread hatred and resentment."[3] This is mind-boggling. It is impossible to push the utopia of the internet further into naive sentiment.

MONEY: LINGUISTIC UNIT OF THE CITIZENS OF THE WORLD?

Is this the result of middle-class ideology? Will we forget our local roots and sacrifice the sense of belonging to a region or a country? Will we join an ultraliberal global economy, the common denominator of which would be the international objectivity of money? Is it possible that the concept of citizen of the world – which remains so abstract and theoretical, even in the minds of the intellectual elite – will give rise to a real and widespread sense of belonging? Belonging to what? And as opposed to what? To create a sense of belonging, do we not need at least one other social community to which we don't belong? Will this belonging be defined in relation to the inhabitants of another planet – aliens? Or in relation to the kingdom of ants, or monkeys? Would the opposing social communities be those hooked up to the internet, and proud of it, and those who are not, utopia's forgotten? Is there a will to power of the information-rich of developed countries over the information-poor of developing countries in this idealistic vision?

If we could wipe out the real cultural differences and conflicts that so disturb our utopian philosophers and captains of industry, would the economy then become the sole bond of a humanity preoccupied with calculations? The daily struggles and confrontations over territory, language, and jurisdiction, the tribal disputes, the fragmentation of major confederations, invalidate such a thesis – even though we are seeing a certain amount of political and economic unification. It would be a big leap to make in just a few years. And it is far from proven that one day we could forgo these identity micro-networks, which constitute the references and the parameters of our relationship with the world.

THE GREAT CENTRAL COMPUTER:
BIG BROTHER?

Political democracy, not market democracy, can only occur in communities that are of human scale – cities, regions, or nations. In these communities, the right to vote can be exercised as part of a relationship of proximity. We need only try to imagine what world-wide democracy would be like to understand this requirement: it could only be a centralist and bureaucratic dictatorship. A global government would be totalitarian, a techno-structure echoing nightmare science fiction scenarios; it would be a Great Central Computer giving orders to control the masses, itself controlled by the arbitrary decisions of a few superhumans. Even if the globalist utopia today promotes transnational values, there can be no democracy without nations and without the solidarity of proximity.

TWENTY-SECOND PARADOXICAL LAW
The concepts of citizen of the world and global government promoted by digital globalization are political sophistry and paradoxical non-sense.

Globalism and communism are concepts with the same planetary ambition, and this ambition is shared by globalization. Such concepts are the successors to the religious conquests of Islam and Catholicism and the capitalist colonial conquests of the great empires. They all betray the same compulsion for expansionism, the same will to power and conquest, the same reliance on mythical tales, although the strategies and the discourse have changed through the eras, sometimes resulting in positive changes, and sometimes in destruction.

MARKET UNIVERSALISM

Coca-Cola, Erfrischung ohne Grenzen ("Coca-Cola, refreshment that knows no borders"), read advertising billboards in the summer of 1999 in Weimar, the city in the former East Germany where Goethe lived and the Nazis established the Buchenwald concentration camp. And a renowned athletic shoe manufacturer boasted, "On planet Reebok, there are no boundaries."

Wearing a watch made in Japan, socks made in Guatemala, a cap sewn in Vietnam, a cotton shirt produced in India, shoes manufactured in Italy, and each inhabiting his or her own little inner Africa, the citizens of the new world can finally live happily on a shoestring. Commerce has always been internationalist. And with the internet, as Jeremy Rifkin points out, we can ask whether there is still a perceptible difference between communication, communion, and commerce.

RELIGIOUS UNIVERSALISM

Globalism and Catholicism are universalist philosophies, with their own sets of beliefs and virtues to justify their expansionism. Christianity and then the Catholic Church were founded on the universal uniqueness of God, the same god who created all human beings from a single stock – beings, including savages in far-off countries, who must therefore all be converted to Christianity. The Catholic Church has always been globalist in its message and in its organization; it constantly reaffirms a discourse of Truth, convinced of its righteousness, and it is therefore intolerant, even though it has managed to appear generous and humanitarian. Islam has done the same. All of these universalist churches, by definition, have sinned repeatedly through their fundamentalism, the primary horror of the human spirit, and one that is still found in almost all major religions – whether in the United States, Europe, or the Arab countries. Buddhism has the virtue of being innocent of this.

PHILOSOPHICAL UNIVERSALISM

The idea of globalization, so widespread these days in media and market discourse, is not really new. It has its roots in the rationalism and the universalist philosophy of the eighteenth century. The father of Greek philosophy, Socrates, despite the fact that in his time political discrimination was the norm, already believed that every man, slave, foreigner, or Athenian patrician had equal access to a universal truth through the application of maieutics – the Socratic mode of inquiry. In this sense, he was one of the primary founders of Western rationalism and, in spite of himself, its concomitant will to power.

Seventeenth-century Western thinkers were divided between Montaigne, who admired relativism, reminding us that truth can vary from one side of the Pyrenees to the other, and Descartes, who was convinced that common sense is common to all and undoubtedly aware of the political universalism that this simple epistemological statement leads to – he wanted man to thereby make himself "master and possessor of nature."

EMMANUEL KANT

Kantian rationalism took up the idea of the universalism of pure reason, of morality, and of a priori forms of sensibility. Consequently, Kant did not avoid the problem of *On the Various Races of Mankind* (1775) and developed the *Definition of the Concept of a Human Race* (1785). The philosophy of the Enlightenment and the idea of a universal history led Kant, following the French Revolution, to prophesy the establishment of a universal republic: "The greatest problem for the human species to the solution of which nature compels it is the establishment of a universal civil society administering the law." Kant devoted his ninth proposition to "A philosophical essay to compose the universal history of the world according to a plan of nature, which aims at the perfect civic union in the human species."[4]

This belief in universalism has therefore been a constant of Western philosophy, its tendency towards political ethnocentrism and its hidden vice – something we also see with other philosophers throughout history, such as Fichte.

JOHANN GOTTLIEB FICHTE

Fichte expressed these ideas powerfully two centuries before the mass media propagated them daily:

from the beginning of history down to our own day, the few landmarks of civilization have extended themselves abroad from their center, that one individual after another, and one nation after another, has been embraced within their circle, and that this wider outspread of culture is proceeding under our own eyes. And this is the first point to be attained in the endless path on which humanity must advance. Until this shall have been attained, until the existing culture of every age shall have been diffused over the whole inhabited globe and our species become capable of the most unlimited intercommunication with itself, one nation or one continent must pause on the great common path of progress and wait for the advance of the others; and each must bring as an offering to the universal commonwealth, for the sake of which alone it exists, its ages of apparent immobility or retrogression. When that first point shall have been attained, when every useful discovery made at one end of the earth shall be at once made known and communicated to all the rest, then, without further interruption, without halt or regress, with united strength and equal step, humanity shall move onward to a higher culture of which we can at present form no conception.[5]

THE WARS

These ideas made the rounds with the expansionism of the French Revolution, the conquering colonialism of the nineteenth century, and the general intellectual and political currents. The horrifying world wars and colonial wars; the Cold War between the capitalist and communist blocs; the Vietnam and Korean wars; the ethnic genocides in Asia, Africa, and Europe, which went on until the end of the twentieth century; the official abolition of apartheid in South Africa; and the fall of the Berlin Wall shook up and then reinforced the idea of globalization to the same extent. International institutions such as the United Nations, UNESCO, the International Monetary Fund, the World Trade Organization, and the World Health Organization, among many others – in particular, humanitarian and ecological organizations – as well as the creation of the European Union, the introduction of the euro, and the deployment of free trade zones, have all given concrete expression to this idea. Yet the fall of the Soviet Empire, the partition of Czechoslovakia, the wars in Yugoslavia, Indonesia, Northern Ireland, and especially Israel raise reasonable doubts about the trend towards globalization, while offering additional justification to its advocates.

TECHNOLOGIES AND THE ECONOMY

Air transport; mass media and electronic telecommunications; the flow of immigrants from developing countries to developed ones, and the resultant mixing of cultural origins; stock market and financial speculation; humanitarian, epidemiological, climate, and environmental concerns; the growth of the multinationals; the internationalization of the markets and of economic and financial trade; and the spread of English as a language of utilitarian communication have all decisively consolidated this tendency towards globalization. In fact, the philosophical concept of universalism inherited from the Enlightenment found its logical result in the political idea of internationalism before giving way to the current concept of globalization, which has much greater economic and utopian resonance.

INTERNATIONALISM

The ideology of internationalism has been promoted by leftist intellectuals and political currents. The Socialist International and the international pacifism of Aristide Briand come to mind, in contrast to the nationalism of the right. On the eve of the war of 1914–18, debate in France was heated. Internationalism was therefore a political ideal of the left, the dream of a more fraternal, possibly more egalitarian, humanity.

THE PARADOX OF THE GLOBAL VILLAGE AND THE DRAMATIC RETURN OF LOCAL IDENTITIES

The idea then evolved with the communication technology revolution and the explosion of the mass media. McLuhan's inspired prophesy of the global village, as paradoxical as it might have initially appeared, is coming true before our very eyes. The more globalization progresses, the more the search for local identities and cultural roots, the preservation of marginalized languages, and the celebration of difference are modernized and promoted as compensating and necessary values in a new global-local equilibrium (synthesized in 1994 by Frank Feather, in *The Future Consumer*, with the term "glocal": "Think globally, act locally").

The universalist ideologues who hoped and prayed for a global, homogenized, uniform, and increasingly undifferentiated society – or, as Marcuse would have said, an increasingly one-dimensional society – could not have thought of this dialectical law of equilibrium, according to which the more our life space becomes global, the greater our tendency as individuals or as local or cultural communities to revive distinct identities, to cultivate cultural differences, to regain our roots, and to demand political autonomy. We saw France, a country extremely centralized due to its Jacobin tradition, begin to move towards regionalization and decentralization under the regime of de Gaulle, which, at the end of the twentieth century, has resulted in a resurgence of local languages – Breton, Basque, Corsican. And the creation of the European Union facilitates and even encourages the local autonomy of Catalonia, Walloon, Slovakia, Scotland, and perhaps tomorrow even Corsica, the Basque Country, and Northern Ireland.

Quebec's claim to independence from the Canadian federation reflects the same global tendency and responds to the same demand for renewed local convergence within an enormous collectivity that too often sacrifices local and distinct interests for the global vision of its political centralist structure, upsetting a fragile, but necessary, equilibrium of powers. The apparent indifference of Europeans to the construction of their union, demonstrated in the widespread abstention from the 1999 European parliamentary elections, is not so much an expression of opposition to the idea of the European structure, which is no longer under threat, but rather an expression of a message in counterpoint. The electors clearly expressed their desire to ensure that their local, regional, and national preoccupations not be sacrificed to the European concept, which is undoubtedly virtuous, but somewhat theoretical and more concerned with its own affirmation than with their daily lives. In fact, the emphasis on international news over local news in the media is declining in reaction to the evolving interests of readers.

FROM GLOCAL TO TODAYMORROW, OR PRESENT FUTURE

That which applies to space also applies to time. We need to invent an equivalent of McLuhan's global village or Feather's glocal for the concept of time. We have to invent a new vocabulary to adapt to a new experience of time. Using the model of glocal, we can take "today" and "tomorrow" and create the contraction "todaymorrow," a concept that binds together references to the present and the future; or we could call this dimension of social time the "present future," giving slightly more weight to tomorrow, in deference to our current ideology.

Because decision makers must take into account both the present and the future, short-term efficiency cannot threaten sustainable development. However, the present can no longer be sacrificed to the future. Short-term management is required, but it should not be short-sighted, and, conversely, we cannot think only of the future and neglect short-term efficiency. When the government of Canada cuts education and health spending and provincial transfer payments, creating daily crises, and then proudly announces a surplus of $15 billion (as it did in 2001), with which it plans to repay the public debt out of respect for future generations, we are at the heart of the issue of todaymorrow, or the present future.

TWENTY-THIRD PARADOXICAL LAW
The time/tense of digital globalization affects us, as does the glocal space of the global village, according to the double constraint of the present future – the todaymorrow.

THE PERVERSE EFFECT OF
THE UNIVERSALIST DISCOURSE

The expansion, and undoubtedly the success (even relative), of globalization is based on inequality: the rich grow richer and the poor grow poorer. In other words, fragmentation is the necessary consequence of the will to power. There is a major distortion in this shift in meaning of the concept of universalism. Today, universalism covers the will to globalization and associates the discourse of globalization with international commercial and financial conquest. This change in the values of universal humanism is difficult to justify. The concept of globalization, which was apparently inaugurated during the Davos conference of 1993, is above all an economic notion. It is tied to the global free trade demanded by ultraliberals. This internationalism resonates as the planetary triumph of capitalism, in sharp contrast to the Socialist International, which has been marginalized.

STOCK-MARKET-TRANSMITTED DISEASES,
OR SMTDS

We often hear about ITDs, or internet-transmitted diseases, but there are also SMTDs: stock-market-transmitted diseases. As with

ITDS, contagion can be instant, and the pandemic is just as difficult to stop. The same corrupting effect occurs in the dreams of stock market speculators, bankers, and owners of multinationals. The free speculation in international currency; the relocation of textile and electronics industries to countries where labour is cheap; the dynamic of the communicating vessels, which causes financial crises to circulate from one country to another, resulting in universal contamination, have developed the globalization of markets more than the globalization of people and values.

This vision of globalization is therefore very incomplete. Global integration by multinationals is really an economic pseudo-integration that reinforces the power of rich countries and provokes the social disintegration of poor countries because it gives rise to drastic anti-inflationary economic policies, orchestrated in particular by the International Monetary Fund and in accordance with an ultraliberal tendency towards international trade – which is simply the law of the strongest and the richest. Poor countries, forced by their debts to align themselves with the logic of rich and dominant countries, are home to growing numbers of poor, destitute, and exploited people.

ECONOMIC COLONIALISM

These disparities, which are a sign of a new phase of colonialism – economic colonialism – are in keeping with a well-known ideology of powerful countries: rich countries have supposedly reached a higher level of religion, rationalism, progress, development, and (today) digital technology, and their duty is to impose these via the commercial (formerly the religious, moral, rationalist, and military) force of universalism. The internationalist project is formulated and legitimized in the name of civilizing values combined with ultraliberal ideas. This supposedly universalist democracy is made up of international financial institutions – such as the International Bank for Reconstruction and Development, the International Monetary Fund, and the World Trade Organization – which dictate laws to developing countries.

It would be going too far to say that we exploit poor countries for the benefit of rich countries and the rich minorities of poor countries in the name of idealism, moralism, simplistic rationalism, or development. People are probably not all that selfish and twisted. There are many efforts made on behalf of the destitute for purely humanitarian reasons. But it would also be simplistic to maintain that rich states offer generous and compassionate aid devoid of mercenary ulterior motives.

THE WORLD TRADE ORGANIZATION

They say the road to hell is paved with good intentions. The words of Mike Moore, a recent director general of the World Trade Organization (WTO), a former prime minister of New Zealand, and a man of modest origins, make you wonder: "the very poor, the less developed countries still don't get the access they need for their products, and the technical assistance to fully engage so that they can sit at the table of our global family and share equally and fully ... I am focusing on Seattle, ensuring that the smaller guys who have felt locked out have a chance to engage and benefit from what is a system that has driven ... the most sustained increase in living standards in the history of our species."[6] Moore would need Herculean strength to escape the rigid logic of the ultraliberal system – and the image of one big family is just a smokescreen for paternalism and ethnocentrism. The WTO does not have the same mandate or the same representation as humanitarian organizations, and the charity of the rich will never wipe out misery. The placards of the demonstrators at the Seattle meeting of the WTO evoked an old maxim: He who sows misery harvests anger. The bitter failure of that 1999 meeting reaffirmed it.

INCREASING AND SHAMEFUL INEQUALITIES

Those who sing the praises of globalization forget that in the year 2000 the fortunes of the three richest men in the world surpassed the GNP of the thirty-five poorest countries, which have a combined population of 600 million. At the beginning of the twenty-first century, a billion people on the planet were unemployed or without regular employment (some 50 million in Europe), and it is estimated that close to 30 million die of hunger each year. The 1999 report of the United Nations Development Programme (UNDP) offered an account of the situation in Africa; twenty of the fifty-three countries on that continent are engaged in internal or external conflicts. The UNDP pointed out that the drop in price of raw materials and the volatility of financial markets are the rich countries' joy and the poor countries' sorrow. It established that, in 1997, 20 per cent of the world's population had 86 per cent of the world's GDP and 74 per cent of phone lines at their disposal. The debt of poor countries to rich countries is astronomical. Tanzania, which has a low human development index (HDI), but one that is still higher than that of many more disadvantaged countries, devotes nine times more money to repaying its debt than to health, and four times more than to education. It follows that only those with the means can feel they are citizens of the world. States the UNDP report: "The collapse of space, time and borders may be creating a global village, but not everyone can be a citizen. The global, professional elite faces low borders, but billions of others find borders as high as ever."[7] To defend a globalization with a human face is to denounce the dominant neo-colonialist ideology that rules over this new structure of social inequality.

THE BLACK HOLES OF GLOBALIZATION

In Mexico, "Subcommander" Marcos's Zapatista guerrillas have become champions of society's discarded; Marcos poses as the spokesperson of the subcontinents. The injustice of poverty and the scandal of exploitation obviously stir up identity-related resistance as well. The globalized and computerized world is full of black holes, populations absorbed by their own poverty, that no longer even send out signals. This globalized world of communication, of transparency, of e-commerce, of airlines, a world that has become so small for the rich, is full of distant continents and forgotten and abandoned inner-city neighbourhoods whose names do not appear on the globe of globalization. This globalized world has become more unequal than ever, divided between predators and victims, between gangs and those who try to sell their own organs to survive.

Globalization is a mirage of businesspeople out to conquer markets. It is not a cultural concept, even less so a concept of civilization. But, as always, the myth gives moral legitimacy to the slogans and actions of the dominant.

THE CULTURE COMMODITY

Likewise, still in keeping with the integrative rationality of the ultraliberal model, dominant countries want to include cultural industries in the market economy. As a result, they are waging an attack on cultural difference. America makes no distinction between trade in meat and trade in books. It exports its culture on the trade route opened by commodities; it's the best way of consolidating its international trade. It has always been thus: the trade of commodities is also the trade of humans, and it is one of the vehicles for the circulation of cultural objects. But culture must remain a site of freedom. Ongoing efforts must be made to exclude it from market pressures, which have already ravaged it so much. Adding the legal constraints of a foreign imperialism should be prohibited.

The culture exception is a concept of resistance forged by those who want to protect their identities and cultures. This resistance to the homogenization that would result from a market stranglehold on culture must be perpetuated. American culture is, of course, remarkable – as is German culture, Italian culture, and Mexican culture: the point here is not to criticize it. At stake are the importance, the richness, and the diversity of human cultures. They must be protected at all costs from the cultural hegemony that is the goal of the powerful. Once again, the myth of globalization shows itself to be extremely perverse. Anyone who travels knows that despite the spread of norms and standards, we are still living in a multipolar world, and we must hope that we will continue to do so for a long time. We are still living in a world of cultural, religious, economic, and social diversity so profound that the concept of globalization seems superficial. Anyone who ventures from Mexico into the Islamic world, from Japan into the African world, from France into the Indian world, or from Australia into the Vietnamese world would agree. The *Wall Street Journal, Die Welt,* and *La Prensa* provide only very limited information about the globe.

THE INTERNET AND
THE CREDO OF GLOBALIZATION

Pierre Lévy, when he proclaimed the advent of a unified civilization thanks to the internet and trade, was updating the discourse of Kant and Fichte: he stated that one of the major themes of his book *The Virtual Economy* was "unity of the human race." In a fit of philosophical passion, he detected in humanity "a complete anthropological mutation" based on "collective intelligence"; he predicted that all of this would end with "The Convergence of

Homo Economicus and Homo Academicus in Cyberspace."[8] Bill
Gates (a great admirer of the Wright brothers) may insist that the
internet, like the invention of flight, makes the world smaller by
"bringing people, languages, ideas, and values together,"[9] but globalization is still the myth of the rich, who benefit from it, and the
unrealistic economic dream of ultraliberals rather than the manifestation of a real anthropological evolution. The internet doesn't
carry as much weight as the disparity of the world. The new global
social fabric forecast by Nicholas Negroponte is just a utopian
dream of the rich. Internet companies are not ready to impose a
new social fabric on humanity, even an electronic one; it remains
a completely foreign graft to 90 per cent of humanity, and it can
only be rejected.

TECHNOLOGICAL APARTHEID

To those who claim that the internet has an internationalist calling,
that it has already circumnavigated the globe and that it will spread
everywhere, we must respond: Really? Everywhere? These people
ignore the fact that there are countries where a cell phone costs
the equivalent of twenty-five fifty-kilo bags of corn. The myth of
global communication – the myth of the rich – is revealed for what
it is when we consider that the number of phones barely increased
in Africa between 1996 and 1998; the slight increase (the number
of people with phones rose from 0.5 per cent to 2 per cent of the
population) was attributable to the cell phone, which requires less
infrastructure, but which is still a very urban phenomenon. Furthermore, the average cost of a rate plan and communication
charges is as high as 43 per cent of per capita income. The International Telecommunications Union forecasts a rate of five lines
per hundred inhabitants for black Africa, and one pay phone per
thousand inhabitants by 2010. On the eve of the year 2000, there
were only 2.5 million wire-line telephones in sub-Saharan black
Africa. The African market offers fake cell phones, plastic shells
that people buy to show off. Such irony arises from the discrimination at the heart of global communication – it's digital apartheid.

   In 2001, connecting to a sixty-four-kilobits-per-second (Kbps)
FTP internet-dedicated phone line still cost US$3,000 a month in
Vietnam; in Chad, Mali, and Ivory Coast, connections are so diffi-
cult due to a lack of infrastructure – accesses still do not often go

beyond 128 Kbps or 256 Kbps for the entire country – that sending a simple e-mail can be a major feat. And here is another consideration for those who continue to insist that the earth is round and communication is global: according to UNESCO, in the year 2000, approximately 20 per cent of the world's adult population was illiterate and 113 million young people were not educated, 110 million of them in developing countries.

> **TWENTY-FOURTH PARADOXICAL LAW**
> Digital technology, while apparently the instrument of global integration, in fact creates societal fractures and a technological apartheid that separates the info-rich and the info-poor.

THE CHALLENGE OF THE INTERNET
FOR DEVELOPING COUNTRIES

After having roundly and rightly denounced the neo-colonialism of the globalization that is creating a digital divide, we should consider the remarkable advantages that developing countries could draw from it. Faced with the excesses of globalization on the one hand and the virtues of cultural diversity on the other, we should not endeavour to keep digital technologies from being implemented in poor countries. We must not deprive these countries of the internet any more than we should deprive them of the telephone or the television simply because these communication technologies were initially created in developed countries. We must instead help the inhabitants of poor countries appropriate new technologies and take control of them locally.

The internet is similar to the African tam-tam. Internet messages, like tam-tam messages, are transmitted via a simple code of binary communication – 1 or 0 – with protocols to identify the sender and the receiver. Due to the speed of transmission and the processing and memory power of computers, this new electronic tam-tam has prompted a communications revolution. And unlike books, the internet re-creates multi-sensory communication, blending image, sound, movement, and interactivity – it is much closer to the African tradition of oral communication. It is therefore the internet's calling to be a popular, efficient, immediate, and user-friendly method of remote communication in countries with the financial means to support it. The challenge for developing countries lies in implementing the technological infrastructure required for internet use to spread.

Satellites, short-wave communication, and low-frequency radio, combined with wireless telephony, could eventually make it possible for developing countries to skip the long and expensive step of cabling that developed countries had to take. But this infrastructure has not yet been set up, though it is the top priority in all developing countries. Without it, the hoped-for catch-up cannot occur, and technological apartheid will deepen.

Developed countries, which talk so much about globalization, will have to offer efficient technological aid to developing countries to build their infrastructures and their networks. At the same time, there must be the political will in developing countries to put an end to public or private, foreign or local telecommunications monopolies as quickly as possible because they slow progress through prohibitive pricing.

PROMOTING ACCESS TO INFORMATION

The development of digital communication networks could quickly promote not only e-mail discussion groups and individual exchanges, but also wider access to all the sources of information available on the Web. Billions of pages of information on scientific, economic, professional, technical, social, political, and cultural topics are now found on the Web, free of filters or censorship. It is an extraordinary source of knowledge and development that also allows people to enrich the pool instantaneously by adding their own material – research and publications, information on a wide range of activities, on cultures, on foreign countries. This is a revolution of major strategic importance. We have entered the era of information and knowledge societies. Developing countries need to be able to seize this opportunity, but to do so, as I have said, they must have infrastructures and equipment and access to the basic training required to take advantage of this incomparable tool.

OPENING ONESELF TO THE WORLD

The internet has a transnational calling. It does not stop at borders, and it is difficult to control. It therefore allows everyone to travel the world over, to discover other cultures and other values; and, conversely, it gives everyone virtual access to their own countries, to their own cultures – whether they be small nations, local little-known cultures, or marginal social groups. What will ensue from these exchanges is an enrichment of the mind, an extremely productive cultural and social bonus. On-line real-time translation software will permit everyone to read Web sites in Arabic, Spanish, Chinese, Japanese, Finnish, or Vietnamese, which are currently inaccessible to those who do not speak those languages. One hopes that the internet will spread throughout the world like television, which can now be found almost everywhere – on a houseboat in the Mekong Delta or in a straw hut with a beaten-earth floor in a Yucatan village.

PROMOTING DEMOCRACY

Democracy is a daily challenge, not just for poor countries but also for rich ones. We are well aware that the free circulation of information is one of its most effective foundations. And that is precisely what the internet encourages: it allows non-governmental organizations to denounce crimes against humanity and violations of human rights, to lead effective campaigns for the liberation of political prisoners (who still number in the thousands worldwide). The internet also helped protesters to mobilize in Seattle and elsewhere to denounce the globalization politics of the WTO and the IMF. A planetary critical consciousness can be strengthened and expressed through the internet. Free access to the internet is therefore a gauge of the existence of democracy in each country.

TAKING ACTION:
MICRO-INITIATIVES AND MICRO-COMMERCE

In the largely rural developing countries, local leaders could have access to the advice, specialized support, models of development, and environmental, professional, and legal information necessary for the success of economic, commercial, and social micro-initiatives that are decisive factors in the improvement of working conditions and local life. Agricultural, craft, or fishing co-operatives could be created with the help of professionals who cannot stay on-site because they are providing the same services to other villages. Daily follow-up could be done remotely by sending digital photos that show, for example, the damaging effects of a parasite on a plant, the installation of a piece of equipment, or the topology of a site. In other words, in situations where there not enough qualified people to go around, the internet could be a precious form of aid.

That's not all: commercial management can also be monitored remotely. The internet can be employed to manage inventory and the transport of goods to be sold in cities or exported; this is particularly useful in the case of perishable foodstuffs. Many farmers in developed countries manage their production and sales via the internet. Again, however, they have the advantage of access to training and the necessary communication infrastructures, which are still lacking in the developing world. Not all leaders of developing countries have recognized the urgency of setting up these infrastructures, and developed countries cannot be of much assistance until they do.

THE POOR MAN'S COMPUTER

In India, at the beginning of this century, there were fewer than five million personal computers for a population of more than a billion. But India is also home to many who are skilled in computer science, and for this it is recognized around the world. The state of Karnataka harbours its own Silicon Valley, near Bangalore. This is where the Simputer Foundation is working to perfect a little computer for the rural masses, potentially priced at less than $200, which would have an internet connection and a smartcard to enable on-line transactions. Due to the diversity of official languages in India, it will also have a multilingual on-line translation system. As small as an electronic agenda, the Simputer would take ordinary batteries, like a radio, overcoming the problem of the lack of electricity in rural areas. It will be equipped with a touch-screen, icons, and a multilingual voice command system, making it usable for the illiterate. The creators of the Simputer also hope to sell the licence for their "poor man's computer" to other developing countries and maybe even acquire the technological expertise for a new generation of dumbed-down pocket computers.

This seems to me an inspiring example for all. We cannot allow the gap between developed and developing countries to keep widening. Aside from the moral injustice of it, such a situation risks becoming explosive, as we see in the news every day. We need to reshuffle the deck. New methods of acting and co-operating must be put into place in developing countries, and these countries must learn to take charge and to collaborate with one another.

The small minority of people who are connected to the internet have a weighty responsibility: they must help to broaden access to digital communication networks, which can be built fairly quickly if there is a true desire to do so. But this desire assumes knowledge of these new technologies and an understanding of their incredible potential. This knowledge and understanding are not yet widely enough shared by political leaders with decision-making power. Digital apartheid will only grow worse if the brain drain is not stopped. The UNDP's 2001 report reveals that the Americans plan to recruit 100,000 computer developers in India in the coming years – they have already implemented a special process for obtaining work visas for them. This organized brain drain will strengthen the technological potential of the United States and deprive India of human resources and some $2 billion in annual revenue. The trend is spreading: rich countries welcome Chinese, Iraqi, or Iranian computer programmers. Even Canadians are being pilfered – each year, Canada stands to lose some 70,000 computer programmers, lured by the salaries and technologies offered in the United States.

And in 2005, we even saw the MIT lab launch a $100 laptop with the intention of marketing it to millions of people around the world. One of its notable features was a hand crank for generating power in places where electricity is undependable or unavailable.

THE GLOBAL ARBORESCENCE
OF THE INTERNET

Developed countries must not view the growth of the internet in developing countries as an extension of their own vision, practices, and info-rich markets. If they do, they will again fall into a post-colonial logic, an approach better adapted to the advancement of developed countries than to that of developing countries. We have to start by analysing the priorities, social practices, and cultures of each developing country. In short, we have to start with the basics and establish internet practices that are appropriate to a country's specific needs, which are usually very different from those of developed countries.

We must imagine the growth of the internet in developing countries as an arborescence rooted in the cultural and economic soil of each such country, and not as a big tree rooted in the north that extends its protective branches around the world, embracing developing countries. The image of the northern, protective tree implies that emerging countries can only adopt the internet in its shade, can only gather the fruits of globalization that it allows to fall from its branches out of compassion or calculation.

16: Wired Schools and Virtual Universities

It seems the mind is becoming virtual.

A SOCIETY WITHOUT SCHOOLS?

Author-guru Peter Drucker predicted a society without schools or universities. Drucker had in mind on-line teaching, teaching in virtual space, teaching that would render useless the physical premises of schools and universities. And he was not the only one to think so boldly. In 1995, Brian Carlson, a professor of artificial intelligence at Dakota State University, made the following predictions: "In 2010, courses will be broadcast using cable TV, computers and the information highway. School buildings will have been replaced by meeting places where children and adults will come to learn from each other rather than endure the torture of classrooms."[1]

A GREAT PEDAGOGICAL HOPE AGGRAVATES THE CRISIS

The digital monster has arrived in the midst of a profound and widespread crisis in mass education systems. The failure of these systems is generally acknowledged to be massive. Will the monster act as a saviour? Or will it be just one more shock that will further destabilize the system and aggravate the crisis?

In only a few short years – since 1998 – most wealthy countries have made serious efforts to wire their schools. There has been

almost an international competition to modernize, to enter the
knowledge society, to appropriate its symbol: wired education for
the new generation. The initial challenge for governments was
purely financial. Even before we considered connecting schools to
the internet, we were looking at CD-ROMs, and titles started popping up in every field and format. Although the CD-ROM did not
meet with commercial success, all of this interactive content was to
find new dissemination on-line.

The abrupt arrival of digital technology in schools was at first
seen by most teachers as a sudden and brutal intrusion, a shock –
one for which educational institutions were completely unpre-
pared. But if schools were as wired and educational methods as
electronic as we then assumed, we would now be experiencing an
educational revolution. Today we know that the adaptation process
will be a long one. It was still barely underway in 2001 in most
schools due to a lack of funds, lack of technicians, lack of multimedia educational materials, and lack of new teachers with the
necessary conviction and training. And five years later, in 2006, we
are not much further along. But perhaps the revolution has been
slow in materializing for more fundamental reasons. The internet
is considered an interesting teaching tool, but no more interesting
than books or audiovisual materials. Above all else, education
requires human exchange, and therefore teachers. We must not
confuse education with the dissemination of information – even
digital. We must not confuse teaching with Net surfing.

TWENTY-FIFTH PARADOXICAL LAW
Cyberpedagogy, which promises to be cheaper and more effective,
actually costs more and destroys the foundations of traditional
pedagogy.

Let's consider the main paradoxes raised by the cyberpedagogical
shift:

FIRST PARADOX OF CYBERPEDAGOGY
It's more expensive.

A pilot project using CD-ROMs conducted in 1996 at the Cité des
arts et des nouvelles technologies de Montréal, called Le Cyber-
monde, left no room for doubt. Groups of two or three children,

each group allotted a computer, participated in the project with their regular teachers. The teachers, who had selected the CD-ROMs in advance, sat down to work with the children, but since children are faster than both computers and adults, a few minutes after the session started they were off and running. As teachers led their groups on large, carefully prepared navigation screens, the excited children burrowed into the arborescence of active links that appeared on their screens, or they froze the screens by clicking on anything that moved. There were cries of "It's not working!"

It became apparent that as well as the expensive equipment, teachers would need one teacher's aide per computer to supervise the children, which budgets obviously wouldn't allow. In the end, multimedia pedagogy requires much more teaching personnel than traditional pedagogy. This is an unexpected paradox, but one that seems inevitable, short of blocking the software and depriving students of the interactivity that is, after all, the main appeal of such a revolution in educational methods.

Technicians are also needed to regularly clean up hard disks quickly saturated by accumulated traces. The more recent use of the internet and educational Web sites does not resolve the problem; it will persist as long as computers are anything more than basic terminals with little memory; and memory increase will, of course, create new problems.

SECOND PARADOX OF CYBERPEDAGOGY
Its rapid pace eliminates the temporal slowdown traditionally required for learning.

Pedagogical exchange involves slow-moving, steady, circular time, which oral exchanges between people allow. The dance of the internet is no substitute for this, even if it seems more attractive at first glance. We must also take into consideration the time required to produce and test new educational materials and to train teachers to use new digital technologies. There are many complex and expensive challenges involved in the educational "progress" that a number of countries claimed to have achieved several years ago. We must learn to take our time in the field of education. It is far from proven that the accelerated time of the cyberworld is appropriate to the spirit of learning. If we are not careful, we will encounter insurmountable difficulties and crushing pedagogical failures.

THIRD PARADOX OF CYBERPEDAGOGY
It demands a new way of thinking to teach the old way of thinking.

In classical culture, teaching was based on linear thought, causality, the requirements of identitarian logic – therefore, on written language, grammar, and rigour – but also on memory. Students were taught how to break down a problem in order to understand it, to push questions further, to find classical references, and to recite. Conversely, cyberpedagogy involves associative thinking, interactive arborescence, hybridity, an obsession with the new, and a loss of interest in memory (all knowledge is stored and accessed effortlessly). Valuing speed, it neglects language and grammar and adopts a telegraphic style. It prefers the game to effort; the superficiality of surfing to the patient exploration of difficult questions; events to permanence; and colours, appearances, scintillation, and movement to plain truth. It consumes and erases thought. Classical culture preserved and demanded respect.

The digital tools of cyberpedagogy were suddenly imposed on a form of teaching that was still fundamentally classical, a form based on values diametrically opposed to those cyberpedagogy embraces. This naturally resulted in confusion, conflict, rejection, and contradiction. In the eyes of some, this imposition was like the ransacking of the temple by the barbarians. And, in effect, it was.

FOURTH PARADOX OF CYBERPEDAGOGY
It is playful and it breaks down the austerity and authority of institutionalized education.

Knowledge has always been equated with authority, and the role of the teacher has traditionally been associated with knowledge. Teaching is the opposite of entertaining: we play in the schoolyard; we do serious work in the classroom. This has always been the architectural concept of school. Cyberpedagogy does away with the sacred aura of this opposition. It introduces play into the temple of education and makes it a cardinal virtue. Edutainment is becoming the hallmark of the new pedagogy, which assumes a certain amount of autonomy on the part of the student, resulting in a dramatic loss of power for teachers and requiring them to reinvent their role and status to accommodate digital technology. The blackboard is now a relic. It has been supplanted by a multitude of little cathode ray screens. And the teacher's chalk has been replaced by the mouse, which is controlled by the fickle hand of the child.

THE KNOWLEDGE MARKET

The world is changing. We need new pedagogical values for a new world. Pedagogical approaches do not materialize out of thin air: they reflect the culture they draw their references and their structures from. But now, for once, pedagogy is ahead of a culture, because it is linked to new science and technology, which are the source of the civilization change we are experiencing.

The worldwide corporate e-learning market was forecast to grow at a 35.6 per cent CAGR (compound annual growth rate), from $5.17 billion in 2001 to $23.74 billion in 2006. The US corporate e-learning market – considered to constitute the major part of this market – was forecast to grow at a 36.4 per cent CAGR during the same period, from $3.6 billion in 2001 to $17.18 billion in 2006.[2] From the vantage point of 2006, the state of these fragmented markets is actually very difficult to evaluate. The overall market is certainly still growing and profitable, but we have to distinguish between public and corporate on-line education, consider on-line training, take into account educational levels and sectors, and compare evaluations (not always updated in the same year) in various countries using different methodologies. Utopian enthusiasm is cooling. Large investors grasp the complexity of the situation – the market is fragmented, localizing content is costly – and they doubt that growth will be spectacular and reap handsome rewards.

However, the education market is still one of the issues that the World Trade Organization confronts as it opens the world economy to the free circulation of merchandise. It is significant, for example, that at the Summit of the Americas to discuss free trade held in Quebec City, Industry Canada, and not the provincial departments of education, had the mandate to deal with education.

Knowledge as a market? An industry for the knowledge economy? In the land of the mind – of Molière, of Descartes, and of free education for all – this sounds like the clarion call of the barbarian hordes. While we're at it, why don't we privatize all education and teach only immediately profitable subjects – in other words, concern ourselves with professional training rather than the fundamental values of education? For some, this is grounds for scandal, or at least a fundamental social debate. We could be witnessing education being turned into a commodity, and the fox could be left to mind the chickens. Of course, the debate about free and public education versus private education is not new. What is new is that the debate is now about profit. Education could become a focus for dot.coms and venture capitalists. There are already education trade shows.

Actually, digital technology is not inherently tied to commodification. In 1998 and 1999, in France, the socialist government invested more than US$1.5 billion in digital technology for education, to which it added $1.3 billion in 2000. The money was used primarily to purchase equipment to connect schools, develop interactive content, set up distance education programs, and train teachers.

E-LEARNING

There are major contracts involved, not only for private equipment companies but also for on-line content development companies. In Canada, the Open Learning Agency, based in British Columbia, offers distance courses that are recognized by public institutions. Similar initiatives are increasingly found in developed countries. Google lists hundreds of e-learning portals, like Online Education, KnowledgePool, DigitalThink Inc., CyberU, ThirdAge School of Online Learning, Learndirect, Learn.com, Distance-Educator.com, ActiveEducation, Tutors-Online, e-learn, Cyberclasses, Adult University, iLearn.To, AvidLearn.com, Knowledge Anywhere, Cyber-Works, Get Smart Online, National College, Internet University, TalentEd Virtual Enrichment Program, WebCourse, Online College, Virtual Learn, Internet U, and miStupid.com. This list speaks volumes about the commercial aspirations involved.

In 2000, Vivendi Universal Publishing launched Enseignants.com, an education portal. The site was designed mainly by publishers, authors, and teachers in recognition of the fact that technology alone cannot educate. The site's low-pressure sales pitch would hardly offend anyone, but its profit objectives were clear. It offered local content on any platform the user might choose, and since its launch it has been available in three languages and many countries: France, Germany, Great Britain, Spain, Portugal, Brazil, and the United States. The enterprise was hoping for 1.8 million visitors per month – close to 300,000 subscribers and some 40 million pages visited within two years. The site was very ambitious, because it had to target three different groups – teachers, parents, and students – and cover a wide range of material, some of which went beyond the educational and touched on daily life. The home page offered a menu of games, reference materials, language resources, education, edutainment, and life skills resources; it also had a store. Access was free at the beginning, but as soon as possible it intended to charge for most of its value-added services. The company, which invested almost US$25 million in this portal, expected to break even by the end of the second year. Its business plan was split between subscriber revenue (44 per cent), direct sales (46 per cent), and ad revenue (10 per cent). This was considered a power grab in the field of electronic education, where smaller publishers were still concentrating on CD-ROMs and free portals. Even though the market was not yet ripe, there was heavy pressure on families to subscribe to such portals; they promoted themselves as being as essential as dictionaries or encyclopedias. Pedagogical sites were cropping up everywhere, so competition was tough, but success seemed inevitable. Since then, of course, the business has evolved; but teachers and children in developed countries have continued to refer with growing frequency to on-line content and pedagogical resources.

In the face of competition, the industry is restructuring. Providers are buying each other out, and they are merging to invest in pedagogical innovations and build larger educational portals capable of gaining greater visibility. In the United States, the four main players in the knowledge industry (Kaplan, Knowledge Universe, Pearson, and Sylvan) share a market of several billion dollars and are investing millions. Almost 100,000 schools, colleges, and universities offer courses via the internet. The business of on-line education could become as important on the Web as e-commerce, and probably more quickly.

EDUCATIONAL SERVICES

Students of the Lycée Français de New York find their homework assignments listed on the school's Web site. On-line educational aids are suggested with their assignments, which they can submit on-line. More and more in wealthy countries, general education colleges have Web sites full of useful information. A number of sites, however, offer more sophisticated electronic experiences.

They provide access to virtual libraries, course descriptions and complete courses, discussion forums, on-line mentoring, professional orientation, and psychological assistance; they also include student newspapers, give information on campus events and internships, and even list student job opportunities. In these contexts, the internet makes it possible not only to deliver services but also to create virtual communities within the institution that have an extremely positive role to play.

WEB SITES ASSISTED BY HUMAN ENGINES

You can't stop progress, so a number of companies already offer not only human learning assisted by computer but also computing services assisted by the human presence of professors and experts. On-line cyberteacher services answer children's questions or deliver specific lessons. These are not sites for computer-assisted learning, but human-assisted educational sites, and they have existed in the US for some time. You can consult Askme.com, Webhelp.com, Looksmart.com, among others. The idea was adopted in France (Cyberprofs.net, Woonoz.com, and ysangar.fr) and Switzerland (WeTellYou.com). In general, these sites operate on schedules adapted to their student customers – from five to eight in the evening. But several also target the general public and professionals, placing experts in specific fields at their users' disposal. They are reaching foreign countries with local experts and on-line translation systems. Woonoz Canada and WeTellYou.com are now accessible in Quebec. If the customer has complex questions that require research, the site bills for it. Thus we have sites for legal, psychological, and financial consultation. Soon we could have pay-for-use medical consultation sites.

PROFESSIONAL TRAINING ON-LINE

IBM conducts a quarter of its internal training via the internet. Manpower, a professional placement company, has developed the Global Learning Center, which offers more and more on-line courses in office automation. Siemens and Motorola, like all other major companies, have their own universities to train personnel through multimedia digital technology.

According to the *Wall Street Journal*, the amount invested by companies in on-line training went from $550 million in 1998 to $4 billion in 2001; and International Data Corporation put the figure at $14.5 billion for 2004. There is still great potential for more. This is a growing share of the $58 billion companies devote annually to training. By investing in on-line training, companies are not reducing their training costs, because digital technologies are very expensive, but they are increasing the effectiveness of their training.

In several countries, companies are required to devote 1 per cent of revenues to employee training, and this has prompted many institutions that offer e-learning to seek certification. The new professional training cyberbusinesses are proliferating like dot.com companies did in the good old days, and they are thriving.

DISTANCE EDUCATION AND THE OLD CORRESPONDENCE SCHOOLS

Distance education on the internet sometimes leaves the client feeling lonely, but salespeople for sites offering this service maintain that the student is at the centre of the learning process and not the teacher; and the student can benefit from flexible schedules, locations, and rates of learning, all of which used to be impossible. However, the essential failure of solitary on-line learning reminds us of the similar failure of correspondence education. As early as 1926, John Noffsinger, in his study of correspondence courses financed by the Carnegie Corporation, noted a dropout rate of almost 90 per cent, and he observed that private correspondence schools attached much more importance to sales than to pedagogical follow-ups with students. Dropouts brought the schools regular profit, called "dropout money" (money that is not refunded if the student drops out), and thereby reduced teaching-related expenses. Even though on-line teaching appears to be more lively and user-friendly because it is interactive and uses multimedia, and even though it has a much more reasonable dropout rate, the risk of failure is very real, and it threatens all of the e-learning companies.

David Noble, a professor at Toronto's York University, conducted an in-depth study on the phenomenon, and he points out that it brought American universities to the brink of scandal in the 1930s.

In a 2000 article entitled "Le lourd passé de l'enseignement à distance" ("The Dark Past of Distance Education"), he says that the same profit motive drives companies today – perhaps even more so – and he asks whether we will soon witness a debacle in distance education, in spite of the new powers of the internet.[3]

DISTANCE EDUCATION NETWORKS

The internet developed as a communications network in the university milieu before attracting the interest of the general public. In the 1970s, many academics were already in the habit of communicating with each other via modem, through networks such as ARPANET, established in 1969, and then, beginning in 1986, through NSFNET. The university communities that these networks created gave birth very early on to on-line universities – initially American, but also the Open University of Great Britain, and then the African Virtual University.

In France, the Numéris network for distance education acquired extensive expertise, which it then applied to the internet. It was responsible for major initiatives, such as the Digital Campus, and the University of the Third Millennium, which makes professors' courses available through RealVideo on its Web site for a modest registration fee. In Canada, the Canadian Virtual University (CVU), inaugurated in 2000, brings together twelve Canadian universities. Its site has announced that CVU "will offer students a choice of 1,500 university courses, including 160 online courses, that can be combined to complete 100 recognized university credentials without ever stepping into a classroom."[4]

CYBERUNIVERSITIES

Are partnerships between IBM and the University of Wisconsin, or between America Online, Online learning.net, and the University of California a good idea? Noble reports that these major universities are selling their names and their reputations to private companies, and they are also investing large sums in the stock market.[5] In effect, there are many differences between the current situation in universities and that which existed in the past; we must expect abuses and the failure of many private e-learning companies.

We must also recognize that universities in developed countries already function largely on internal on-line networks removed from any commercial system – these networks accommodate interactions between professors, between professors and students, and interuniversity relations. This hybrid situation that blends real relationships and electronic links, that facilitates much more fluid and immediate human communication, is of obvious benefit in a pedagogical context, and it has become indispensable in university research communities, which increasingly bring together people scattered throughout cities and countries.

As university students must work independently, they don't tend to view electronic communication as an isolating phenomenon: they see it as a means of bringing people together – for example, the professor and the student. E-mail is direct, immediate, and informal. We might even argue that due to the speed of these exchanges, people are brought closer together in the intersubjective space of their relationships.

The École des Hautes Études Commerciales de Montréal, a pioneering school of advanced business studies, launched the Virtuose program in 1997. It requires each student to have a laptop computer, and the school has more than 6,000 high-speed internet connections. The institution encourages professors to renew their pedagogical content and tools and urges students to use digital technologies, to surf the Web, to consult their student files on-line, to submit their assignments on-line. At home, as in class, students work primarily on their laptops. In this way, technology compels everyone towards much greater involvement.

IN PRAISE OF VIRTUAL UNIVERSITIES

- Virtual universities support the development of communities of researchers, professors, and students and encourage connections among these three types of players in the new university.
- Virtual universities provide access to all research and to on-line courses and libraries.
- Virtual universities connect a multiplicity of universities in different cities and countries.
- Virtual universities connect outlying or remote areas with urban centres of knowledge and allow them to participate in the university community.

- Virtual universities are a wellspring of communication and social integration.
- Virtual universities do not discriminate socially, racially, or linguistically; they are open to the contributions of everyone; they combine and hybridize the origins of knowledge; they welcome all cultures and energize their fusion.
- Virtual universities are a dynamic meeting ground for many forms of expression and creation. Their rhizome-structured sites open interactive paths for many forms of exploration, navigation, exchange, discussion, and discovery.
- Virtual universities encourage the regular creation of new multi-media content and ongoing pedagogical innovation; they ensure that general information, news bulletins, and event postings are up to date.
- Virtual universities are ambassadors for the talent they harbour, promotional and recruiting agencies for their own students and teaching staff; they are also forums for debate about the society in which they participate.

Again, we must want them, create them, and sustain them. Virtual universities cannot be a mere bureaucratic or academic project, a compromise among all the constraints, among all the interests at play, among all the human and institutional conflicts – nor can they be the product of a commercial business plan. Human intelligence must preside over them, and the mind must flourish within them. Virtual universities are part reality, part utopia, and part vision, and that's the way they must remain if they are to succeed. Imagining such a virtual university is a mind-boggling project. But it is a societal project, as realistic, strategic, and efficient as the creation of a campus or a multimedia city. Its leverage is guaranteed as the platform of the future for generations to come, as a centre of identification and reference for humanity.

THE KNOWLEDGE INDUSTRIES

In the United States, the term "knowledge industry" has been in use for some time. Google listed thousands of knowledge industry Web sites and references in 2001 – such as Mitsui Knowledge Industries, Kiwifruit, Tourism Not Knowledge Industries, and Knowledge Workers/Industries. Can we then speak of a worldwide proliferation of knowledge factories, workers, warehouses, and sales and marketing employees? Why not? We have become used to hearing about the proliferation of cultural industries; the extent of it no longer shocks anyone. Can we also refer to the markets of these knowledge industries? Such talk has become standard fare: experts tell us, for example, that the Canadian education market was $844 million in 1999, an increase of 11 per cent over the previous year, and it was optimistically estimated at $1.3 billion for 2003 (compared to $22.4 billion in the United States). We are also told that the education market of the Asia Pacific Region is experiencing the strongest growth of any market – in the order of 20.5 per cent per year. Such figures no longer shock us.

In a different vein, I once heard the president of a pharmaceutical company talk about "the cancer and AIDS markets." To him, these "markets" made it possible to obtain large venture capital investments to finance research on these afflictions. No market, no financing, no research. This is why palliative tritherapies are the subject of more research than AIDS vaccines. Vaccines would bring in less money than tritherapies and would end up killing the market. Cynical logic? Yes, and it is the dominant logic of our civilization, which is increasingly based on the rationality of short-term profit.

Is the situation the same in the field of knowledge and education? The fact is that the democratization of education has created a demand of an entirely different order than the one the world experienced at the beginning of the twentieth century. How do we tackle this enormous demand created by the new information and knowledge society? These days, we agree that knowledge is a more important asset than gold or natural resources. But where is the spirit? I see only markets and industries. In short, the knowledge market is booming. ThinkEquity Partners, which participated in the 2001 World Education Market in Vancouver, stressed the importance of market capitalization for on-line training companies, which it believed would become increasingly profitable – the next dot.coms in the making.

We are investing in knowledge, we are trying to derive profit from it, and the digital network of the internet has opened up markets to develop and exploit it on a global scale. We still have to be able to compete, so we invest massively in promotion and marketing, find niches, adapt content to customer base, and offer better-quality products than the competitors, all the while controlling expenses. Education, research, and the field of knowledge have entered body and soul into the logic of economics and consumption. Is this the temporary price we must pay for a democratization of knowledge and education? It's hard to believe, and it throws our humanist reflexes into turmoil.

But, looking at it more closely, is the situation as shocking as all that? The publication of books – even works of philosophy, the Bible, or the catechism – is a matter for the book trade, which requires publishers, distributors, publicists, and buyers, and which makes a profit. This process is what makes books available to us, and it does not diminish the value of the philosophical reflections they contain. Is the fact that we can now read Kant for free on the internet a tragedy or a boon? Should I complain to find in the French series *Que sais-je?* little standard volumes on almost any question that could interest me? Is it shocking that they all have the same number of pages? Does the fact that they are produced in huge print runs for massive distribution compromise the quality of their content? No – we should save our indignation for real scandals, and there is no shortage of these in the world today.

On-line distribution networks only broaden the traditional markets of the knowledge industry reached through print, radio, and television. They are not worse or distorting. The difficulty that the new digital knowledge industries present lies rather in the technological quality of the transmission networks and in the quality of the new electronic and multimedia writing. These new networks may seem to herald the demise of literature that lacks broad appeal, like poetry or challenging essays, or even the demise of the printed book, but nothing of the sort will happen: these networks may actually ensure wider promotion and distribution of traditional offerings. Once we accept the new logic of the knowledge industry we are left to hope that the internet will broaden the knowledge markets, offer good tools for research and on-line consultation of virtual libraries, and strengthen linguistic and cultural diversity.

A ONE-DIMENSIONAL CONCEPTION OF ECONOMICS

We still need to examine our ideas about these knowledge industries in the United States more carefully. In the US, the dominant ideology – centred on the economy, competition, and profit – could be qualified as one-dimensional. It unhinges the calm and realistic analysis we have proposed. We must therefore note that the expression "knowledge industries," because it belongs to the economic sphere, conveys a dangerously narrow vision in the North American context, which is saturated with somewhat fundamentalist capitalist reflexes. The Web site of the American Distance Education Consortium (ADEC), which lists the thirteen American universities that have developed the most significant virtual activities, points in particular to the role of the Western Interstate Commission for Higher Education (WICHE), whose mission it is to make the economic corruption of the business-driven virtual university explicit. WICHE claims to work for the benefit of governments, companies, and citizens. It emphasizes that digital technologies are the most effective agent of change in social organizations, and governments can use them to promote market efficiency by establishing a more affordable and accessible network for services for the public and private sectors. The originators particularly insist on the need to link education and the job market more closely and to create a better educational context for companies. They also promote the importance of developing the market for pedagogical tools and content and removing borders between states so that the education markets can operate freely.[6]

Under the banner of commercial competition and adapting education to the immediate needs of companies, the American knowledge industries are limiting themselves to a narrow vision of the potential of new technologies. They forget the primary virtues of general education, which involve the quality of the mind and the critical spirit, and instead target professional development adapted to the short-term needs of companies according to the evolution of the markets. They also forget that such needs will change constantly over the course of these companies' lives and the lives of their employees, and that a good mind open to learning is worth more than an uncritical, cookie-cutter mind. Good minds offer a more lasting guarantee of success for companies and for the American economy – not to mention for humanist values.

THE STANDARDIZATION OF KNOWLEDGE

It's a well-known fact: the knowledge industries and their on-line dissemination contribute to the standardization of knowledge according to dominant models of thought. We should not over-dramatize this phenomenon, but neither should we deny the fact that the rich diversity of cultural approaches is in danger of being curtailed. We are depriving ourselves of one of the main advantages of advanced education, while knowledge industrialists concern themselves with foreign markets and the World Bank encourages poor countries to concentrate their limited resources on primary and secondary education and to connect to the portals of universities of rich countries for higher education.

At the colloquium Des Amériques solidaires pour le droit à l'éducation ("Americas United for the Right to Education"), held in Quebec in 2001, one of the experts in attendance, Maurice Tardif, highlighted the fact that higher education is the US's fifth largest export and noted that American universities send off educational packages that in no way meet the needs of the population of South American countries. Most of the content is in English – prepared for Americans, not for export.

As relevant as this criticism may be, the fact remains that knowledge disseminated on-line by universities can be a significant aid to higher education and research. Look at the example of MIT: in 2001, it offered free on-line access to 500 courses as part of a larger initiative entitled OpenCourseWare, and it intends to offer more than 1,500 such courses.

DIGITAL TECHNOLOGY AT THE SERVICE OF PEDAGOGICAL INNOVATION

Well-balanced judgments made about the role of new digital technologies take context into account: education or professional training, speculative commerce or respect for the pedagogical relationship. This revolution, which has barely begun, must not be judged definitively after only a few years of rather hesitant and often exploratory trials. Academics and entrepreneurs should work actively on developing the role of digital technologies in the production of high-quality and competitive multimedia training material, an effort that needs special financial support. I believe that such initiatives will contribute to a network of on-line services that will benefit the general population, students, professors, and researchers; they will stimulate interpersonal exchanges and disseminate knowledge, research, and pedagogical innovation.

THREE GUIDING PRINCIPLES

First, computers and Web sites will not replace teachers, but they will increasingly offer teachers and students at all levels invaluable pedagogical support, which will likely revive quality, motivation, and therefore the pleasure and effectiveness of pedagogy. The essential thing, the winning formula, is the combination of real flesh-and-blood teaching and digital pedagogical tools.

Second, there is nothing to stop human beings from progressing and tomorrow's educators from being better than their predecessors. The tools of cyberpedagogy must also be substantially improved without delay. This will draw a much greater commitment from students and teachers, proportionately improving the pedagogical relationship. All the exercises, images, references, and suggestions for additional research that teachers could want will be available to them on-line.

Third, the development of the knowledge industries does not necessitate embracing a narrow economic ideology or sacrificing high-quality education for short-sighted commercial vision. We must at least distinguish carefully between the requirements of education, which is a thing of the mind, and professional development or training, which must legitimately be adapted to the needs of companies.

17: Cyberpathologies and Cybertherapies

Where are the cyberdoctors of the cybersoul?

CYBERCOMPULSIVES

The current generation of teenagers – cybernatives, as compared with cyberimmigrants – has a good many binary addicts within its ranks. But we should not underestimate the number of adults – male and female – who are also in the grips of this addiction. Many of those who enter cyberspace end up becoming cyberaddicts or cybercompulsives, frequenting discussion groups, or chats, or engaging in on-line multi-user games. They are connected twenty-four hours a day, waiting for e-mails, engaged in network games, cell phones on. They spend hours in chat rooms, sometimes getting up in the middle of the night to converse with fellow Netizens in different time zones. Little by little, acute internet dependence sets in, which can require extensive clinical therapy. And this dependence puts them at risk of attracting sexual cyberpredators, who may seduce them into agreeing to meet in the real world.

CYBERDEPENDENCE

The growing power of cyberspace, a place where desire rules, will eventually undermine the value of reality – the real world's disappointments and frustrations invite escape. An inability to differentiate between the real and the virtual sets in at the dawn of a new civilization founded on artificial intelligence and the fusion of the real with the virtual. This loss of contact with reality will lead to mental illness and eventually to certain forms of violence.

This world breeds confusion between the real and the virtual like a new founding paradigm. It forms the very foundation of this new phase of the human journey. We should not be surprised that the new generation is the most profoundly affected by the industrial and cultural growth of this new mode of thinking and frittering away time. The resulting social pathology finds an ideal breeding ground in young people, whose minds are still malleable, sensitive to the imaginary, and whose consciousness of the principle of reality is not yet fully formed. Defenders of the new technologies remind us that children have always loved fairy tales and the often cruel characters that populate them – wicked witches and sharp-toothed wolves – and that negative representations are necessary for the construction of a child's reality. They forget, however, that in this new civilization the virtual is rapidly appropriated by the young, while adults struggle to adapt to it. And appropriation of the virtual can also precipitate – especially in children – a dangerous slide towards de-realization, an obliviousness to the laws of reality. The proof? How else do you explain the massacre of children by children in North American and European schools?

However strong the forces of the irrational and the imaginary become in our world, the ability to distinguish between the real and the virtual remains a fundamental principle of survival, even if it is a question of degree or nuance. It must be respected, cultivated, and taught – if it isn't, the consequences could be deadly. The fascist works of dramatic art produced under Hitler and Mussolini have taught us this. The stakes are high. The tragedies will multiply if politicians, and therefore the general public, neglect the predictable spread of this social pathology. The solution lies not in installing weapon detectors in schools but in teaching the appropriate values and cultural models.

Some hide away in cyberspace to escape a reality that has hurt them, that scares them, or that is colourless compared to the virtual. On a psychological level, the phenomenon is not new – it has parallels with mystical and drug experiences. Pierre-Paul Renders's film *Thomas est amoureux* (2001) tells the story of a thirty-two-year-old agoraphobic named Thomas who shuns all human contact; he has not left his home for eight years and communicates with the outside world via internet and videophone. He has become completely dependent on technology. Renders portrays this character as an addict cut off from reality and imprisoned through addiction in digital space. This brings to mind David Cronenberg's *Videodrome* (1983), the central character of which is swallowed up by a cathode ray tube. One of the original aspects of Renders's film – which, despite its deceptively ordinary title, was the first of its kind in digital culture – is that it presents a computer screen on a full-sized movie screen. This is where Thomas's cyberworld is deployed; we hear his voice, but we never see him. One day, however, the psychologist assigned to Thomas by the insurance agent who takes care of him registers him on a dating site without his knowledge, and he falls in love – first with the beautiful Mélodie, and then with Clara. The psychologist then puts him in touch with a prostitution service for the disabled, and this time Thomas becomes attached to a woman named Éva, to the point where he finally leaves his cybernetic bunker to meet her. It is love in its real, physical manifestation that saves this soul adrift in cyberspace, not the internet – even though it is the digital intermediary.

CYBERTHERAPY

Does the internet, which can create a state of cyberdependence, also offer cybertherapy? It does, but its effectiveness is not yet known. On-line psychoanalysis is performed either through interactive questionnaires or interpersonal sessions in which people undergoing analysis talk about themselves via e-mail. On the American site www.couchconfessions.com, the psychoanalyst disseminates sessions with patients in audio/video and allows patients to consult archived cases and be part of future sessions, duly announced. This is somewhat similar to the advice to the lovelorn published in newspapers and presented on the radio. The site draws those who want to discuss their fantasies or perversions or sexual dysfunctions, and they, in turn attract voyeuristic virtual visitors. And why not? Other systems are being developed that will be more private and professional.

On-line therapy sites are multiplying without much ethical control, and the big names of the various schools of psychoanalysis are voicing their criticism of the phenomenon. Some doubt the value of treatment when the therapist never encounters the patient face to face and cannot even be sure of that patient's identity or sex. They wonder also about the consequences of a written as opposed to an oral mode of expression and about the limits of guaranteeing confidentiality on the internet. John Suler, who has published many articles on the internet since 1996 collected under the title *The Psychology of Cyberspace*, likes to tell this joke: "How many psychologists does it take to do computer-mediated psychotherapy? None! The computer can do it all by itself!" He adds, "the reason why that joke is (or isn't) funny is important. Maybe, like many jokes, it reveals something we're a bit anxious about. Are computers and the internet taking over our lives? Are human relationships being infiltrated and dehumanized by machines?"[1]

Another recognized specialist, Michael Fenichel, who has studied the specific qualities of on-line psychotherapy extensively, lists the difficulties, but also contemplates the advantages. One particular advantage is anonymity: nobody is shy or ashamed in cyberspace. Everyone can express their fantasies freely in cyberspace, confide without holding anything back from their analysts, and they may therefore make faster progress.[2]

INTERNET/SUBCONSCIOUS.COM

Founded in Montreal in 1997 by Jean-Pierre Rochon, Le Psyinternaute ("the internaut psychologist") is a site that treats all forms of cyberdependence, in particular that related to on-line sex and gaming.[3] There are more and more sites offering information and psychological or psychoanalytic help, such as www.technostress.com, Concernedcounseling.com, Headworks.com, Kimberly Young's Center for On-line Addiction, psychservices.com, psychonet.fr, netaddiction.com, alaphobie.com, psynergie.com, psychomedia.qc.ca, redpsy.com/infopsy – the list goes on and on. The increasing attention that heads of psychoanalytic and psychotherapeutic institutions are paying to on-line therapy leaves no doubt as to the magnitude of the challenge, which calls into question Freudian psychoanalysis. At the same time, we are witnessing a proliferation of sites for psychological and spiritual support, which seem to respond particularly well to the predicament of surfers who are escaping the suffering of the real world and who find a warm and sympathetic welcome in the church of the cyberworld.

What creates internet dependency is not the perversity of the technologies themselves but the escape from the real world that they enable. The internet is a drug like any other, a psychotropic substance that allows us to elude a frustrating and painful reality. The source of the ailment must therefore be sought not in the type of drug used but in the life of the patient. It's the origin of the subconscious pain that must be treated, not the abuse of the psychotropic substance. This viewpoint is shared by one of the most important specialists in drug addiction, Dr William Lowenstein,[4] and by Jean-Pierre Garneau of Montreal, who launched the site www.redpsy.com. Still, the nature of the drug is also interesting in itself because it is not a chemical substance, but rather a rational communication technology: a psychotechnology. The virtual world that it provides access to seems at first glance much more normal and real than the world glimpsed through hallucinogens.

TWENTY-SIXTH PARADOXICAL LAW
Despite its technological nature, the internet acts as a psychotropic drug and activates the unconscious.

18: Internet Curiosities and Follies

*You have to visit the amazing amusement park
of cyber-Prometheus.*

THE GREAT INTERNET NAVIGATORS

Today we surf the Net as in times past they navigated the high
seas. We have always sought fortune. Pirates may lie in wait, but
– for our ship owners or cybernauts – the anticipated profits are
worth the capital risk. The daring Christopher Columbuses of the
electronic age, captains of the new economy, are venturing out
onto the World Wide Web at the head of their Navigator and
Explorer armadas, trailed by their Oracle, Excite, Magellan, Galileo,
Copernicus, and Yahoo! caravels, carrying with them the hopes
of Spanish and Portuguese kings of our times – Wall Street and
NASDAQ investors. Sails to the wind, our cybernauts seek favour-
able currents. They have discovered continents, islands, and
niches[1] and have named them America Online, Lycos, Cyberia,
Delphy, AltaVista, Galaxy, and Prodigy; they have established
ports and called them InfiniT, Sympatico, GlobeTrotter, Freenet,
Earthlink, and Wanadoo. Exploring the new virtual routes to
India and El Dorado, they encounter fanciful and hybrid crea-
tures: Gophers, MIME, Eudora, Dreamweaver, Xmetal, Quark-
Xpress, RealPlayer, and the occasional monster, bug, virus, or
terrifying worm. We are sailing at a good clip, we tell ourselves,
towards cyberglobalization. The old economy needed ships on
every ocean. The new economy is not built on the trade of atoms

(merchandise, cargo), but on the circulation of bits – the digital atoms of the information society.

NAVIGATING IN SEARCH OF AN ISLAND

PrivateIslandsOnline.com lets you navigate the ocean of the Web in search of your dream island to discover, rent, or buy. Digital photos allow you to assess its charms. The site provides all the relevant information about more than a hundred of these little floating paradises at prices that range from thousands to millions of dollars.

ITDS: INTERNET TRANSMITTED DISEASES

The internet journey towards the promised land is not without its dangers; we will be threatened by evil spirits, monsters, viruses, worms, and diseases. Be careful: if you are contaminated by the Excite or Melissa viruses, or the Chernobyl virus (launched on the thirteenth anniversary of the Chernobyl nuclear disaster and reportedly affecting more than 60 million computers in a few days), you could lose your computer's software and all of its memory. The virus Happy 99 permanently erased e-mails. And new viruses appear all the time, each with a name more poetic and seductive than the last: I Love You did incredible damage by exploiting the human impulses of cybernauts in need of affection (and more); Homepage came on its heels. Every day brings a new one, particularly to those of us who use the most widespread e-mail software, such as Microsoft Outlook. Happytime arrived from China in 2001. Before you could even open it, this virus infected your hard drive on dates that added up to thirteen, for example 8/5 or 7/6. Once installed, it could freeze your entire system. One final example: the virus Sircam distributed all the chapters of this book and all the files on my hard drive at random to everyone in my electronic address book. Even if we can say that now, in 2006, we are no longer preoccupied with virus threats, thanks to an abundance of firewalls and protection providers, we must still remain vigilant if we are to avoid the cyberpirates and hijackers who can penetrate the networks of banks, credit card companies, or insurance and tax institutions on a quest to steal our money or our identities, not to mention the strategic secrets of government defence departments.

INTERNET MEDICINE AND PHARMACOLOGY

We are now witnessing an explosion of medical and pharmaceutical information and diagnosis on the internet. It is not overstating the case to say that this aspect of digital shock is transforming the therapeutic relationship of trust and authority that has always prevailed between patient and physician. Doctors have to regularly contend with the questions and objections of patients who have conducted their own internet research and created cyberdiagnostics based on their symptoms. They already know which medications they require; some avoid waiting to see their physicians (who, in countries without government-subsidized health care, charge substantial fees) by purchasing medications on-line. Pharmaceutical companies and even physicians have therefore taken to the internet themselves, setting up shop. They offer free consultations, sell drugs without prescriptions, and thus provide a parallel medical service with little if any regulation or public control. Patients don't even know if the cyberdoctor they are consulting with via e-mail for a fee is an authorized physician or pharmacist. There are also many soft or parallel therapies, whose purveyors verge on charlatanism, that are not recognized in the real world and therefore pullulate without restriction in the cyberworld.

Is cybermedicine dangerous? Yes – quite often it is. But even if the internet is permissive and encourages fake medical services, it also offers a wealth of helpful medical information, which may help patients to better understand their problems. Furthermore, it may prompt a behavioural evolution among physicians reluctant to lose their traditional authority, professionals who are disinclined to waste precious time explaining medical alternatives to their patients. These physicians will find themselves obliged to develop a real dialogue with their internet-informed patients, who will ask more and more precise questions and request detailed answers. Physicians themselves are now searching the Web for the latest information on drugs, medical research, and therapies; they will also increasingly use e-mail to follow up on patients undergoing treatment. All of this constitutes a long-overdue revolution in the field of medicine – it has already profoundly altered medical practice within the space of a few years. It remains for us to ensure that the necessary public and professional controls and regulations are put in place – a daunting task from our current vantage point. Again the internet is revolutionizing and democratizing a highly traditional and rigid social institution: medicine.[2]

MAJOR SCARES AND RUMOURS

Major scares punctuate this period of world change and the new millennium. We saw this clearly with the transition to the year 2000. Will the world born of the big bang disappear in a big bug? Disaster scenarios involving a computer apocalypse have evoked popular fears of a world controlled by the Great Computer. The big bug would be a major threat in a world of pure computer simulacra, as we sometimes imagine the cyberworld. Cyborgs would die by the thousands as a result of cyberhacker intrusions into the encrypted systems of central institutions.

The year 2000 scare was compounded by the cyberhacker scare (cyberhackers wanted to destroy strategic world security sites) and the terrorist scare (triggered by the 9/11 attacks). While the scares targeted mainly American powers, they revealed an ancient fear in the gut of society that would resurface at the slightest digital signal. Rumours, which multiply so rapidly in cyberspace, prove the existence of this latent anxiety. They are called hoaxes, and they come in all forms – from the simple prank to the falsified announcement of a new virus. There are comprehensive lists of them on two specialized sites: vmyths.com and andoaxbuster.com. Many an alarmist message has been circulated, received, and forwarded by Netizens eager to warn their friends of such hazards as drivers who hunt down and shoot decent law-abiding motorists at random, or tropical fruits that harbour deadly diseases, or snakes that lurk in the city's sewer system. Influenced by the real existence of computer viruses and worms, these flurries of alarm at times come close to mass hysteria. The dissemination of catastrophic announcements on the internet is a symptom of the agitation and acute nervous tension that are becoming chronic among cybernauts – a state that can lead to social pathologies.

Is the language of computers gaining so much importance that it is contaminating biological designations? E. coli is not a computer virus. Its name might suggest it, but it is an often-deadly bacterium, very much alive and notorious for its resistance to antibiotics.

CRYSTAL WEB:
WHEN THE MEDIUM IS THE MEDIUM

When McLuhan taught us that "the medium is the message," the internet didn't exist. It would undoubtedly have enthralled him and prompted him to take his provocative musings even further. My loose adaptation of his famous expression must therefore be considered an homage to his genius. But clairvoyants have taken the concept literally: to them, a cathode ray screen is as good as a crystal ball. The internet offers more than two million astrology references in English, French, German, and Spanish and as many horoscope references as one could ever hope for. Clairvoyants and mediums seem to have modernized, and they have quickly taken possession of cyberspace – there must be some sort of affinity between the two. Surfers with valid credit cards can learn about their futures. Will they fall in love or strike it rich, in the real world or in the virtual world?

THE DIGITAL GOLD RUSH

When digital shock really set in, people talked about the internet as the site of a new gold rush. The phenomenon was so powerful that the expression had to be taken literally: we saw gold mining and natural resource companies, struggling due to the decline in world prices, buy internet service companies to boost their own stock prices, and with great success. After buying NorstarMall.ca, Sikaman Gold Resources saw its share price rise immediately; American Gem bought Northern Securities for a foot in the door of e-commerce; Dejour Mines invested successfully in InstantDocuments.com; and Cristobal Resources merged with Netgraphe. The phenomenal growth of electronic communication technology has created such fervour and is so disruptive of received ideas that its shock effect is equivalent to the discovery of the New World.

Cyberspace has also become the site of a treasure hunt. In Quebec alone, more than $100 million lies unclaimed in banks. Through oversight or death, or are the heirs unknown? The Public Curator established a Web site to inventory all cases of escheat in

the hope that some holders of forgotten funds would come forward
to claim their balances. The Bank of Canada is doing the same; it
has approximately 800,000 unclaimed balances, for a total of some
$160 million. The city of Chicago, the banking institutions of
which house more than US$30 million in dormant accounts, also
launched a search site, and many other public institutions have
followed suit. The Chicago site alone received close to 500,000
visits from potential heirs the world over, people with immigrants
to the United States in their family trees. They can now consult the
National Archives and Records Administration, as well as many
genealogical sites where they can refine their searches, on their
quest for relatives and lost fortunes.

ELECTRONIC CAFÉS

The attention that the media suddenly paid to the internet aroused
the interest of the general public. In Montreal, the Café Électro-
nique – which I opened with partners in 1995, the first of its kind
in Canada – quickly became a meeting place for the curious, a
place to announce new products (CD-ROMs or on-line services), a
place for government and private sector press conferences. Foreign
delegations and television stations from many countries came to
visit, and for two years Radio-Canada taped its first TV series on
wired society at the café. Almost every day, young entrepreneurs
came in to ask us whether they could open another electronic café
as a franchise in some distant location – in Paris, in Buenos Aires,
in Australia, in Qatar. Real estate promoters solicited us to breathe
life into old buildings under renovation by setting up new electronic
cafés in them.

Cybercafés multiplied. Soon there were about fifteen in
Montreal. In London and Paris, huge twenty-four-hour internet
cafés equipped with 300 to 400 computer stations began popping
up. They were wired forums, meeting places for alternative types,
cyber–night owls, compulsive computer gamers, members of the
Net generation who fit in better in the cyberworld than the real
world. But the spread of the internet in developed countries quickly
undermined the cybercafé trend.

In developing countries, however, the trend took off. In 2001, it
was undoubtedly Irbid – Jordan's second-largest city – that held the
record, with no fewer than 150 internet cafés. They lined one

thoroughfare, extending several hundred metres, offering their clients use of internet-connected computers at the modest hourly rate of seventy cents. Irbid is a university town with a camp full of Palestinian refugees. The young and the poor, those who could not afford a phone much less a computer, flocked to these cafés to surf without restriction and to meet in an atmosphere of liberty and modernity.

THE ACROSS-THE-LANDING WEB

A curious phenomenon is that of the across-the-landing Web: the e-building. In 1999, several residents of an apartment building in Lyons got together and installed a local area network so that they could play on-line video games at home. After playing, they would meet for a drink in one participant's apartment and discuss their games. The network became a sort of building newsletter, greatly improving communication among residents. One is tempted to suggest installing this type of network within a single family dwelling to improve domestic communication.

This use of technology to re-establish simple interpersonal connections points to the solitude of city residents. It is not true that in the third millennium we communicate better than we did in the past. We communicate much more easily in certain respects, but with much more difficulty in others. The power of communication technology must not be confused, as it increasingly is, with the quality and intensity of the content of communication.

FROM THE WEBCAM TO THE WORMCAM

One of the most significant phenomena of this search for communicational fusion, which might ease the loneliness caused by major urban agglomerations and which are a symptom of a lack of affection, are Webcams – cameras connected directly to the internet. They make it possible to watch your children remotely when they are at home with a sitter and you are at work. Many daycares now have them to reassure parents that their little ones are happy and well cared for. Internet devotees set them up in their homes in the hope that they will attract an audience for their day-to-day lives. For promotional reasons, the company Electrolux mounted a Webcam in a Swedish family's fridge, displaying their dietary habits to the planet. Korean company Daewoo offers the Magic Mirror, an LCD touch screen installed on the outside of the fridge door that inventories the fridge's contents, tells its owner what is missing based on consumption habits, and places internet grocery orders for home delivery.

A Dutch computer programmer has placed cameras throughout his apartment, making it possible for the entire world to monitor who rings his doorbell, what his cat eats, what he puts in his fridge, what he throws in the garbage (the camera reads barcodes from discarded packaging and the computer interprets them) – even his visits to the bathroom. And MIT students have put Webcams in their washers and dryers.

The French TV show *Loft Story*, presented by M6, a channel with a limited audience, made big news in 2001 when it suddenly garnered more than seven million viewers, beating out the leading channel, TF1. It did so by adopting the American concept of reality TV launched by such shows as *Big Brother, The Real World,* and *Survivor. Loft Story* presented eleven young people holed up in an apartment for ten weeks under the omnipresent eyes of several cameras. M6 chose to show the complete video takes only on the *Loft Story* Web site, particularly the most intimate scenes, which are obviously very popular with Web surfers. The pair who could rise above the inherent promiscuity, lack of privacy, and voyeurism of the situation would win a house worth US$700,000, the winner determined by audience vote (almost four million viewers voted regularly). The plot device of this real-time soap, rebroadcast in its entirety on the Web, was to eliminate privacy and place relationships under stress. Because the group was made up of five women and six men, couples would form and then break apart, greatly enhancing the drama and adding the lure of sexual voyeurism. The show was an immediate and massive hit in France – it became a sort of extreme public-square ritual and triggered national debate. *Le Monde* devoted a front-page headline to it, and controversy raged among presidents of TV channels, intellectuals, psychiatrists, and political leaders. It was global exhibitionism and global voyeurism, a real-time striptease via Webcam for an internet audience.

Certain Webcams have a tourism-related and promotional vocation; they are placed in zoos, in cafés, at the Place de l'Opéra in Paris, on beaches in Thailand, along ski trails in Colorado and the Alps, at the Montreal Biodome, and so on. Web telerobots also let you paint remotely using a robot, and you receive the framed painting by mail.

Arthur C. Clarke and Stephen Baxter's 2000 science fiction novel *The Light of Other Days* introduces the reader to a world of wormhole technology where information can be passed instantaneously between points in the space-time continuum. In it we encounter an electronic camera that infiltrates the world like an earthworm: the Wormcam.

DOMESTIC AND GLOBAL

The Home Phoneline Networking Association is a group of companies that offer new software for networking all the electrical appliances in your home – the washing machine, the TV, the fridge, the garage door – using a phone line. Once again, the myth of fusion rears its head. What is it for? Microsoft, which offers Universal Plug and Play for the same purpose, believes that it's beneficial to have such a domestic network, which you can program to suit your needs and control remotely. It will make you a powerful magician, master of an intelligent home, lord of the manor. Soon, your hands-free phone will serve you refreshments using simple chip-assisted telepathy.

Webcams and the domestic integration of the global communication network, home automation, and creature comforts? Why not! But Webcams for global remote surveillance is a whole other issue: "In the first quarter of the 21st century, it will become possible to find, fix or track, and target anything that moves on the surface of the Earth," announced the chief of staff of the US Air Force in 1997.[3] The National Security Agency and the National Imagery and Mapping Agency analyse all digital communications on the planet as part of the Global Information Dominance program. This is a lot less pretty than Webcam networks – it is a product of cyberwar.

EXTREME INTERNET

The imagination invested in this communicational and global cyberspace merits the attention of anthropologists. The fact that newspapers religiously report trivial events gives the impression that we are living in a world where the imaginary and the irrational are more widespread than ever. For example, in 1999, Agence France-Presse reported that four volunteers were "shut away naked in separate rooms for 100 days with only a credit card and a computer in an experiment intended to see whether they could survive using only the Internet. Starting at 10:30 local time the only contact the volunteer nudists had with the outside world was via e-mail … to have … items necessary to their survival delivered to them. Scholars will be studying the effects of the experiment."

Researchers, using the theory of the memory of water formulated in 1988 by French homeopath Dr Jacques Benveniste, intend to prove the effectiveness of homeopathic treatments transmitted via the internet. But can the memory of molecules actually be transmitted in this way? Nobel Prize-winner Brian Josephson tried to find a way to do it.

For the Search for Extraterrestrial Intelligence project, researchers from the University of California in 1999 called in 100,000 cybernauts. Using a network of computers, each performing a minute part of the processing, they worked to create the equivalent of a super-powerful computer capable of decoding the information collected by the radio telescope Arecibo, in Puerto Rico, the largest in the world.

The internet will also help you choose a sperm donor. The Canadian Press reported in 1999: "Thanks to a Toronto sperm bank's on-line catalogue, women can choose the pedigree of the donor. Accordingly, donor 1131, of Scottish and English ancestry, is likeable, kind, and generous. None of the men in his family suffer from premature baldness, he wears glasses and has freckles on his shoulders … 'It borders on eugenics,' says a sociologist."

The Quebec firm My Virtual Model has carved its niche and made its reputation by offering clothing shoppers a virtual model on the Web, eliminating the need to try on clothes and permitting shoppers to buy on-line without leaving home. A number of retail chains have adopted this system and have increased their sales appreciably. The company's director of marketing maintains, "We are developing a model that will become a sort of electronic identity. People would bring their clones to portal sites that host a variety of retailers. It's a different way for merchants to sell their merchandise by letting consumers try out the product without really having to try it on."[4]

In 1999, concerts and the first cyberopera in history were offered on the Web. "The image was tiny and the sound lo-fi when a production of Verdi's 'Aida' from Verona, Italy, made history Friday as the first opera to be broadcast live over the Internet."[5] This cyberopera, filmed during the seventy-seventh Verona Opera Festival, brought 50,000 to 100,000 Netizens together on a site created by IBM. Of course, there were sound problems and the singers' movements were jerky and the dark images were no larger than five centimetres, but, as the general director of the Houston Grand Opera enthused, "This is a fascinating precedent" – the internet "will no doubt become the main delivery system for in-home fine arts performances." This fetish-like enthusiasm was not shared by everyone: one music critic remarked, "Listening to music on a computer speaker is like taking a bath with your socks on."[6]

Cinema formally encountered the internet in 1999, when the first feature film to be premiered on the internet was announced: Metafilmics' *Quantum Project*, which was thirty-two minutes long. And now full-length features with excellent image definition appear on the big screen, thanks to advances in streaming technology.

THE INTERNET, THE NAZIS, AND THE KU KLUX KLAN

Racist, extremist, and Nazi sites are proliferating on the Web. The Simon Wiesenthal Center, which investigates Nazi-related crimes, counted no fewer than 2,000 neo-Nazi sites in the United States in 2000; their number doubled in a year. The perpetrators are often European, but since they are prohibited from operating in Germany, they use American sites, because US law protects freedom of expression without discrimination. According to a report to the Council of Europe from the Swiss Institute of Comparative Law, a German company called Only Solutions counted some 50,000 swastikas in cyberspace, 85 per cent of them on American sites. A study conducted in 2000 found 4,000 racist Web sites, 2,500 of them in the US.

Those who fight fascism have created sites denouncing neo-Nazi sites – for example, Nazis Raus von Internet. But there are also sites maintained by skinheads and other groups that advocate racism and anti-Semitism. Commercial resistance to such initiatives is relatively rare. The auction site eBay prohibited the sale of extremist-group paraphernalia, but it only did so in 2001, and under public pressure.

CYBERGANGS

The impunity that racist sites enjoy in cyberspace is so great that it should come as no surprise that criminal gangs have set up shop on the Web and are using their sites for promotion and recruiting. The Crips, a very active Los Angeles gang, has a site on which it shares its guiding principles of absolute freedom and invites visitors to get in touch – to find out more, you simply click on the dancing colt at the bottom of the screen.

The Hells Angels have an impressive site that testifies to their international presence. The site sells branded merchandise and invites visitors to contact their local Hells branch. It is regularly updated. Rival gangs the Bandidos and the Rock Machine are not to be outdone; their sites are emblazoned with Gothic and blood-oozing fonts. The Outlaws have skulls crossed with gun barrels on their home page menu, along with a list of upcoming events.

MR WEB.COM

In 2000, Mitch Maddox, a Texan who remained housebound for months to show that you can survive with only the internet, changed his name to DotComGuy. And in 2001, a young Israeli Netizen named Tomer Krissi managed to get permission from the authorities to change his name to his Web site name: he is now called Tomer.com. His site features a reproduction of his new passport and credentials: First name: Tomer. Last name: .com. Profession: computer programmer. Nationality: Israeli. Born: 28–07–1975. He remarked that his site had opened up the world to him, because anyone who knew his name would know he had a site they could visit. Tomer.com went on to say, "I see surnames, which have meaning as archaeological artefacts, and I wanted to give mine some significance for myself in the year 2001 ... Say I meet a girl, for instance, and don't get her number. That could have been a missed opportunity, but now it won't be, because she'll always know where to find me."[7] Such identity changes make it clear that internet fetishists believe they have begun a new existence as citizens of digital cyberspace.

THE SAGA OF THE TWINS SOLD TWICE
ON THE WEB

In the United States, there are hundreds of sites that offer children for adoption. In 2001, a twenty-eight-year-old woman put her twins up for sale on the Web. They were bought for $12,000 by an American couple, then their mother took them back and sold them for a higher price to a British couple. The two families, British and American, laid claim to the children, as did their mother, who insisted that she did not receive the money promised her by the agency – called Caring Heart – that made the Web sale. The resulting mess was difficult for the police and the justice system to sort out. This is but one high-profile child-selling case; babies are now routinely bought and sold in cyberspace, and the money that changes hands is referred to as a "file management fee." Most people who engage in this business probably have nothing but good intentions, but the fact is that there is little protection for the children. There is no legislation that expressly prohibits mercenary trafficking, which, if it is widespread in the real world, is even more so in the permissive space of the virtual world.

ANOREXIC NATION

In the US, there are several hundred Web sites promoting anorexia, a new philosophy of the body that seems to be winning over young people who are reacting against the obesity epidemic that is undermining the health of Americans. War has broken out between the National Association of Anorexia Nervosa and Associated Disorders and the militants of the emaciated aesthetic. The association has asked Yahoo! to remove 115 "pro-anorexia" sites from its servers. Anorexic Nation is one of the 400 sites advocating extreme skinniness; others include Dying to Be Thin, Fading into Obscurity, Anorexia Goes High Tech, and Twisted Body Image.

INTERNET GUILLOTINE

A few years ago, an unfortunate Netizen (although he has a nice smile in the photo on his site's home page) invited us to pay to watch the amputation of his feet live on the internet. He was disabled and looking for a way to finance a prosthesis, because his insurance company had refused to cover it. He asked surfers to send him twenty dollars each, hoping 200,000 would come through for him. "Welcome!" his site announced. "Prepare yourself for an adventure like you have never before experienced. In an unprecedented event ... LIVE via webcam access ... you can watch me amputate my legs with a homemade guillotine on November 30, 2001! Yes, you read that correctly!" This declaration was illustrated with drawings of severed feet and a guillotine; there was also a credit card payment form. According to the site, by June 2001, 144,675 visitors had dropped by.[8]

DEATH.COM AND GHOST SITES

A Norwegian with incurable cancer decided to record his deterioration on a daily basis on a private TV station's Web site. His aim was "to help other cancer victims and their friends and families," because "sickness and disease are taboo subjects in Norway today. I don't want it to be like that."[9] Other entrepreneurs are exploiting the niche of virtual cemeteries. The applicant signs a pre-death contract – or the applicant's loved ones sign an after-death one – for a long-term burial plot in a cybercemetery. You can select your location and a decor that suits your taste and budget, and you can post an on-line obituary notice (it can even be a multimedia notice, if you so choose), which will ensure that you are remembered for cybereternity. Since the cemetery is indexed on search engines, those who wish to commune with you after death just have to type in your name in order to access your virtual tomb. And it would be wise before dying or making funeral arrangements to record your last wishes on the site, which guarantees their authenticity and confidential dissemination.

As noted earlier, electronic memory is paradoxically very short. Steve Baldwin was aware of this and decided to open an on-line cemetery for Web sites that have gone to the great beyond. In his "cemetery," you can view final screen shots of over a thousand sites that have disappeared from the internet. Baldwin pointed out that everyone looks at today and tomorrow, but no one looks back. While he believed that there were many sites that deserved to die because they were so idiotic, he still found it depressing how many had passed on. "Our goal," he explained, "is not to laugh at the fallen, but to preserve their last image before all traces of these sites' existence are deleted from history's view." Baldwin's creation was dubbed the "Museum of E-Failure" – an exhibition honouring the Web's golden age of design.[10]

SEXXXX.COM

First, let's reassure ourselves: cyberspace must be completely healthy and normal, because the only sites that really make money on the internet are porn sites. In other words, digital shock has not destroyed the world's oldest profession. Another sign of health: virtual dating agencies are very profitable. Of course, the explosion of eroticism on the internet is not based on anything new. Voyeurism was not born with digital civilization. The difference is that with the internet, the genre is now characterized by an unlimited inventiveness, which is indicative of the extreme obsession with sex that seems to plague humanity. The storage of porn images on the Web will undoubtedly require a larger and larger digital silo.

A few charming examples? In 1999, the Russian television network M-1 launched the Naked Truth channel, which not only delivered the naked truth but also built anticipation for it through a striptease that progressed during the broadcast. In a similar vein, but this time on an internet station, a Web TV show called Nakednews.com was launched in December 1999 in Toronto (despite that city's reputation for Puritanism). The show offered daily news, which would have seemed serious if its anchors were not delivering the news of the day while stripping to their birthday suits. These "journalists" were initially all female, but men have now joined their ranks at the request of a number of regular Web viewers. There were more than 200 applicants for the anchor jobs at the launch of the free station, and some six million people eager for fresh news visited each month.

It is fair to say that the amount of sex surfing on the Web, compared to searches devoted to commerce, tourism, or education, is explosive. One of the major advantages of cybersex, or virtual sex, is that although it gives free rein to the most outrageous fantasies and perversions, it is safe. You can't catch venereal diseases or AIDS on-line. One of the major risks, however, is posed by pedophilia sites, which victimize children. A lesser danger is that porn sites hide viruses or cookies that make it possible for those who plant them to use your telephone line to make long distance calls.

Anyone can have the experience. When you access a porn site on the Web, you open your door – your screen – to a flood of Web sites for all tastes and appetites, from the most charming to the most perverse. It's a veritable shock for the cybervirgin (someone having the experience for the first time). A cascade of interconnected porn sites assaults you immediately; these sites will ask for your e-mail address and credit card number to more effectively hold you captive. The devil, master of diabolical programming, has electronically attached these sites with cyberglue, and they wind through cyberspace like a string of pearls. The panicked surfer who closes one site will see another pop up on his or her screen. The glue is so strong that many of these sites refuse to obey the closing click; others vanish initially but keep reappearing. Escaping from the cyberbordello becomes an onerous task. You succeed in closing all the sites that have accumulated like layers of a mille feuille on your screen; you are finally free and safely back in the real world, having closed the hatch and even the computer. But an unpleasant surprise awaits you: when you restart your computer, you see that one of those clingy porn sites has become your home page by default. And the cascade starts again as soon as you try to close it: Pandora's box is not so easily shut. You are trapped, and in order to extricate yourself, you have to clean the very guts of your computer, searching through your browsing history and rooting out the parasites on your browser.

Fortunately, only cyberpimps seem to have adopted these parasitic techniques, but e-commerce entrepreneurs could conceivably enter the game. Since no one is publicly denouncing this state of affairs, we must conclude that some people find it advantageous and others simply don't want to admit that they have navigated those blue-tinted waters and been cyberviolated in the process.

And, of course, you will receive daily e-mails offering you drugs or "natural" means to enlarge your penis; the senders can also help you solve erectile dysfunction, or furnish you with a replica of a staggeringly expensive watch, or even a fake university diploma. Intelligent robot searchers and cookies have you permanently in their sights.

THE BANANA.COM CYBERREPUBLIC

In 1942, during World War II, Great Britain built an offshore platform in the shape of a star ten kilometres off its southeast coast in order to bolster its anti-aircraft defence system. In 1967, "Prince" Roy Bates, the former military entrepreneur who had purchased the platform and named it Sealand, proclaimed it a principality, with embassies and its own currency. Bates has made Sealand a haven for cyberworld companies that want to escape the restrictive laws of the real world. In 2000, he gave refuge to cyberrebel Sean Hasting, president of HavenCo, whose site (havenco.com) offers an extraterritorial and libertarian cyberzone that provides hosting beyond the reach of the law. Publicly, anonymously, or under a pseudonym, HavenCo clients can have their databases, pornographic material, or financial transactions securely hosted. A fiscal e-paradise? Perhaps, but there are limits – the laws of HavenCo exclude anything that could provoke an immediate reaction from British authorities, like child pornography, tax evasion, or cyberterrorism.

PRISONS.NET

Prison inmates will increasingly be able to surf the Web and escape into cyberspace. In the more permissive institutions, they will also be able to exchange e-mail, create their own Web sites, enter chat rooms, conduct small trade, look for jobs before their release – or even remotely order crimes to be committed. In many instances, internet activities are strictly limited, but indications are that they will be progressively liberalized. In Quebec, the site www.souverains.qc.ca links to Bordeaux Prison and connects prisoners with "real" life. We can assume that the prisons also have cyberguards who scrutinize the Web activities of their charges, just in case. Those interested can visit many prison Web sites, whether they be in the United States, Russia, India, France, or Germany, where the remarkable Tegel Prison Web site (www.planet-tegel.de), based in Berlin and designed by the inmates themselves, offers an impressive virtual visit for potential candidates or tourists; it also serves as an excellent model for Web site creators.

THE ODOURS OF THE WEB

The Web makes it possible to diffuse scents remotely, just as easily as music and images. It has existed in principle for several years, but now it's operational. A digital file specifying the exact chemical composition of a fragrance is light enough to circulate on the Web.

Those interested in partaking of this technology simply have to equip their computers with a digitally commanded perfume generator, which is hardly more complicated than a colour printer. Thus equipped, they can waft the perfumes that they receive into the air around them – whether they are at home, in a perfume store, or at a cosmetics trade show. For the launch of a French perfume in New York, this innovation would guarantee a media sensation.

The company AromaJet offers IPSmell and the Pinoke diffuser. In 2000, it announced that it had diffused odours from Plano, Texas, to Sydney, Australia, in a few seconds. AromaJet is particularly interested in olfactory accessories for on-line games. The company TriSenx provides sensory experiences on the Net using technologies that stimulate taste and smell: "Trisenx will make numerous online experiences more real, from e-commerce and interactive entertainment to education and communication ... the Internet finally comes to its senses!"[11] The California firm Digiscents,[12] which markets the iSmell peripheral and Scentware, can diffuse millions of new smells that it creates by combining 128 basic distinct essences; its odours can accompany the dissemination of Web home pages, images, videos, and ads. And why not diffuse pheromones to accompany porn sites, or diffuse the smell of the ocean or of the subway to accompany scenes in a film?[13]

DIGITAL GADGETRY

The digital universe puts itself in the palm of the hand of the new cyberman, who has been so suddenly endowed with new powers. Magazines promote all sorts of gadgets, each more useless than the last, that compete on the basis of connectivity, miniaturization, design, and magical illusion. These include foldable wireless computer keyboards that you can slip into your pocket and digital watches – including one model by Casio that connects wirelessly to the internet, allowing you to listen to MP3s; and another, the Wrist Camera, which is also a digital camera; and the WatchPhone by Samsung, which is a phone if you bring it close to your ear. On it goes: talking robots, dildos that you connect to your computer to experience intimate sensations to the rhythm of the Web video that you're watching, internet-connected jewellery that communicates (exhibited at the famous CeBIT trade show in Hanover, Germany) – audio caps, microphone earrings, and mouse rings. And Sony has launched the first portable TV that lets you connect to the internet. Soon you will get it on your wristwatch.

FUTURISTIC INNOVATIONS

Other inventions are more fascinating, and more likely to revolutionize our way of life. Smart keys can prevent your house from being robbed or your car from being stolen. The Vista4 system, developed by the Quebec company Net Creation, made it possible to select films from the internet and watch them on a large TV screen – until it was declared illegal. The M2A Imaging Capsule, developed by Israeli company Given Imaging, which you swallow like a pill, films the inside of the body for medical diagnoses.

Researchers at the University of Stuttgart, Germany, have developed fibres that can be woven into clothing – fibres capable of capturing solar energy to power the electronic equipment (laptop computers, cell phones, internet-connected TV-glasses) that is integrated into that clothing. These fibres are machine washable, which solves one of the problems posed by interactive fibres and wearable computing.

What emerges from all of this is that digital technology unleashes the imagination, giving rise to all kinds of fantasies, whether they be related to voyeurism, clairvoyance, homeopathy, or escape. The cyberworld is an alternative space where we can shed real-world constraints, where we can act on our urges anonymously and without consequences.

TWENTY-SEVENTH PARADOXICAL LAW
The digital realm, despite its technological nature and its basic binary code, releases the most fantastical imaginative processes in all areas of human activity.

19: Cyberviolence and Cyberwar

The futuristic technology of cybergames contrasts strangely
with the primitive behaviour of the players.

A GAMING CIVILIZATION

Gaming has become a central activity and reference value of cyber-society. Thanks to new digital technologies, we now produce a parallel world daily – a virtual world or cyberspace not only of simulation, games, dreams, excess, escape, and utopia but also of venture capital investment and gaming-based profit. To counter reality, which can be burdensome and painful, we secrete a game opiate through which we escape to a world without responsibility, a world that offers us the simulation of power, the chance to win denied us by the real world, and the experience of failure without consequences. When we win, we're euphoric; when we lose, we know it's not for keeps.

In just a few years, the digital gaming industry has matched the sales of the Hollywood film industry. Much of its success is based on gratuitous violence inflicted on virtual targets using a laser gun that offers the illusion of being a superhero. Is this an electronic rehash of the catharsis attributed to the great Greek tragedies? Is it the opiate of the frustrated seeking violent revenge – a revenge made all the more pleasurable by the fact that it's consequence-free? From the dream of wealth sold to the poor through slot machines or lotteries and the dream of physical power sold to the young through video arcades emerges the sad reflection of a reality that is economically arduous and hard on the ego.

Digital technologies have strengthened the technical power of these dream machines. We are a long way from games such as marbles, cards, ludo, or hopscotch. Most digital games deal in money and death. They arouse deep, destructive urges in the solitary player sitting in front of the computer screen, beyond social control. These violent games, offered in virtual spaces via cathode ray helmets, or played by several players over on-line networks or in theme parks, can last for many hours. They exploit the digital capabilities of 3-D imaginary spaces and the interactive movement of electronic characters that depict evil figures.

Why are there so many games on the market? Why have they become increasingly violent? Why has an artificial, elementary, instinctive parallel world met with such incredible commercial success? Because digital gaming allows us to escape the gravity of the real world in a spiral of speed and reflex. It gives us a negative reflection of the burdens and irrational forces of the real world – a reflection of the difficulty of partaking in that world. The success of the gaming industry is proportionate to the vindictive power of the real world; gaming enthralls those who cannot otherwise share in that power.

CYBERWAR AS A GAME

In televised statements, American military leaders – seemingly reasonable adults – set a disgusting example by bragging that bombarding Iraqi or Serb targets was like playing Nintendo. They shouldn't be surprised when their children also play "Nintendo," murdering their classmates and teachers in cold blood. These robots – or cybernanthropes, as French Marxist sociologist Henri Lefebvre was already calling them in 1968 – act mechanically, with no cultural or emotional awareness, responding to human passion with technique. They are wilfully ignorant of the fact that reality is not merely an algorithm, that the cyberworld interferes with the real world, that we cannot kill in the cyberworld without affecting the real world.

According to many specialists, the violence of video games has a cathartic effect and even contributes to the building of the child's personality. Gerard Jones examines this in his 2002 book *Killing Monsters: Why Children Need Fantasy, Super Heroes, and Make-Believe Violence*, and many other studies underline the negative influence of this deployment of violence in children's culture. While we should not accept that the answer is a simple choice between 1 or 0, yes or no – it instead depends on the individual child, game, and family context – we should remember that too much of anything is still too much.

We witnessed a cyberwar game between the Chinese and the Americans in the spring of 2001, provoked by the forced landing on Chinese soil of an American spy plane. According to Vigilinx, based in New Jersey, and i-Defense, based in Virginia, Chinese hackers reacted by trying to paralyze the White House by bombarding it with e-mail. More than twenty other government sites, and even some business sites, were targeted. In retaliation, American hackers launched e-mail attacks on some twenty Chinese sites. (When the dust finally settled, there were media reports that according to i-Defense, pro-American computer hackers hit 350 Chinese sites, and Chinese hackers hit 37 American ones.)

TWENTY-EIGHTH PARADOXICAL LAW
Though it is virtual, digital space is much more vulnerable than the real world.

Cyberwarriors destroy their adversary's communication network, as we saw with the first American strikes (graphite bombs) on Serbia during the 1999 war in Kosovo. They aim to throw the enemy's communication networks into disarray as opposed to wreaking massive physical destruction. (It's interesting to note that the internet arose from the desire to create a digital communication network with no centre, which would be difficult to destroy in the event of war.) Cyberwarriors also manage global communication – they control the stories that are circulated – by having more strategic information than their adversary. Cyberwar is waged by small groups (elites) that can communicate perfectly among themselves rather than large numbers of massively armed troops.

THE DEVIL'S SITE

Algerian military dissidents in the Algerian Free Officers Movement created a mysterious Web site using the initials of the national popular army: anp.org. On it, they denounced the depravity of the regime, revealed the true results of the national election, and presented readings of Algerian events that differed from official versions. The dissidents saw themselves as cybercommandos. Their site is an interesting one, due to its positioning and success, which forced the Algerian government to take notice of it. When the Algerian government denounced them and accused them of collusion with the enemy because they had opened their site to foreign countries, they defended themselves by asserting that they had done what was necessary at the time – they would have gone to the devil's site in order to fight for their country. The Israeli-Palestinian conflict has also been transformed into a cyberwar, for which NetVision and Amman alwababa.com, the largest Israeli and Arab suppliers of internet access for public services, companies, and ordinary citizens, paid the price.

There is no doubt that every country must now protect against terrorist attacks on its internet network, because such a network is essential to coordinating its activities. The internet, first thought of as a non-hierarchical structure that would be invulnerable to traditional attack (it has no command centre at which bombs could be targeted), has one Achilles heel: it is bidirectional. Every originating or relay point in the network can be targeted by any other point within it. The network is therefore extremely vulnerable because it is open to the world and can be attacked from any other point in the world. So how do we seal it up? What impenetrable firewalls do we use to protect our vital computers? Can't seasoned terrorists decipher the codes, enter the Pentagon, and even order Pentagon computers to attack or self-destruct? Cyberterrorist attacks can be much faster and more insidious, unpredictable, and dangerous than missile attacks. And they no longer depend on military strike force; they rely instead on the mathematical intelligence of isolated or marginal terrorists. Control, negotiation, and decision making are becoming much less reliable courses of action. We are living more and more dangerously.

FROM THE BUNKER TO THE WALL OF FIRE

Here is one perverse effect of an increasingly sophisticated technology: there is no virtual bunker for the internet. Underground armed concrete bunkers are much more effective against bomb attacks than the firewalls protecting strategic computers are against internet terrorist attacks.

In 2000, Bill Clinton's specialist in the fight against terrorism clearly acknowledged this when he said that foreign military powers were exploring the possibility of cyberattacks on American

infrastructures: electricity production, telecommunications, transportation. And as if in response, ultranationalist Russian leader
Vladimir Zhirinovsky insisted, "we can bring the entire West to its
knees with our Russian computer specialists. Let us put viruses into
their secret programs ... and they will not be able to do anything."[1]
All of this echoes statements made by the director of the FBI before
the US Senate the same year: "while we have yet to see a significant
instance of 'cyber terrorism' with widespread disruption of critical
infrastructures, all of these facts portend the use of cyber attacks
by terrorists to cause pain to targeted governments or civilian populations by disrupting critical systems."[2] As a result, Clinton asked
the Senate for a 2000 budget allocation of $2 billion for the fight
against cyberterrorism. Experts say that the computer system of a
plane in flight could be remotely targeted and the plane brought
down, because all the vital functions of a plane are computerized.

Since then, terrorist groups, including Al-Qaeda, have been
exploiting the internet, directly or indirectly, to commit information terrorism. Fundamentalists and terrorists – even those based
in remote areas – are becoming experts in digital technologies.

VIOLENCE, GAMING, AND ENTERTAINMENT

The media have changed the world. They have transformed it into
a spectacle in which the distinction between games, entertainment,
and violence is effaced. Violence combines with the media to
achieve its objectives, and at the same time it is made common-
place within this daily spectacle. Mass media was born with the
rotary press and television, and its power has become such that the
entertainment economy – for which phenomenal growth is forecast
in the twenty-first century – is using it as a model. Perhaps the baby
boomers, who are going to enjoy a long and relatively healthy
retirement, will partially and belatedly bear out the predictions of
sociologist Joffre Dumazedier, who forecast the rise of leisure in
wealthy countries. Certainly, entertainment has become a major
profit sector in such countries. As situationist Guy Debord pointed
out, we distract ourselves in an imaginary world, a fake world, a
world of media and spectacle that substitutes itself for the real
world and often conceals the real world's misery. The sets and
trappings of popular TV series take on new life as installations in
theme parks or hotel casino complexes, and this phenomenon has

attained a new level with digital technologies, in which violence can so closely resemble television entertainment.

Violence has achieved incredible expressive force in the entertainment industry. The best (or worst) example of this is found in the electronic games marketed by American and European corporations. When they are accused of encouraging violence, their promoters insist that these games have the beneficial cathartic effect of Greek tragedies. At the 1997 edition of the gigantic American e3 Trade Show, a leading video game publisher put up posters in its booth bearing slogans like "It's better to pretend to kill ten people in a game and to really kill one in the street," and "Violence is in all of us. Games set us free of it."

With violent television dramas reaching record audiences, public opinion has begun pointing a finger at the fictional violence industry. It causes real violence, the public maintains, particularly among young people, who are major consumers of games and television. Among the young, violence is trivialized, while within the US adult population the crime rate is dropping dramatically. This trend forces us to think hard about cyberviolence and its repercussions. The fantasies of cyberpower offered to young people, who naturally identify with the new electronic civilization, blur the line between the game and the real act, between arcade laser guns and firearms that kill for real. The violent games of the digital world do little to appease our violent impulses; instead, they liberate them and make them familiar.

CYBERVIOLENCE

The profound transformation of our values and representations of the world, supported by the excesses of the new priests of the cybermyth, involves fear and violence, even though computers seem much gentler than the old industrial machines. The violence – particularly terrorist violence – is proportionate to the identity-based resistance of groups who feel economically and culturally under attack from the arrogant American myth and its evangelists. The American embassies and the great financial edifices of New York have suffered the dramatic consequences of this, and the suffering will continue. The violent attack against the spirit and the material interests of groups marginalized by the triumph of e-capitalism has, in turn, engendered violence.

Within privileged countries, there are many who have not embraced the new electronic civilization – due to their religious convictions, or political traditionalism, or fear of change – and so they take refuge in cults that run the gamut from fundamentalism, to archaism, to Scientology. A number of the founders of these cults seem to have perceived the virtues of the new capitalism and have learned to exploit the naïveté of their followers, who are rendered helpless by the speed and the violence of the changes they are witnessing. Some of the cults are pacifist, others are violent, yet others draw their members into suicide pacts. Cults like these will likely continue to flourish due to the loss of influence of major religions and the destabilization of our image of the world.

CYBERCRIME

Not all is rosy in cyberspace. The internet has opened itself up to the activities of criminals as it has to those of the businesspeople and artists who quickly understood its potential. We no longer speak only of software, but also of crimeware.

Bank servers are as vulnerable as those of the Pentagon, and there are more fraud artists tempted by the lure of easy money than there are determined cyberterrorists. The amount of money circulating on such networks is vast, and the carefully encrypted code numbers – notably credit card numbers – attached to the files that contain it are not very difficult for a seasoned computer programmer to decrypt. Fraud is rampant. The banks protect themselves up to a point, and the insurance companies take care of the rest.

KPMG Consulting conducted a perception study in an effort to understand the attitudes of companies engaged in e-commerce. Its report, published in Quebec in 2000, notes first of all that companies and financial institutions do not readily admit to having been victims of fraud because they want to avoid tainting the credibility of their supposedly secure transaction systems. The report also lists a number of crime categories: protection racketeering (when cyberblackmail is perpetrated by someone who has managed to copy a computer database, or who threatens to block an e-commerce site – witness the simultaneous blocking of Yahoo!, eBay, and Amazon in 2000); misappropriation of funds; hacking of marketable files, such as music or other cultural works; theft of strategic information, like confidential medical or tax files; and distribution of destructive viruses.

In 1994, the French government instituted the Brigade centrale de répression de la criminalité informatique (the "Central Brigade to Crack Down on Computer Crime"); and in 1999 it established the Office central de lutte contre la criminalité liée aux technologies de l'information et de la communication (the "Central Office to Fight Crimes Related to Information and Communication Technologies") and the Centre d'alerte de secours sur l'internet (the "Emergency Internet Alert Centre"). All of these bodies were intended to help the state fight computer attacks. The creation and multiplication of such institutions testifies to an awareness of the dangers and difficulties involved in mastering the situation. Most countries now have police experts dedicated to the task, but their numbers are insufficient, given the dramatic rise of cybercrime. In 1999, in France alone, there were approximately 4,000 officially reported computer crimes, while the US Federal Trade Commission on Internet Fraud received 18,000 complaints that year. Also in 1999, the FBI estimated computer fraud on the stock exchange at $10 billion (the Securities and Exchange Commission, the agency that monitors the stock exchange, receives on average 300 fraud complaints per day). And Internet Fraud Watch recorded more than 10,000 complaints that year – an increase of 42 per cent over the previous year. Many of us receive e-mails from African or other countries announcing that we have won $50 million in a government lottery or that we have inherited millions from an unknown uncle; all that we have to do is send several hundred dollars to facilitate the cash transfer or to purchase an "export permit." This particular cyberplague is spreading – it's still a threat in 2006.

Gangs and drug dealers are using the internet more and more often to launder their money, moving funds through a series of banks located in banana republics. Some of these banks don't even really exist – their addresses are the island countries of the virtual world of the internet. From their comfortable quarters in cyberspace, they process the cash flows of their very real clients.

The globalization of the internet requires co-operation among international investigation and crackdown services, and this is why the cyberpolice now hold international conferences. A G8 of cybercrime was organized in Paris in June 2000 on the theme of providing security and confidence in cyberspace. Three hundred representatives from the world's wealthiest countries and Russia met, among them police officers, judges, industrialists, and politicians.

In 2001, the Council of Europe established a European convention to fight cybercrime. It granted the police broad powers of investigation and authorized them to conduct investigations of internet service providers, who are required to keep a history of the files that flow through their services (at first, they had to do so for a period of only sixty days, but this was later extended). This convention merits mention because it is the first international treaty to establish crime monitoring on the Web. To forge the agreement, a compromise had to be reached with the defenders of privacy, who wanted safeguards.

The cyberpolice also work to locate sites with pedophilia content or that are racist or terrorist in nature. But there are not yet many laws for them to employ in their efforts to characterize virtual crime and obtain convictions, because cybercrime leaves so few traces – no digital fingerprints, no DNA – and it can be committed from foreign countries or from anonymous or immediately abandoned computers. Police investigations have demonstrated that criminal gangs, like those involved in prostitution networks, are proliferating on the internet in a disturbing way. Cyberspace is as vast as the planet. Its laws are still incomplete or non-existent, and its free flow remains unhampered. Within the space of just a few years, cybercrime has become a major challenge for the police, who must now be computer experts on top of being good detectives.

The 2006 RSA Conference, held in San Jose, California, attracted some 14,000 experts in computer and network security. Most of them were pessimistic, admitting that the good guys are losing the battle. Alex Shipp of Messagelabs declared: "My company scans 13 million e-mails a day, and of that e-mail we stop between 3 million and 10 million messages a day because they contain some kind of malware (malicious software). Of the malware we're seeing, 99.9% is crimeware – something where the bad guys are trying to steal money from the end user. We're detecting one to five new species of virus a day and seeing 100 to 200 new phishing sites appearing every day." Jeannette Jarvis, security systems product manager at Boeing, commented that "Crimeware is sky-rocketing, even as the stream of new viruses holds relatively steady … But the biggest threat to us are targeted attacks. We have seen targeted attacks coming from China that are specifically looking to transmit engineering data and other intellectual property to the attackers."[3]

Why has this crime explosion occurred in cyberspace? Because its victims are so easy to access, its perpetrators enjoy anonymity, and the cyberworld breeds a sense of unreality that encourages transgressions and violence. It has become an often unsavoury place, an outlet for vice, a playground for abusers. In the digital world, we can act immediately, remotely, according to our desires. The principle of pleasure triumphs over the principle of reality. We can indulge our most primitive instincts with near impunity and entertain the illusion that we are truly acting because the distinction between the real and the virtual is transient. This situation incites all manner of transgressions and violence, which will inevitably spill over into the real word.

TWENTY-NINTH PARADOXICAL LAW
Because of its virtual nature, the digital realm encourages transgressions as well as the destruction of the reality principle and the elevation of the pleasure principle; it fosters a transition to action, delinquency, and criminality in the real world.

20: Electronic Primitivism

*The extraordinary digital adventure
is still in its primitive infancy.*

THE DISCOVERY OF
A NEW ELECTRONIC WORLD

At the dawn of the third millennium, science and technology are turning our modern cultures upside down. The new communication technologies, under the influence of multimedia digital convergence, are reinstituting an interactive multi-sensory experience that for the five centuries since the invention of print was subjugated to a simplistic linearity. We are rediscovering the aesthetic virtues of primitivism, and, in many respects, the beginnings of this new civilization evoke an electronic primitivism. The icons on our computer screens are the African masks of the new millennium. We are at the dawn of a great civilization.

Bill Gates recently said that we will soon arrive at the end of the beginning of the digital era. By this he meant the beginning of a period of consolidation following the madness of the dot.coms. He added that he thought "this next decade is the big one. This is the decade where your involvement with computing will be very pervasive ... anything you want to do, there is no hardware limitation that will hold this back – with one exception, and that's the cost of broadband communications primarily to the home."[1]

ELECTRONIC NEO-PRIMITIVISM

I will venture, on the strength of several convergent observations, to talk about neo-primitivism in relation to this new civilization of electronic communication born with the third millennium. First of all, we should recognize that as amazing as they may seem to us, the new electronic technologies are still fairly primitive. Connecting a computer to the internet or installing a CD-ROM is still a labour-intensive process, one that recalls the galena radios of yesteryear, which required the user to engage in much experimentation before he or she could actually hear anything from them. Within a single generation, current technologies will appear to us as primitive as the first mid-twentieth-century computers that used accordion-folded perforated cards.

THE INTERNET AND
THE AFRICAN TAM-TAM

Electronic language corresponds much better to African drumming than it does to printed language – indeed, to writing itself. This is not only because it can be multi-sensory, but also because it has a binary base (1 or 0) and its identification and authentication protocols are very similar to those of the tribal tam-tam. Before transmitting a message from one village to another, the drummer announces that a message is coming using a specific rhythm comparable to the electronic signature that authenticates the identity of the sender. And the drummer uses "bruitiste" language, alternating sound (1) and silence (0), building their sequences and their rhythms according to a structure that is very similar to the binary language of the computer and nothing like phonetic language. Furthermore, the binary nature of computer language is much more primitive than the rhythmic codes of the African tam-tam. It's the processing power of computers that makes the difference, not the structure of the language.

In traditional societies, communication was multi-sensory and part of the collective rites. Contemporary multimedia re-establishes, through both mass media and self-media (a distinction established by René Berger before he had even heard of the internet), an integrative collective communication that attempts to cross cultural divides and promote a common popular culture of the dominant middle class.

Writing and print separated individuals and social groups; the new electronic media bring them closer together, often in spite of themselves. Of course, you would have to subscribe to the myth of communication to believe that these new technologies can create a harmonious, transparent global society, one that is egalitarian, peaceable, and devoid of class differences. But the movement towards re-establishing communication as a group of collective rituals is very real, and the interactive mechanisms offered by artists, television, the internet, and touch-screen public information kiosks contribute to this.

COMPUTER SCREENS AS STAINED GLASS WINDOWS

The bluish and ethereal light that emanates from our computer screens is otherworldly. Contemporary cathode ray screens bring to mind the stained glass windows of the Middle Ages. Like these windows, they are two-dimensional filters with no realistic depth that draw the spirit towards another world – in times past, the world of God; today, the world of the virtual. The figures that they display – vividly coloured cut-out icons with outlines like black lead – show us illuminated paths to other places. Our cathode ray stained glass windows are the transitional interfaces between the real and the virtual, and they control the rites of initiation. We slip into the fusing light of the cyberworld, and we are absorbed the way we were once absorbed by the divine Great Whole.

It is interesting to visit stained-glass sites to explore the analogy further. And notice that the cathode ray screen is a much more effective medium than the art book when it comes to diffusing light through stained glass.

THE INTERNET IS A CHURCH

The physical rituals of the contemporary e-world are religious. We don't get down on our knees, of course, but we assume a position of meditation and concentration before the tabernacle-computer. When we click to open the door, the cathode ray window blazes to life in response to our call and guides us towards the cybergod. We make contact.

We are no longer alone. Virtual communication evokes the symbolism of communion. Through our physical posture and a remote digital connection, through our initiate's knowledge of the requisite gestures, through the rites of Windows or other shared software, through the magic click of mouse on icon, we commune with fellow cybernauts in the electronic light of the cybercommunity. And this cybercommunity enfolds us – infinite and omnipresent, near and far. Our gestures are subjected to the invisible judgmental gaze that follows us in all of our navigations. We commune with the virtual community of each site, of each chapel of the Digital Church. And we find intensity and comfort within those communities; we are moved and connected.

So we should not be surprised to find in cyberspace so many religious portals and on-line centres for meditation and spirituality. The faithful can attend mass via their home computers using RealAudio. On-line confession is destined to become common practice, once confidentiality can be assured. There are already some religious sites where you can confess your sins and clear your conscience. (And in the US, there is a police site called Self Arrest, where you can cop to your crime and turn yourself in.)

ELECTRONIC ICONS AND PICTOGRAMS

At times, cathode ray screens also bring to mind old parchments and books of spells from the Middle Ages, with their coloured illuminations. A language of cathode ray pictograms and icons has appeared with the advent of mass communication and screens, and it hearkens back to African masks and the stained glass of the Middle Ages, without rivalling their beauty. It's true that the phenomenon had already manifested itself in public signage – traffic and highway signs, consumer product symbols, and so on. In the century of speed and globalization, we needed to reintroduce a pictographic language that could be instantly and universally understood, especially for market and public security purposes. The pictogram has reasserted itself to the detriment of phonetic writing and language diversity. Pictographic language has also re-emerged, in a more complex and almost multi-sensory form, in

comic books. Apollinaire, with his *calligrammes*, and later the lettrist
poets, were aware of this. Again, we think of the intuitive McLuhan,
who asserted this return of iconic and quasi-sculptural language;
and in the 1970s, Jean Cloutier addressed the subject of an audio-
scripto-visual language in *La Communication audio-scripto-visuelle, ou
l'ère d'Emerec*. The message is a massage (tactile).

A NEW MODE OF READING
FOR A TACTILE LANGUAGE

Electronic communication has reinforced this trend considerably.
We know that reading on the screen is much slower than reading
on paper. Studies show that in the inflationary mass of all sorts of
communications, grabbing the attention of the audience requires
effective visual or auditory signals, a task for which phonetic language is no longer sufficient. We must use boldface, italics, underlining, or large characters; we need to employ cut-and-paste,
typographical surprises, original page layouts, and colours. Web
page creators know that surfers only read a tiny portion of the text.
They jump like kangaroos from site to site, page to page, sentence
to word, image to hyperlink, clicking on anything that moves. Studies show that only 16 per cent of cybernauts read any text attentively
on their computer screens.

THIRTIETH PARADOXICAL LAW
The sophisticated visual language of the digital realm revives the icons
and pictograms of primitive languages.

21: The Magical Click and the Digital Imagination

"Oh, man is a God when he dreams, a beggar when he thinks"
(Friedrich Hölderlin, *Hyperion*).

THE MAGICAL POWER OF THE INTERNET

The strength of the digital realm lies not only in the exceptional technical performance of things digital, for which the phone, radio, and television – now much easier to manipulate and more user-friendly – had already prepared us. Technical power responds to a human drive for power, but the internet also makes the dream of planetary communication within the global village resonate within us, and it draws another powerful symbolic force from this dream. Why does the internet impress us more than the phone? No doubt because it emerged more suddenly and more universally. It was decades before the phone was widely adopted. Its penetration was technically difficult and therefore slow; its technological power is still limited to a single voice, while the digital technology of the internet makes multimedia possible and is infinitely more powerful than electromagnetic transmission. Plus, the internet can reach us anywhere in the world, or almost anywhere, even without cabling.

THE DIGITAL ACT: THE CLICK

On the internet, a magical click makes electronic purchases or shoots messages off to distant locales. And that click is generally irreversible – click in haste and repent at leisure. The click can make things appear or disappear; it can create or permanently erase. Its simplicity, speed, and effectiveness are magical qualities that reveal the extent of its power. And this magical click opens the door to the cyberworld the way "sesame" opens Ali Baba's cave.

THE DIGITAL PHONE

Will utopia soon be achieved? Will the cell phone, which an increasing number of us carry at all times – the wallet on the left and the cell phone on the right in a man's jacket, and everything jumbled together in a woman's purse – soon replace everything that fills our bags and pockets, including wallet, social insurance card, credit cards, business cards, driver's license, electronic agenda, pen, and key ring? Manufacturers such as Nokia, Ericsson, Sonera, Motorola, Alcatel, Siemens, Cisco, and Lucent aimed to have one billion cybermen and cyberwomen carrying cell phones by 2005.

The mobile phone, or cell (a hybrid word bridging technology and life), stands to be the big winner in digital convergence. It combines some outstanding qualities:

- It is portable. Its hardware has been remarkably improved and miniaturized; it's getting smaller and lighter as its performance improves.
- It is on the cutting edge of wireless connectivity, being the only piece of digital equipment that has dispensed with the tangle of often-incompatible cables, wires, and outlets, with which other equipment – televisions, computers, and all sorts of transmitters and receivers – is still saddled.
- It is the subject of advanced research into developing efficient batteries for very long autonomous use.
- It is mobile. Due to its wireless connectivity, whether analogue or digital, and to the network of satellites currently under construction, it will soon be connected everywhere in the world. This is a mighty, almost magical power, both for communication and for the security of people and things. How many people in distress have already been saved by a cell phone?
- Not only will it soon be connected everywhere in the world, but it will also provide access to everything: databases and personal communications.

- It will allow non-industrialized countries (African nations, for example) to skip the long and costly step of building cabled infrastructures. This is an extraordinary benefit for emerging countries and for isolated, inaccessible, or hostile regions of the globe.
- It has a keyboard, a screen, a miniaturized computer with software and memory, and a sound system. And it has an integrated handset transceiver with an antenna. You can insert cards into it – smartcards – to add electronic money, memory, or specific software. Manufacturers are developing high-definition colour screens the size of the cell phone itself. The keypad will soon be replaced by a voice-command function using voice-recognition software. Plus, you will be able to integrate countless peripherals – connect the phone to a large computer, printer, or fax, use it as a Walkman, or link a micro-camera and send the pictures you take. As with a computer, you'll use the Naviroller to click on a menu to retrieve the files you want.

The cell phone, with its high-definition screen, is already capable of receiving audio/video streaming, including short films. As a result, the phone function that dominates today will lose its importance. The cell phone will instead become a complete, portable, miniaturized computer, with a multi-functional, universal interface that, among other things, will allow you to:

- establish phone communication between two people anywhere in the world at a very low cost or no cost at all, with quality that rivals that of the traditional telephone, and soon in internet mode (IP protocol)
- access all the services of the internet and make many of your purchases via e-commerce from anywhere in the world
- order drinks and other items remotely from public vending machines and pay for purchases using e-cash, putting an end to plastic credit cards
- open the door of your house, office, or car
- remotely control your home automation system
- remotely control your TV
- ensure your physical security with a satellite GPS (global positioning system) and an alarm
- monitor your health with programmed indicators (blood sugar, blood pressure, and so on)

- access practical information related to travel, professional activities, leisure, and more (for example, financial services, weather updates), thanks to wireless application protocols

Each person's digital identity, assigned at birth, will be the number at which he or she can be reached by cell phone or land line. Does this make you shudder a little, the way Huxley's *Brave New World* did? Perhaps it shouldn't, because this lifetime ID number will allow you to do so much, as I have mentioned – pay for things anywhere using your digital phone and access your medical file in an emergency, among other things. And, as a security measure, the phone will be able to recognize your finger and voice prints. This powerful interface could therefore serve the best and the worst ends.

Government auctions of frequencies, now a common occurrence, have resulted in licence purchases in the billions of dollars. The market holds much promise. Thanks to a universal standard, which will become recognized, and high-bandwidth, third-generation cell phones (3Gs), the mobile phone will provide efficient access to an increasing number of internet services, and the frontiers of possibility will recede once again. It's a major step, and one that will supposedly make our lives easier. Have we discovered the magic wand that will allow us to communicate instantaneously anywhere in the world – to know, say, control, buy, or sell anything; to have fun, get help, and (soon) vote? It seems that way, at least for those who have electronic money in the bank.

In any case, here is the technological extension of the most powerful human being we can imagine at the beginning of the new millennium. And the magical cell phone will be shaped by brilliant ergonomists to fit perfectly into a man's or a woman's hand – the magic is within reach. But be careful not to lose your cell phone. It would be like losing your heart – unless your cell phone can find you by using a transmission chip implanted under your skin.

BUT MY BODY IS NOT A SMALL BUSINESS

The digital simulacrum that we are currently constructing within the empire of computing is taking on incredible force. Of course, the economy is the ultimate domain of numbers. And democracy itself is becoming digital, dependent upon the numerical results of elections and public opinion polls. My body is also numbers. When the doctor sends me to the hospital, I am given long forms to fill out. These forms are replete with numbers – numbers that provide a detailed account of my white blood cells, the primary metals and minerals in my blood, my blood pressure, blood clotting rate, age, temperature, and so on. The doctor will tally up these numbers to determine the state of my health. It's as if I were a company undergoing an audit to determine my financial health. Any deviation from the statistical standard is significant. The doctor will prescribe drugs to ensure that I regain that standard, and therefore an acceptable level of health, just as an experienced company manager will take measures to ensure that the accounts are balanced and the company regains its financial health. And yet I am not an equation, a logarithm, or a statistical table. I cultivate difference. My body is not a small business. Still, my body, my company, my country's economy and its social equilibrium are all healed through numbers: more calcium, less cholesterol, more investment, fewer employees, an increase of a quarter of a point in the central bank interest rate, a 1 per cent reduction in my income taxes, an increase in the unemployment rate, a decrease in blood pressure ...

Now my DNA is read as a barcode, and the line on my electrocardiogram resembles the zigzag that tracks the market value of my stocks. The images of my body are computer-generated in hospital on cathode ray screens, like the false colour images of distant celestial bodies or varieties of plankton in the oceans, monitored by satellite.

THE WORLD HAS BECOME
AN ELECTRONIC SPREADSHEET

Why do we interpret almost all phenomena – biology, genomes, physics, chemistry, the economy, social and political life, nature and the infinitely large or infinitely small universe, even our psychological and intimate lives – with numbers, still more numbers, and only numbers? Is there anything left in the world that cannot be translated onto a computer screen, into computer language, via numbers, quantities, numerical sequences?

THE NEW TRINITY

The hold of numbers over our universe, an almost totalitarian hold, reflects a singular mode of thinking, exclusive and dominant. And this excess of ideology needs to be demystified, because the digital realm is also a very powerful instrument in the hands of what appears to be the new religion of the twenty-first century – a religion based on the trinity of the economy, science, and technology. This trinity is not inherently bad. It is perhaps by far the least objectionable of the possible power trinities, and it is as valid as the Holy Trinity: the Father, the Son, and the Holy Ghost.

BUT WHERE HAS THE MYTHICAL NARRATIVE OF THE CONTEMPORARY WORLD GONE?

Now, when the metaphor of the digital simulacrum has occupied our mental space and evacuated all reference to the story of the origins of the world, it is no longer enough to consider numbers as symbolic attributes of the original mythical narrative. We could see narrative and numbers as the two traditional expressions of the myth. Numbers originated well before Pythagoras, in the Indo-European tradition. But it is safe to say that the mythical force of numbers is found ritually in almost all known early societies. Numbers are often symbolic and ritualistic attributes of mythical forces, the stories of which explain the origin and the meaning of the world.

The widespread tendency to translate the aspects or virtues of a mythical figure into numbers is tied to the very rhythm of nature – to the alternation between day and night, to the cycle of the seasons, to the stages of life, and to the five cardinal points of primitive societies. Why did God need six days to create the earth? Why does the number 3 come up so often in myths, all the way up to the Hegelian dialectic? Three describes the family structure: the mother and the father beget the child. And the cycle of the moon suggests the number 7. Chinese mythology and the musical scale also invoke this number. The four elements are a basic illustration of the main aspects of nature, itself deified. Numbers have therefore been invested with symbolic virtues, condensing the forces of the mythical figure into a simple language. We could think of numbers as the symbolic figures of narrative that persist even after the oral tradition of the original story that carried them has been lost.

Cultural production is also split between the tradition of story-telling and the tradition of numbers. Music, architecture, all the visual arts, and dance are above all expressions of numbers, whereas literature, opera, the theatre, and film spring from the narrative tradition, even though narrative and numbers merge in many works. The digital arts themselves, which are dominated by numbers, certainly do not exclude narrative. As well, numbers seem to speak by themselves. They are displayed in ascending or descending equilibrated curves, and statistics establish the norm. The absence of difference or the growth in a curve take on the value of virtue and explanation. The metaphor of the rise of a growth curve on the stock market, for example, or the popularity of a political party, describes an economy or the management of public affairs as positive. But what do numbers tell us about the origin or the destiny of the world? What meaning do they give the human condition?

THE MYTH OF TECHNO-SCIENCE

The mission of explaining the world to us seems to have fallen to techno-science. Science is built on, and expresses itself, in numbers. And its language, distilled by the processing power of computer technologies, seems increasingly capable of explaining everything. But what meaning does science give to the world? What values does it instill, and what dominant ideology does it found? It seems to be taking the place of religion as a discourse of truth. Is that really what Marxism had in mind for us, according to the theory of scientific dialectical materialism? Will capitalist thought adopt such a belief as well – one that is already very much in evidence in science fiction? Can we say that science is the myth of the digital simulacrum? And if this is the case, a question arises: What myths drive or underlie both contemporary science and technology and the virtual world that they engender?

THE MYTHS OF THE CYBERWORLD

We know which Marxist myths of socialist democracy also presented themselves as models of democracy. We now need to decipher the new myths of the cyberworld utopia that aspire to replace them. The cyberworld is paved with good intentions, as was the communist utopia, but it will not necessarily be as nightmarish – although it, too, presents itself as a new Eden, and the virtues it sings of are as worthwhile as those that inspired Marx and Engels. And, upon reflection, the magical thought that the cyberworld expresses, which conceals its technological and market totalitarianism, makes it truly worrying at times.

THE FUTURE OF THE PAST

Although our eyes are turned obsessively towards the future, we must also look to the past in order to orient ourselves. We must recall the great creators of the Renaissance, symbolized by Leonardo da Vinci, because they faced such challenges in their own time.

Although they dominate our era, magical thinking, the irrational, and technological and scientific power, left to their own devices, create an explosive mix. This is why new cultural and political means must again be found to overcome the dangers of the human journey and pursue a path towards the unknown. The unknown can seem primitive and savage. The archaism of the soul, which has resurged with the advent of the digital realm, never disappeared. Today it expresses itself in never-before-seen modes of power that excite the wolflike instinct for power that we all harbour.

22: The Digital Golden Calf

Numbers are neither inherently good nor inherently bad,
but we must denounce our cold worship of the digital golden calf.

THE NEW CARDINAL POINTS

It's no understatement to say that our universe has changed a lot
of late. And it has lost its bearings. Quantum science and the
imperialism of the new economy have awakened parallel and chaotic universes. The five cardinal points of the primary numbers
have drifted with the internationalist current of our political geography. They have become Reality, the Imaginary, Arrogance,
Distress, and – at the centre of them all – Money.

The illuminated towers of impudent Hong Kong soar into the
night like computer cards to write their binary sequences of arrogant *ex votos*. At the same time, in the same world (can it really be
the same world?), a torrent of mud buries sleeping families in a
Peruvian mountainside *favela*. Very real mud, heavy and viscous
and suffocating, that seals voiceless mouths. The real world is not
made up of numbers alone. We are not living in an all-digital
realm. Although the digital fascinates us, we must preserve our
instinct for the real, which we still have and which secretly tells us
what to trust. We have to cultivate our critical freedom, because it
tells us what to mistrust.

The earth's rotational axis is shifting with the shock of progress.
It passes through the hands of an African child dying in his
mother's arms, and through the hands of a child of the North who

playfully crosses the space-time of the cyberworld, surfing on a spray of electrons. And the 9/11 terrorist attacks on the Pentagon and the World Trade Center will go down in history as the terrible symbol of a fractured world.

THE COUNTER-SHOCK OF POVERTY

The way the world is going is scandalous, and the scandal is becoming digital. Everything is measured and displayed in numbers on the screens of the new civilization: the temperature and the level of air pollution, the prices of things, the time, our physical and financial health, our taxes and profits, our ages, our work hours, the number of characters in this book, the speed of my car, the altitude of the plane I travel in, the barcodes of every consumer object, my phone number and the duration of my calls, the number of my genes and chromosomes, the tally of those born and those who will die of AIDS or malnutrition, the binary system of sexuality, 1 or 0. And those who would like to counter quantitative logic and numbers with qualitative thought – the spirit of things, the subtlety and nuances you can't put a number to – must admit that the qualitative world also expresses itself through numbers.

But we should not fault the numbers themselves, even though their omnipresence is becoming oppressive – they permeate the very air we breathe. It is true that they control government policies, the decisions of banks and multinationals, our daily activities, but they also reveal to us daily on the control panel of the vessel of humanity the glaring injustices that afflict our planet. It is their cold logic that appalls us, digital logic, to which we sacrifice ourselves over and over again as though to a golden calf. Because this cold and cynical logic of immediate profit and financial speculation seems to widen the gap every day between the rich, who get richer, and the poor, who get poorer. Over-consumption and malnutrition are developing at the same rate, with a little corruption thrown into the mix. How can we correct this explosive situation? Will digital technologies help us, as the optimists maintain? Or will they instead impose the imperialism of the North on the countries of the South?

In the great battle of ideas, technology seems to have won. Those deep and thoughtful souls who fear the future seem to have been vanquished by the carefree futurophiles. But to what point will people accept this logic as inevitable? The pendulum of time never stops swinging. And from which cardinal point will the one who holds the jokers appear?

THE CHILDREN OF THE CYBERWORLD

We have all noticed that our children are getting along in the cyberworld much better than we are. We navigate its surface, but our children frolic in it like dolphins. They were born into it and have no first-hand memory of the old world that came before. They will inherit this new world, and they will not contest that inheritance.

Children like to play, and they learn through play; in this, the cyberworld has fulfilled their desires and needs. We have witnessed the proliferation of consoles and joysticks, teddy bears with chips, interactive Barbie dolls, intelligent mice and rattles – all of which combine digital technology and rainbow-coloured plastic to delight and educate our little ones. These playthings are now so varied and plentiful that they constitute a universe in and of themselves – not counting the thousands of CD-ROMS and computer games for children.

A UNIVERSE OF GAMES
AND DIGITAL SEDUCTIONS

We have been witness to a lovely encounter between an awakening generation and a newborn digital simulacrum that presents itself to us not as the far-off and austere beyond of a transcendental religion, but as a universe of games and seductions. What will the consequences be? Heedlessness does not seem to have found a niche, but shifting from the cyberworld to the real world, when the time comes to submit ourselves to the principle of reality, might not be easy. The dialectic of the digital simulacrum and the real world has not yet enacted its final movement.

THE DIGITAL GARDEN

The city of Bury St Edmunds, England, has installed an internet-connected bench in its Abbey Gardens. Local people go there with their laptops to surf surrounded by trees and flowers. "Park it, plug it and the World is all yours with this wired bench," the city announced.

As the children awake, the solitary navigator dreams of resting a moment on that bench. I go to the gardens and settle in. The clear summer light filters through the brilliant green foliage. Birds flit back and forth in the sunshine. My sense of time diminishes, and I forget the text on the screen. There is no longer depth or distance, only a soft electronic surface. I fall asleep and dream in the digital garden. I believe I know everything, understand everything, love everything. And suddenly it's night. Like a child afraid of the dark, I run in panic towards the digital light.

23: The Thirty Paradoxical Laws of the Digital

The paradoxical laws that give the digital simulacrum its structure are so numerous that they leave little doubt as to the importance of the imaginative domain from which they draw their values and allegorical expression. Generally, a paradox is either the registration of crisis, the dialectical engine of change, or the expression of the societal desires and utopias that we project into the future of the human adventure.

Listed here are the paradoxical laws of the digital realm, a sampling suggestive of the imaginative domain at work in the social, scientific, technological, political, psychological, artistic, and economic fields; they may also serve as a guide for those who want to analyse their predominant trends. Furthermore, one could state many corollaries to these laws, which I present without any claim to Spinoza-like rigour, since it would be intellectually misguided to attempt to reduce the burgeoning and elusive imaginative domain to series of laws and constructs. The imaginative domain does not fall within the scope of inventories and Cartesian logic – on the contrary.

FIRST PARADOXICAL LAW
The regression of the human psyche is proportionate to the advance of technological power.

SECOND PARADOXICAL LAW
Though it appears in gentle guise, the digital revolution has unleashed a radical and brutal force due to its suddenness, its acceleration, its

globalizing logic, and the immediacy of its expansion into all fields of activity.

THIRD PARADOXICAL LAW
Digital technologies evolve more quickly than our ideas.

FOURTH PARADOXICAL LAW
The digital realm, which presents itself as a realistic, utilitarian, and futuristic approach to the world, is in fact a new manifestation of traditional transcendental idealism.

FIFTH PARADOXICAL LAW
Once again, human intelligence is inclined to devalue itself and to renounce its own abilities in favour of a supposedly superior intelligence – this time around, the so-called artificial intelligence of the digital realm.

SIXTH PARADOXICAL LAW
The digital simulacrum appears not as a new attempt to interpret the universe as it is given to us, an attempt that would take its place in a historical series of analogies – magical, religious, naturalistic, vitalistic, organicist, mechanist, and so on – but rather as a powerful new instrumental device that can radically change the world according to human desire.

SEVENTH PARADOXICAL LAW
The cyberworld presents itself as a symbolic space of global connectivity that is apolitical, asocial, and ahistorical, but, in fact, it acts as a socially integrating virtual superstructure that gives power and legitimacy to the new middle class, whose image of the world it expresses and whose dominant ideology it forms.

EIGHTH PARADOXICAL LAW
The cyberworld acts as a virtual outline of the new world reality we are developing. It already constitutes this new reality's basic paradigm in real time and its allegorical metaphor.

NINTH PARADOXICAL LAW
The more powerful and sophisticated digital technology becomes, the greater the risk that the artificial memory it is meant to protect will become ephemeral.

TENTH PARADOXICAL LAW

The digital itself constitutes an extremely powerful and universal tool of interpretation and communication, able to express all languages and all manner of content. Because it is also the network for all communication networks, it has imposed itself with immediate and undeniable success, thus confirming McLuhan's paradox "the medium is the message."

ELEVENTH PARADOXICAL LAW

Despite the unifying and globalizing tendency of its underlying technology and symbolism, the cyberworld will increasingly reflect linguistic and cultural diversity and even contribute to their promotion.

TWELFTH PARADOXICAL LAW

Digital technologies are a powerful agent of cultural and spiritual development. They recover, disseminate, and record all previous cultures. They generate new cultural products and ensure their propagation. Computer language leads to a new aesthetic. The cyberworld comprises and institutionalizes a new cultural space-time that is exceptionally dynamic and communicative.

THIRTEENTH PARADOXICAL LAW

Digital technologies have triggered an explosion of new artistic creation, and they reconcile art with society. They restore the primitive social function of art and call into question the classical and modern fine arts system, which bestowed value on the object and on the unique signature and entailed a market, collectors, and museums.

FOURTEENTH PARADOXICAL LAW

The more that digital arts destroy the stable visual space of classical art and explore the accelerated and destabilizing flux of time and the circumstances in which we are caught up, the more they will lean towards iconic expression, thus renewing links with the tradition of primitive arts.

FIFTEENTH PARADOXICAL LAW

Although the digital realm is based on a simplistic and reductive binary language – 1 or 0 – the resulting new information society depends on imagination and creativity, which henceforth will comprise the principal capital of the new economy.

SIXTEENTH PARADOXICAL LAW

As the digital convergence of the media becomes more established, we rediscover the irreducible specificity of different media and the social uses that distinguish them.

SEVENTEENTH PARADOXICAL LAW

The digital realm favours a fundamental and dynamic new human equilibrium that valorizes opposite poles: even as globalizing tendencies are expressed, tendencies towards fragmentation assert themselves in opposition. On the social level, this translates into an intensified repositioning of the individual in the heart of a communication network oriented towards globalization; and on the political level, into the identity-oriented repositioning of small social groups (villages, communities, regions, countries) facing global groups (federations, large continental free trade zones, international organizations).

EIGHTEENTH PARADOXICAL LAW

Cyberspace has become the political playing field of two opposing conceptions of liberty: on the one hand, a libertarian utopia; and on the other hand, groupthink – the hegemony of ultraliberal ideology.

NINETEENTH PARADOXICAL LAW

The digital realm, which presents itself as a space for individual and commercial freedom that eludes control and even encourages piracy, has in fact the technological potential to become a space for the most radical digital control we can imagine: all information circulating and the profiles of users can be traced, situated, and kept on file.

TWENTIETH PARADOXICAL LAW

The monetary and the digital are two complementary forms of the same language of numbers, which becomes the raw material of the new economy.

TWENTY-FIRST PARADOXICAL LAW

Monetary flow is both the degree zero of human solidarity and the accelerator of the imaginative economy – the i-economy.

TWENTY-SECOND PARADOXICAL LAW

The concepts of citizen of the world and global government promoted by digital globalization are political sophistry and paradoxical non-sense.

TWENTY-THIRD PARADOXICAL LAW

The time/tense of digital globalization affects us, as does the glocal space of the global village, according to the double constraint of the present future – the todaymorrow.

TWENTY-FOURTH PARADOXICAL LAW

Digital technology, while apparently the instrument of global integration, in fact creates societal fractures and a technological apartheid that separates the info-rich and the info-poor.

TWENTY-FIFTH PARADOXICAL LAW

Cyberpedagogy, which promises to be cheaper and more effective, actually costs more and destroys the foundations of traditional pedagogy.

TWENTY-SIXTH PARADOXICAL LAW

Despite its technological nature, the internet acts as a psychotropic drug and activates the unconscious.

TWENTY-SEVENTH PARADOXICAL LAW

The digital realm, despite its technological nature and its basic binary code, releases the most fantastical imaginative processes in all areas of human activity.

TWENTY-EIGHTH PARADOXICAL LAW

Though it is virtual, digital space is much more vulnerable than the real world.

TWENTY-NINTH PARADOXICAL LAW

Because of its virtual nature, the digital realm encourages transgressions as well as the destruction of the reality principle and the elevation of the pleasure principle; it fosters a transition to action, delinquency, and criminality in the real world.

THIRTIETH PARADOXICAL LAW

The sophisticated visual language of the digital realm revives the icons and pictograms of primitive languages.

Notes

CHAPTER TWO

1 Alfred Jarry, *The Supermale*, trans. Ralph Gladstone and Barbara Wright (New York: New Directions), 77.
2 Ray Kurzweil, *The Age of Intelligent Machines* (Cambridge, MA: MIT Press, 1990); *The Age of Spiritual Machines: When Computers Exceed Human Intelligence* (New York: Viking Penguin, 1999), 51.
3 John Markoff, "Tiniest Circuits Hold Prospect of Explosive Computer Speeds," *New York Times*, 16 July 1999.
4 Ray Kurzweil, "Kurzweil's Law," *KurzweilAI.net*, 12 January 2003.
5 See Qinghua Liu, et al., "DNA Computing on Surfaces," *Nature*, 13 January 2000.
6 "Sci/Tech Biological Computer Born," *BBC News*, 2 June 1999, http://news.bbc.co.uk/1/hi/sci/tech/358822.stm.

CHAPTER THREE

1 Herman Khan and Anthony J. Wiener, *The Year 2000: A Framework for Speculation on the Next Thirty-Three Years* (Washington, DC: Hudson Institute, 1967).
2 Michel Saint-Germain, *L'Avenir n'est plus ce qu'il était* (Montreal: Éditions Québec-Amérique, 1993). (Quotation translated by Rhonda Mullins.)

3 Collins Hemingway and Bill Gates, *Business @ the Speed of Thought: Using a Digital Nervous System* (New York: Warner Books, 1999).

4 Pierre Lévy, *La Machine univers: création, cognition et culture informatique* (Paris: La Découverte, 1987). (Quotation translated by Rhonda Mullins.)

CHAPTER FIVE

1 This famous passage is from Edward Gibbon's *The History of the Decline and Fall of the Roman Empire* (1776–88).

2 See Alejandro Piscitelli, *Internet: la imprenta del Siglo XXI* (Buenos Aires: Editorial Gedisa, 2005).

CHAPTER SIX

1 "Gore GII Buenos Aires Speech," Peace Corps Online, http://peacecorpsonline.org/messages/messages/467/2369.html (accessed 5 January 2006).

2 Katie Dean, "And God Said: Let There Be Net," *Wired*, 18 January 2001, www.wired.com/news/culture/0,1284,41229,00.html (accessed 6 January 2006).

3 Evangelisch-lutherische Landeskirche Hannovers, http://www.evlka.de (accessed 3 February 2006).

CHAPTER SEVEN

1 François-René de Chateaubriand, *Les Mémoires d'outre tombe*, vol. 44 (1849–50). (Quotation translated by Rhonda Mullins.)

2 Jorge Luis Borges, *Collected Fictions*, trans. Andrew Hurley (New York: Viking, 1998).

3 International Technology and Trade Associates, Inc., *State of the Internet 2000* (Washington, DC: ITTA, 2000).

4 Derrick de Kerckhove, *Connected Intelligence: The Arrival of the Web Society* (Toronto: Somerville Press, 1997).

CHAPTER EIGHT

1 Eric Flint, "Introducing the Baen Free Library," http://www.baen.com/library (accessed 13 January 2006).

2 David D. Kirkpatrick, "A Stephen King Online Horror Tale Turns into a Mini-Disaster," *New York Times*, 29 November 2000.

3 Geraldine Faes and Yves Eudes, "Guerre ouverte contre le copyright et le droit d'auteur sur les œuvres écrites," *Le Monde*, 7 June 2001. (Quotation translated by Rhonda Mullins.)

4 Nicolas Bourcier and Marlene Duretz, "Le Pivot malgré lui: Frédéric Grolleau amine la seule émission littéraire du Web," *Le Monde*, 5 April 2000. (Quotation translated by Rhonda Mullins.)

5 Reena Jana, "Whitney Speaks: It *Is* Art," *Wired News*, 23 March 2000, http://www.wired.com/news/culture/1,35157–0.html (accessed 16 January 2006).

6 For more information, see Hervé Fischer, *Le Déclin de l'empire hollywoodien* (Montreal: Éditions VLB, 2004); an English translation, *The Decline of the Hollywood Empire*, is forthcoming from Talonbooks, Vancouver.

7 Gabriel Sigrist, "Webbie Tookay, le top model 100% synthétique de l'agence Elite," *Largeur.com*, 20 September 1999, http://www.largeur.com/expArt.asp?artID=199 (accessed 17 January 2006). (Quotation translated by Rhonda Mullins.)

8 Michel Alberganti, "Ananova, première présentatrice virtuelle des informations sur Internet, " *Le Monde*, 21 April 2000. (Quotation translated by Rhonda Mullins.)

9 See Edgar Morin, *Pour sortir du XXᵉ siècle* (Paris: Nathan, 1981).

10 Nicholas Negroponte, *Being Digital* (New York: Knopf, 1995), 229.

CHAPTER NINE

1 See Hervé Fischer, "ENDNOTE: A Crisis in Contemporary Art?" *Leonardo*, 1 February 2000, www.ingentaconnect.com/content/mitpress/ leon/2000/00000033/00000001/art00014 (accessed 6 March 2006).

2 Jeremy Rifkin, *The Age of Access: "The New Culture of Hypercapitalism, Where All of Life Is a Paid-for Experience* (New York: Jeremy P. Tarcher and Putnam, 2000), 28.

CHAPTER TEN

1 See Institute for Research / Creation in Media Arts and Technologies, www.hexagram.org/

2 Derrick de Kerckhove, *Connected Intelligence: The Arrival of the Web Society* (Toronto: Somerville Press, 1997), xxvii. I develop these ideas in the prologue.

3 See David Rockefeller, *Creative Management in Banking* (New York: McGraw-Hill , 1964); Bernard Arnault, *La Passion créative: Entretiens avec Yves Messarovich* (Paris: Plon, 2000).

4 See Andrew S. Grove, *Only the Paranoid Survive: How to Exploit the Crisis Points That Challenge Every Company* (New York: Doubleday, 1996).

5 Henry Mintzberg, preface to *Artists, Craftsmen, and Technocrats: The Dreams, Realities and Illusions of Leadership*, by Patricia Pitcher (Toronto: Stoddart, 1995).

6 Jeremy Rifkin, *The Age of Access: The New Culture of Hypercapitalism, Where All of Life Is a Paid-for Experience* (New York: Jeremy P. Tarcher; Putnam, 2000), 5.

7 "Testimony of Chairman Allan Greenspan: The Federal Reserve's Semi-annual Report on Monetary Policy," Federal Reserve Board, 22 July 1999, http://www.federalreserve.gov/boarddocs/hh/1999/July/Testimony.htm (accessed 19 January 2006).

8 Unfortunately, this innovative approach was abandoned in 2003 by a new management team. (Quotation translated by Rhonda Mullins.)

9 Rifkin, *Age of Access*, 7.

CHAPTER TWELVE

1 See John Perry Barlow, "*A Declaration of the Independence of Cyberspace*, www.eff.org/~barlow/Declaration-Final.html (accessed 27 February 2006); see also http://homes.eff.org/~barlow/ (accessed 27 February 2006). Barlow is a retired Wyoming cattle rancher, a former lyricist for the *Grateful Dead*, and co-founder of the Electronic Frontier Foundation. Since May of 1998, he has been a Fellow at Harvard Law School's Berkman Center for Internet and Society.

2 See Douglas Rushkoff, *Cyberia* (New York: HarperCollins, 1994).

3 http://yfosa.thinkfree.org

4 See Tsutomu Shimomura and John Markoff, *Takedown: The Pursuit and Capture of Kevin Mitnick, America's Most Wanted Computer Outlaw* (New York: Hyperion, 1996).

5 http://freenet.sourceforge.net/

6 See Faith Popcorn, *The Popcorn Report: Faith Popcorn on the Future of Your Company, Your World, Your Life* (New York: Doubleday, 1991).

7 Keith Regan, "One Year Ago: Study: Women Now Online Majority," *E-Commerce Times*, http://www.ecommercetimes.com/story/12566.html (accessed 24 January 2006).

8 Pierre Lévy, *World philosophie: le marché, le cyberespace, la conscience* (Paris: Odile Jacob, 2000), (Quotation translated by Rhonda Mullins.)

9 www.rushkoff.com

10 "Afghanistan's Taliban Bans Internet," Reuters, 14 July 2001, http://www.rawa.org/internet.htm (accessed 24 January 2006).

CHAPTER THIRTEEN

1 See, for example, http://www.spyworld.com/Snooper_Info.htm.

2 See Reg Whitaker, *The End of Privacy: How Total Surveillance Is Becoming a Reality* (New York: New Press, 1999).

3 For information on anonymous surfing and anti-spyware, see http://www.anonymizer.com.

4 European Parliament, "Resolution on the Existence of a Global System for the Interception of Private and Commercial Communications (ECHELON Interception System)," 4 July 2001, http://cryptome.org/ echelon-epmr.htm (accessed 11 February 2006).

CHAPTER FOURTEEN

1 Jeremy Rifkin, *The Age of Access: The New Culture of Hypercapitalism, Where All of Life Is a Paid-for Experience* (New York: Jeremy P. Tarcher; Putnam, 2000), 1l.

2 See Nicholas Negroponte, *Being Digital* (New York: Knopf, 1995).

3 Rifkin, *Age of Access*, 55.

4 Solveig Godeluck, quoted in "End of the Beginning for the Internet," by Derrick de Kerkhove, trans. Ed Emery, *Le Monde diplomatique*, August 2001, http://mondediplo.com/2001/08/10internet (accessed 7 March 2006).

5 "Remarks by Steve Ballmer and Bill Gates, Microsoft CEO Summit, Redmond, Wash., May 24, 2000," http://www.microsoft.com/billgates/speeches/2000/05–24ceosummit.asp (accessed 8 February 2006).

6 Michael de Kare-Silver, *E-Shock 2000: The Electronic Shopping Revolution* (Basingstoke, UK: Palgrave Macmillan, 1998).

7 "A Framework for Global Electronic Commerce," White House, 1 July 1997, http://www.technology.gov/digeconomy/framewrk.htm (accessed 8 February 2006).

8 See Mike Dash, *Tulipomania: The Story of the World's Most Coveted Flower and the Extraordinary Passions It Aroused* (London: Orion, 2000);

and John Kenneth Galbraith, *A Short History of Financial Euphoria* (1990; repr., New York: Viking Penguin, 1993).

9 Derrick de Kerkhove, "Internet à l'heure du désenchantement," *Le Monde diplomatique*, August 2001, http://www.monde-diplomatique.fr/2001/08/DE_KERCKHOVE/15542 (accessed 7 March 2006). (Quotation translated by Rhonda Mullins.)

CHAPTER FIFTEEN

1 Nicholas Negroponte, *Being Digital* (New York: Knopf, 1995), 183.

2 Piérre Lévy, "The Virtual Economy," trans. Briant Sarris, *Chair et Métal*, 2000, http://www.chairetmetal.com/levy-ang2.htm (accessed 10 February 2006).

3 Ibid.

4 Immanuel Kant, *Essays and Treatises* (Bristol: Thoemmes Press, 1993), 1:419, 429.

5 J.G. Fichte, *The Vocation of Man*, ed. Roderick M. Chisholm (New York: Macmillan, 1985), 107–8.

6 "Business: The Economy New World Trade Czar," BBC Online Network, 1 September 1999, http://news.bbc.co.uk/1/hi/business/the_economy/433576.stm (accessed 15 February 2006); "Launch of Report into APEC: 10 Years and Beyond," World Trade Organization, 24 August 1999, http://www.wto.org/english/news_e/spmm_e/spmm02_e.htm (accessed 15 February 2006).

7 UNDP, *Human Development Report 1999: Globalization with a Human Face* (New York: UNDP, Oxford University Press, 1999), 31.

8 Lévy, "Virtual Economy."

9 Bill Gates, "75th Anniversary TIME Salute," http://www.microsoft.com/billgates/speeches/gatessalute.asp (accessed 15 February 2006).

CHAPTER SIXTEEN

1 Olivier Peuch, "L'Enseignement devient collectif," *Le Monde* 30 September 1995.

2 Mind Leaders Partners, http://partners.mindleaders.com/opportunities/ (accessed 28 February 2006).

3 David F. Noble, "Le lourd passé de l'enseignement à distance," *Le Monde diplomatique*, April 2000, http://www.monde-diplomatique.fr/

2000/04/NOBLE/13691 (accessed 16 February 2006). (Quotation translated by Rhonda Mullins.)

4 http://www.cvu-uvc.ca/release1.html

5 Noble, "Lourd passé."

6 http://www.adec.edu/vuniv/place1.html; ADEC is a non-profit distance education consortium composed of approximately sixty-five state universities and land-grant colleges.

CHAPTER SEVENTEEN

1 John Suler, "Psychotherapy and Clinical Work in Cyberspace," in *The Psychology of Cyberspace*, http://www.rider.edu/~suler/psycyber/therintro.html (accessed 20 February 2006).

2 See Fenichel's Web site: www.fenichel.com

3 http://www.psynternaute.com; Rochon has also published *Les Accrocs d'internet* (Montreal: Libre-Expression, 2004).

4 See William Lowenstein, "New Perspectives for the Prevention and Treatment of Addictions," www.skoun.org/conference_oct2005/talks.html (accessed 28 February 2006).

CHAPTER EIGHTEEN

1 There are many metaphors for this: the new frontier, the cyberworld, and so on. For more on the subject, see Ollivier Dyens, *Continent X* (Montreal: Éditions VLB, 2004).

2 In 2006, the internet offered about 2.3 million e-medicine sites. These provide all kinds of clinical knowledge, discuss a full range of symptoms, describe rare illnesses, promote practice communities, and publicize thousands of private medical centres – including top-quality public hospitals with reduced prices and immediate access to treatment or surgery in the Third World (India or Thailand, for example) for Western patients who do not want to wait months or even years to have medical procedures in their own countries.

3 John A. Tirpak, "Find, Fix, Track, Target, Engage, Assess," *Air Force Magazine Online*, July 2000, http://www.afa.org/magazine/July2000/0700find.asp (accessed 21 February 2006).

4 www.myvirtualmodel.com

5 "Opera on Internet," *Tribune*, 27 June 1999, www.tribuneindia.com/1999/99jun27/world.htm (accessed 21 February 2006).

6 Mary Campbell, "Opera 'Aida' Goes Live on Internet," Associated Press, 25 June 1999.

7 "Israel's Mr .com," BBC News, 12 April 2001, http://news.bbc.co.uk/1/hi/world/middle_east/1271728.stm (accessed 21 February 2006).

8 http://web.archive.org/web/20011205063607/www.cutoffmyfeet.com/main.html

9 "Cyberspace Search for Cancer Cure," CNN.com Health, 17 January 2001, http://archives.cnn.com/2001/HEALTH/01/17/norway.cancer/ (accessed 21 February 2006).

10 Joe Lavin, "Surf the Net Like It's 1999," CCN News, http://www.ccnmag.com/story.php?id=200 (accessed 21 February 2006).

11 http://web.archive.org/web/20010405071633/trisenx.com/aboutus.asp

12 See, for example, www.redzip.com; www.upspiral.com; www.oeza.com.

13 See, for example, http://www.PherX.com; http://www.pheromonesandmore.com; http://www.Pherlure.com; http://www.human-pheromone-reviews.com.

CHAPTER NINETEEN

1 "Russian Touts Computer Virus as Weapon," *Washington Post*, 9 May 2000.

2 Louis J. Freeh, Statement of the Director of the Federal Bureau of Investigation before the Senate Committee on Appropriations Subcommittee for the Departments of Commerce, Justice, State, the Judiciary, and Related Agencies, Washington, DC, 16 February 2000.

3 Wait Gibbs, "*The Rise of Crimeware,*" *Scientific American*.com, http://blog.sciam.com/index.php?title=the_rise_of_crimeware&more=1&c=1&tb=1&pb=1 (accessed 23 February 2006).

CHAPTER TWENTY

1 "Keynote Presentation by Bill Gates, Welcome Remarks by Steve Ballmer, CEO Summit 2001," http://www.microsoft.com/billgates/speeches/2001/05–23ceosummit.asp (accessed 24 February 2006).

Index of Names

Index of Topics